Also by Ruth Brandon

RUTH BRANDON

The New Women and the Old Men

Love, Sex and the Woman Question

Flamingo
An Imprint of HarperCollins*Publishers*

Poem by W.H. Auden reprinted by permission of Faber and Faber Ltd from *Collected Poems* by W.H. Auden. Extracts from *The New Machiavelli*, *The Research Magnificent*, *The Secret Places of the Heart*, and *First and Last Things* reprinted by permission of A.P. Watt Ltd on behalf of the Literary Executors of the Estate of H.G. Wells. Extracts from *H.G. Wells in Love* reprinted by permission of Faber and Faber Ltd and Little, Brown and Company. Quotations from *Experiment in Autobiography* by H.G. Wells, copyright 1934 by Herbert George (H.G.) Wells; © renewed 1962 by George Philip Wells and Francis Richard Wells, reprinted by permission of Little, Brown & Company. Extracts from the Pearson correspondence reproduced courtesy of Dr Sarah Pearson. Extracts from *The Doctor's Dilemma*, *Misalliance*, *Pen Portraits and Reviews* and the Shaw correspondence reprinted by permission of the Shaw estate, the Society of Authors. Extracts from works and correspondence of Havelock Ellis reproduced courtesy of Professor François Lafitte. Extracts from *The Strange Necessity* by Rebecca West reprinted by permission of the Peters, Fraser and Dunlop Group Ltd. Extracts from *H.G. Wells: Aspects of a Life* by Anthony West, Copyright © 1984 by Anthony West, reprinted by permission of Wallace Literary Agency, Inc, on behalf of the author's estate. Extracts from *The Diary of Beatrice Webb*, 3 vols, ed. N. and J. McKenzie, the Passfield Papers, Copyright © 1982-4 The London School of Economics and Political Science, reprinted by permission of Virago Press.

First published in 1990 by Martin Secker & Warburg Limited

This edition first issued in 1991 by Flamingo,
an imprint of HarperCollins Publishers,
77–85 Fulham Palace Road,
Hammersmith, London W6 8JB

9   8   7   6   5   4   3   2   1

Copyright © Ruth Brandon 1990

The Author asserts the moral right to be
identified as the author of this work

Printed and bound in Great Britain by
HarperCollins Book Manufacturing, Glasgow

THIS BOOK IS FOR JAN
WITH LOVE

Acknowledgements

A great many people have helped with the preparation of this book, often with a word or a suggestion which has started a fruitful train of thought and investigation. I should like to thank: Cathy Henderson of the Harry Ransom Humanities Research Center, University of Texas at Austin, for help with Olive Schreiner and Havelock Ellis materials; Susan Boone, curator of the Sophia Smith Collection, Smith College, Northampton, Mass., for help with the Margaret Sanger papers; the archivists at University College, London, for help with the Pearson papers; the archivists, Sheffield County Library, for help with the Edward Carpenter papers; Gene K. Rinkel, Curator of Special Collections, University of Illinois at Urbana-Champaign, for help with the Wells papers. I should also particularly like to thank: Julia Briggs, Owen Greene, Nick Humphrey, Barbara Pearce, Philip Steadman, Diana Vincent-Daviss, and Justin Waddington, without whose diverse assistance this book would have been much the poorer. I am especially grateful to Jan Marsh, who has been unfailingly generous and helpful in every way.

CONTENTS

LIST OF ILLUSTRATIONS

To the man in the street who, I'm sorry to say
Is a keen observer of life,
The word *intellectual* suggests right away
A man who's untrue to his wife.

W. H. AUDEN

I

A DERBYSHIRE IDYLL

I

In the late summer of 1884 two unusual couples arrived to spend a joint 'honeymoon' (although they were not married) in the village of Middleton, just outside Wirksworth in the Derbyshire hills. There was an eager, Jewish-looking girl with shining dark eyes and abundant, untidy, black curly hair. She was accompanied by a pale, stooping, rather sinister-looking man. They took lodgings at the Nelson Arms public house. Their friends, who stayed at a farmhouse at Bole Hill about a mile away, were a small, plump young woman, with a delicate, Italianate, laughing face and a tall, grave, bearded young man.

The pair at the Nelson Arms were Eleanor Marx, Karl Marx's daughter, then twenty-nine, and her lover, Dr Edward Aveling, a natural scientist and devoted follower of Darwin, four years her senior. At Bole Hill was the South African novelist Olive Schreiner, also twenty-nine, whose brilliant and disturbing book, *The Story of an African Farm*, had been published the previous year, quickly making her famous. Her companion (who joined her after his medical exams were finished, when she had already been there about three weeks) was Henry Havelock Ellis, later to become famous as the Sage of Sex.

There was nothing furtive or shamefaced about these couples. The fact that they were not married, although contemporary moralists might have thought it the most significant thing about them, was merely the outward sign of their general commitment to a new approach to life. In this rethinking a new view of relations between men and women played an important part: a part which was usually aired under the generic title of the Woman Question. This, for later generations, has most often been connected with the suffragette movement and the campaign for women's votes. But for New Women like Olive and Eleanor that was never the nub of the question. It was merely one of a whole range of inequities and moral and economic double standards which they saw as being imposed upon women. So the Derbyshire holiday was, among other things, an affirmation that they had abandoned the old restrictions. Olive was already a significant contributor to the debate, the creator of a fictional heroine, Lyndall in *African Farm*, who utterly rejected the pattern of life and assumptions then normally laid out before young women.

This holiday, which represented for all of them a peak of hope and physical enjoyment, remained vividly in their minds. Havelock Ellis, fifty years later, could still remember those days in sensuous detail: 'During this week spent at Bole Hill we would all go for long walks together in the delightful country around. . . . Eleanor . . . was then in full physical, mental and emotional maturity, a vigorous and radiant personality. It is perhaps a bodily trait of her powerful personality that I have never known a woman who on a long summer's day ramble diffused so potent an axillary fragrance [i.e. she smelt strongly of armpits: Ellis was always prone to arch quasi-medical circumlocution]. She was none the less always a delightful personality, intelligent, eager, full of enjoyment, whatever the moods and melancholy she may privately have been subject to. The alleged resemblance in mind and body to her famous father certainly included no trace of his dogmatic and domineering temper. Aveling also proved an agreeable companion on these expeditions, though I recall as characteristic that when we came on notices to warn trespassers he would disregard them with immense gusto and trample ruthlessly over everything in his path. At times he would read aloud to us. He had a good voice and was an admirable reader, with much power of dramatic expression. At Olive's suggestion he once read out some of my own youthful sonnets and put into them a passionate intensity which was quite a revelation to myself.'[1] He recalled other moments, when 'Olive for a moment dropped behind those two to put her arm caressingly round me and Aveling cast a sharp glance back; I see her on yet another walk when for some reason I was unwilling to go along the road she preferred, and she softly sang to herself: "I have a donkey and he won't go"; I see her coming suddenly quite naked out of the bathroom in the house where she was staying into the sitting-room where I was waiting for her, to expound to me at once some idea which had just occurred to her, apparently unconscious of all else.'[2]

★

The New Woman was but one manifestation of that passion for fresh thinking, that search for new ways of approaching life, which swept the whole of the western world between 1880 and 1914. This of course expressed itself differently in different places. A pattern was set then which is still recognizable. In continental Europe the new thought was embodied in artistic and philosophical exploration and adventure, while the Anglophone countries, distrusting these intellectual excesses, preferred to concentrate upon the pragmatic and the practical. Such movements as symbolism, surrealism, cubism, the Vienna Secession, the beginnings of psychoanalysis, marked a definitive break with the old ways of thinking about the self and viewing the world. This was the beginning of an intellectual and artistic universe which the twentieth century would recognize as its own. But while these movements and their initiators were celebrated in the salons of Paris and Vienna, in London they were regarded with the deepest suspicion.

The London view of these things was perhaps epitomized in its treatment of Oscar Wilde, who was fêted in Paris for his intellectual daring at a time when his work was received in London with wariness and derision. When Sarah Bernhardt wanted to play his *Salome* in London she was unable to do so because the Lord Chamberlain banned the work for indecency. Wilde's talent and uproarious wit finally forced itself on to even the London stage, but British society's deep distrust of him, for his intellectual as much as for his social excesses, was shown by the vindictive glee with which it turned upon him after his fall, when in 1895 he was imprisoned for homosexuality. It was enough, after that, even to have been professionally associated with him. Following Wilde's destruction, Aubrey Beardsley, who had had the bad taste to illustrate his *Salome* while Oscar was still the darling of the drawing-rooms, was dismissed from the art editorship of *The Yellow Book* at the behest of a popular lady novelist, who averred that 'She owed it to her position before the British people' to demand his dismissal. 'Beardsley,' wrote W. B. Yeats, who was a member of that circle, 'was not even a friend of Wilde's – they even disliked each other – he had no sexual abnormality, but he was certainly unpopular, and the moment had come to get rid of unpopular persons. The public at once concluded – they could hardly conclude otherwise, he was dismissed by telegram – that there was some evidence against him, and Beardsley, who was some twenty-three years old, being embittered and miserable, plunged into dissipation.'[3] This was acceptable, as long as he kept his dissipation to himself, which is hardly the point of art.

As for the intellectual flourish of Vienna, where, for example, Freud, in the course of formulating his *The Interpretation of Dreams*, could write to his friend Fliess in Berlin marvelling at the sheer intellectual beauty of the work he was doing – that would have been dismissed as showing-off in Britain: a sin almost as heinous as indecency in a land where the all-round amateur remained the ideal. At the beginning of 1900 Beatrice Webb meditated in her diary on the possible outcome of the Boer War – but her musings might have applied to any aspect of the nation's life. Mrs Webb, a despairing enthusiast for professionalism in a sea of amateurs, thought that to lose the war would provide a salutary lesson for her country. 'If we ultimately win, we shall forget the lessons. We shall say once again, "We muddled through all right!" . . . Once again we shall believe that the English gentleman's "general capacity" is equal to the science of the foreign expert. Again our politicians and officers will bask in the smile of London Society and country house-parties, and will chatter bad metaphysics and worse economics, imagining themselves to be men of the world because they have neither the knowledge nor the industry to be skilled professional administrators and soldiers.'[4] It was an attitude that extended itself to all aspects of life, even – especially – including those in which the phlegmatic British had had to adapt their ideas to that post-Darwinian, post-1848 world in which radicalism had abandoned the barricades but was clearly only quiescent, liberalism was everywhere on the retreat, and the orderly picture of divine creation had been supplanted by a universe seemingly governed by random chance.

In this world, where beneath the façade of solidity so much that had been taken for granted seemed to be coming adrift, the disquiet manifested itself in an exploration, or series of explorations, not of the individual but of society. In the early 1880s there suddenly mushroomed a plethora of groups dedicated to the exploration of new worlds, here or elsewhere. At one end of the spectrum the Society for Psychical Research catered for those whom Darwinism had deprived of a religion which would otherwise have been the foundation of their lives, and whose aim was to find scientific proof of the existence of what might loosely be termed the soul. At the opposite end the secularists, led by Charles Bradlaugh and Annie Besant, built on Darwin's foundations to try and destroy once for all the pernicious influence of religion. Political life, too, was lively. While inside Parliament the Liberals destroyed themselves as a force by splitting over the issue of Irish Home Rule, outside it various degrees of socialist, from Fabian 'permeators' to Marxian revolutionaries, now began to organize, ably assisted by the influx of radicals who (like Marx himself) found a last refuge in England after being expelled from other European countries. There were societies for activists and societies for idealists, from militant vegetarians and Rational Dressers to bomb-carrying anarchists, the membership largely interchangeable and (in that small world) mostly acquainted.

It was perhaps not surprising to find the families of the clergy largely represented among those who began to meet together to try and work out the pattern of a possible new world. For who were more intellectually and emotionally cut adrift than the clergy? Of the four who found themselves that summer in Derbyshire, Havelock Ellis had seriously considered entering the church, but found that his beliefs, or lack of them, would not allow him to do so. Edward Aveling was the son of a dissenting minister of liberal outlook, and himself professed a Darwinism so extreme and unbending that it was clear his free-thinking was not merely a rejection of religion but a violent reaction against it. Olive Schreiner was the daughter of Evangelical missionaries from the South African backveldt. She had rejected her family's literalist religion at the age of ten and had suffered the terrible trauma of being immediately rejected by them – a rejection which still caused her, and was to continue to cause her, an infinity of pain. As for Eleanor Marx, arguably the most balanced of this quartet, she of course had no religion, being the daughter of 'Old Nick'5 himself.

Olive Schreiner was in a sense the connecting link of the group. Eleanor Marx, who was her great friend, had persuaded her to come to Derbyshire, and she had persuaded Havelock Ellis – though there is little doubt that Ellis and the Avelings would have got to know each other anyway in the small world of London's radical intellectuals.

This was just one of the worlds which *The Story of an African Farm* opened to its authoress. Literary London was as charmed by the vivid beauty of its style as were feminists by its substance. In the story, two English South African sisters, Em and Lyndall, are living on a farm in the Karroo with a Boer woman, Tant' Sannie, the second wife of their dead father. The novel centres on Lyndall, who is pretty and clever and discontented with the limited life which is all that seems to be open to her. Many of the characters express aspects of their creator, but it is Lyndall who speaks most directly for Olive in her suspicion of the traditional route mapped out for women.

A stranger comes by the farm; he falls in love with Lyndall and she with him. But he goes away, and Lyndall becomes engaged to a dull, not particularly suitable young man who is all that presents, and with whom Em is in love. Then the stranger reappears: he begs Lyndall to marry him. This she will not do.

> 'Who is this fellow you talk of marrying?' [he asks her.]
> 'A young farmer.'
> 'Lives here?'
> 'Yes; he has gone to town to get things for our wedding.'
> 'What kind of fellow is he?'
> 'A fool.'
> 'And you would rather marry him than me?'
> 'Yes; because you are not one.'
> 'That is a novel reason for refusing to marry a man,' he said . . .
> 'It is a wise one,' she said shortly. 'If I marry him I shall shake him off my hand when it suits me . . . As far as I wish he should come, he comes, and no further. Would you ask me what you might and what you might not do? . . . If once you have me you would hold me fast. I shall never be free again.'[6]

What in fact happens is that Lyndall agrees to leave with the stranger, but not to marry him. Her distracted fiancé finally tracks her down to find her dying, with a baby, all alone in a small town, refusing to take any money from her stranger, just as she has refused ever to marry him, in spite of the baby.

This book was begun in about 1878 while Olive was working as a governess in the Karroo, the great semi-desert interior of Cape Province she so memorably evokes in it. This was one of several such posts which she had held since, at the age of fifteen, her family had become destitute and she had had to fend for herself. Her one

aim at that time was to come to England or America and free herself
of this narrowly bounded life to which, ironically, she was always to
look back with such longing. In 1881 she finally achieved her aim of
escape. Her brother Fred had a school in the Isle of Wight, which gave
her some family to fall back on, and some other friends from South
Africa, Dr John Brown and his wife Mary, had arranged for her to
train as a nurse at the Edinburgh Royal Infirmary. She would have
preferred to be a doctor, but since she could not see how she would
raise the money for the long training, she would be a nurse. But after
only three days it became clear that her health would not stand the
strain and Fred had to go to Edinburgh to fetch her. He encouraged
her to try again, and promised to let her have any money she needed to
train as a doctor if she could achieve the academic entrance standards
required. Since Olive was entirely self-taught – she had never been to
school – the chances of this were vanishingly small. Fred advised her to
stick to writing. 'I am not yet beginning my medical studies as both my
brothers think I had better get my books ready for publication before I
begin,' she wrote then to an old friend, Mrs Cawood, in whose family
she had been a governess for some time (besides *African Farm* there
was another novel under preparation, *Saints and Sinners*, which was
to be published posthumously as *From Man to Man*). 'They think
I ought to stick to literature, but I can't quite see it. I am a man with
two loves and don't know which to choose.'[7] She finally decided to
try nursing again, this time at the Women's Hospital in Endell Street,
Covent Garden – the infamous Seven Dials, notorious for its filth and
wretchedness. This time she lasted five days before inflammation of
the lungs struck her down. Her mind was thus made up for her.

In spite of her novel's quality, finding a publisher was not easy.
Quite apart from its originality (something which does not necessarily
make for an easy sale) it was not at all the kind of thing lady novelists
were supposed to produce – neither wholesome nor morally uplifting.
Olive, dreary and disheartened, horribly lonely and hating the English
climate, did the rounds of the publishers. 'I remember when I walked
up Regent Street with *S.A.F.* under my cloak in the rain, thinking
everyone could know that what was stuck under my cloak was
a rejected MS. Oh! so heart-sick.'[8] But by the summer of 1882
the manuscript was accepted by Chapman and Hall, whose reader,
George Meredith, recommended it, accepted Olive's absolute refusal

to tamper with the book in any way, and advised her, when dealing with publishers, 'always to get some friend who was a competent businessman to make the arrangements'.[9] By then, however, Olive had already agreed the preliminary details: she claimed she was paid £18 12s. 11d. for the first edition.[10] *The Story of an African Farm*, by Ralph Iron, came out early in 1883; there were two more editions the same year. By the time the third of these appeared everyone in London knew that the book's author was Olive Schreiner, and so she appeared on the title page, then and subsequently.[11]

The book did not precisely create a sensation: its unorthodox and rather shocking stance prevented it being widely enough reviewed for that. But it was nevertheless quickly recognized as being important. It was very widely read, and discussed in the most diverse circles. Rider Haggard and Mr Gladstone were both enthusiasts for it. A good many people wrote to Olive, having read her book. This was perhaps how she met Eleanor Marx; it was certainly how she met Havelock Ellis.

Ellis read the book early in 1884, and was moved to write to its author, 'partly by my admiration and sympathy, partly also because it seemed to me that the book had attracted almost no attention and its fine quality had remained unappreciated . . . After an interval came a reply in what I afterwards knew to be her best and neatest hand.'[12]

Olive received Ellis's letter in February, and the correspondence continued until May, when she came to London, and it seemed natural that they should meet.

What had they expected? Ellis, of course, by now knew that 'Ralph Iron' was a woman (in fact, as a perceptive reviewer had remarked, that was apparent from the book). He knew from their correspondence that he would like her and that they were in sympathy with each other. 'I still recall the first vision of her in the little sitting-room of the South Kensington lodging-house,' he wrote in his memoirs nearly forty years later, 'the short sturdy vigorous body in loose shapeless clothes, sitting on the couch, with hands spread on thighs, and, above, the beautiful head with the large dark eyes, at once so expressive and so observant.' Olive, however, did not receive a reciprocally satisfying impression. 'She evidently expected much from that meeting. She told me some time later that, at first actually seeing me, her disappointment was so acute that on going into her bedroom to put on her hat . . . she burst into tears.'[13]

Henry Havelock Ellis (addressed by Olive sometimes as Henry, sometimes as Harry) was four years younger than she was, born in 1859. His father was a sea captain, and young Henry spent most of his childhood in the company of his mother and his four younger sisters, with occasional visits from his father. In contrast to Olive's tempestuous and emotional childhood and youth, Ellis describes a rather detached family life: 'for my mother I had always an equable and unquestioning affection, which seems to have been entirely free from any of those complications to which the child's affection for his mother is now supposed to be liable . . . There was no physical intimacy, her love for her children was not of the petting kind . . . Nor was there ever any trace of jealousy on my part with regard to my father. That in any case may indeed have been excluded by the fact that he was such a stranger in his own house. We saw but little of him, and we always accepted him, as a matter of course and willingly, though there was little or no opportunity for warm affection to spring up, for even during his stays in London he had to be away all day at the ship or office, and Sundays were too formal and sacred to be conducive to intimacy.'[14]

When Henry was seven his father decided – 'doubtless for the benefit of my health,' says Ellis in his autobiography, but possibly to try and get to know his small son a bit better – to take him on a long sea-voyage: they were to travel around the world, to Australia and then home via South America. He recounts various mild sexual adventures with other children in the course of this voyage – by the time he wrote his autobiography he had for years been taking a professional interest in such things – and dismisses them all: 'sexual problems had no interest, or rather no existence, for me at this age, and for years after.'[15] He was entranced by Lima, with its Spanish gateways and patios, enjoyed taking a small boat round the islands of Callao looking for starfish and other creatures with another captain's son, and couldn't remember his reunion with his mother when eventually they returned. Then he took up his life where it had been left off, not noticeably changed by the voyage: he was a studious, solitary, intellectual boy who hated games. His adventures all took place in books. He was also a very religious boy, fascinated by the Bible. His mother was deeply Evangelical, and young Henry's greatest influence was the Revd John Erck, a low-church Anglican clergyman. When he left school at the age of sixteen he had no idea what he was going to do: the only possible career that presented itself was that of the church. But there was a difficulty: he had begun to lose his faith. What was he to do? His father was soon to sail for Sydney: he suggested that Henry accompany him. It was a momentous decision.

Captain Ellis's ship, the *Surrey*, was to call at Sydney and then go on to Calcutta. But the ship's doctor told his father that in his opinion the Indian climate might be very bad for Henry's health. It was therefore proposed that he should register as a schoolmaster with an educational agency and stay for some time in Australia.

The young man's first efforts at schoolmastering were not very successful, ending with the collapse of the school at which he was teaching and of the educational agency which was supposed to have him on its books. The head of the erstwhile agency, an old friend of Captain Ellis, then suggested that Henry take a three-month training course and enrol as a teacher in the government service. This he did, 'and shortly after received an appointment as Teacher at the Half-time Schools at Sparkes Creek and Junction Creek, with instructions to proceed thither almost at once'.[16]

This was 1878, the year when Olive Schreiner, living her lonely but happy life in the Karroo, was embarking upon *The Story of an African Farm*. For Havelock Ellis, too, isolated in *his* outback, 1878 was to prove a momentous year as far as his future career was concerned.

Ellis travelled by train to Scone, the nearest railhead, and then by horse to Sparkes Creek. For a couple of nights he stayed with one of the settlers living near the school, but he was not a welcome visitor – the house was small and the family was large. He would have to go and live in the schoolhouse. 'So I put on my tall silk hat and took up my little bag . . . and went my lonely way to the schoolhouse. Now at last I was completely adrift . . . I felt like a lost child.'[17]

The schoolhouse, isolated in the bush, was bare and bleak enough. It had two rooms, opening out on to a verandah in front; one was the schoolroom, with rough desks and benches, one the teacher's room, containing 'nothing but a makeshift bed, formed by a framework of four poles supporting two sacks and resting on four legs which were so insecurely attached that occasionally the whole structure would collapse during the night'.[18] There was a privy out in a shed, a table with a tin bowl for washing in, water from the creek, and drinking water was got from a well near by. A Chinese trader in Scone provided all supplies except bread and milk, which were got from the settler with the large family and small house, whose wife sometimes sent over a peach pie or some similar luxury. Here, quite on his own once his pupils had left, Ellis spent a blissful year. The place was beautiful, the climate delightful, the animals – jew lizards, koalas, and vast herds of leaping kangaroos – a never-ending source of interest. The young schoolmaster spent his time walking, reading and thinking.

One of the things he thought about, a good deal, was sex. Here he first experienced orgasm (while reading Brantôme's sixteenth-century French memoir *Vies des dames galantes*). It was not until after this event that he ever became physically excited by the thought or presence of a woman, but (presumably after it) his memoirs record that 'in the year of my solitary life, as never before or since, there was an immense thirst deep down in my youthful soul . . . for the revelation, in body and spirit, of a divinely glorious woman'. Rather pathetically he adds: 'Now, when I grow old, sweet and gracious women come to me unsought and are ready to pour out the treasures of their loveliness and devotion. Then, when their coming might have meant so much, they never came.'[19]

But sex was not the only thing, nor the most important, on his mind. There was also the question of his philosophy of life, a question which, since his loss of faith, had allowed him little if any peace of mind. 'I had the feeling that the universe was represented as a sort of factory filled by an inextricable web of wheels and looms and flying shuttles, in a deafening din,' he records (using a memorably nineteenth-century simile: Ellis was as much a child of his time in this respect as Freud, with *his* steam-powered metaphors of 'repression' and bursting libido). 'That, it seemed, was the world as the most competent scientific authorities allowed it to be made. It was a world I was prepared to accept and yet a world in which, I felt, I could only wander restlessly, an ignorant and homeless child. . . . The dominant feeling always was that while the scientific outlook, by which I mainly meant the outlook of Darwin and Huxley, commended itself to me as presenting a sound view of the world, on the emotional side I was a stranger to that world, if indeed I would not, with Omar, "shatter it to bits".'[20] Now, almost suddenly, the question was resolved. He described the occasion of it in his journal, 21 July 1878: 'And so I am "converted". The factors in my "conversion" are, 1st, hearing that Mr Erck [the clergyman who had been his main religious influence in England] was about to write to me; 2nd reading Hinton's "Life in Nature", 3rd reading Spencer's "Study of Sociology." But it would be absurd to say that these three things *produced* the spiritual revolution I have undergone. But that I have undergone a spiritual revolution there can be no question. For the last three years I have known nothing but doubt . . . I was living in a vacant universe which I felt to be a machine. I was a living thing groping my way amid dead blind relentless laws, ready at every moment to crush me . . . Four years ago, as a boy, I was religious (for I was always religious), Church of England, and of rather Broad Church tendencies. There came a time when vast questions crowded one after another, threatening to overwhelm me. For I would not shirk them – rather I could not. And so one by one I met them and was conquered . . . And I believe that even then I was following Truth; it was at the command of Truth and not of any phantom that I gave up my beliefs. For I had no right to them. I had found them and adopted them; they were not mine. But if Truth takes away, she poured thousand-fold in my bosom. She took away my beliefs because they were not mine. And thus there is for me no more doubt. I met the waves of the sea of doubt, and battled with them, and never looked back at the lowlands I had left. And I have reached shore now. I have reached a height I had not dreamed of before.'[21]

The book that was the key to this sudden mystical finding of himself – for it was no less than that – was *Life in Nature*, by a now obscure doctor and mystic called James Hinton. Hinton, who was at that time an influential thinker, was mainly known for the way in which his philosophy insisted that man, and especially woman, must be open to love, and the literal way in which he and his followers interpreted this. His aim was to counter the random materialism which seemed to be Darwin's legacy by an insistence that the material had a beauty of its own, and that because something was corporeal that did not mean it did not have its own mystic beauty. ' "You are faced," ' he said to the depressed victim of 'materialistic' science, ' "by a small ingot you believe to be gold and a large mass you believe to be clay, and you are told they are both of the same nature. You jump to the conclusion that they are both clay. *But what I can prove to you is that they are both gold!*" ' This rather vague promise was the core of 'Hintonism', as it was generally known. In his search for some kind of spiritual order which would replace what Darwin had destroyed, Hinton hit upon a kind of Nature-worship which could be seen as a material counterpoint to that notion of a collective unconscious, or spiritual *élan vital*, central to the vitalist thinking which was also (and for the same reasons) so popular at this time. Hinton's concern was not, like that of the vitalists, with the soul, but with the body. He saw life as 'the bright blossom wherein Nature's hidden force comes forth to display itself, the necessary outpouring of the universal life that circulates within her veins unseen'.[22] Hintonism and its interpretation, especially as regards the free enjoyment of sex as a quasi-mystical form of communion with the essence of Nature, caused (as we shall see) more than one flurry in intellectual coteries in the 1880s. But Ellis, isolated among the kangaroos and the koalas, was blissfully unaware of any such controversies. For him, Hinton offered a revelation of how the two worlds which had hitherto been so sadly separated in his mind – the vision of divine life and beauty on the one hand, and the wonderful but soulless concept of mechanistic evolution on the other – might be merged and harmonized. It was a wonderful vision, and one that transformed the world for him. 'In an instant, as it seemed, the universe was changed for me. I trod on air; I moved in light,' he wrote later.[23]

Hinton was also to transform it in a more prosaic way. By September, Ellice Hopkins' *Life and Letters of James Hinton*, for which he had sent, arrived. There was a passage describing how Hinton, at the age of nineteen – Ellis was now that age – on the advice of a doctor friend, entered St Bartholomew's Hospital as a medical student. 'When I got so far a flash of thought, as it were, passed through my brain. I laid the book down and jumped up. I may not be fit to be a doctor, but I shall never make anything else. And then I wondered how ever it was that this had never occurred to me before.'[24]

At the end of his year at Sparkes Creek, then, Ellis returned to England certain of what he was going to do, though with no idea of how he was to get the money to do it. However, the feeling of a miracle somehow connected with James Hinton continued. Some time after his return he got in touch with Hinton's widow, and she and her family very much took to this serious, intelligent, new young disciple. When they heard of Hinton's (albeit unconscious and posthumous) role in deciding young Ellis to be a doctor, Miss Caroline Haddon, Mrs Hinton's sister, who ran a girls' boarding school in Dover, offered to lend him £200 to add to £100 which his mother had recently inherited from an old friend. Thus equipped he enrolled at St Thomas's Hospital, and was in the middle of his long-drawn-out medical studies (he took seven years to complete them) when he met Olive Schreiner. And in spite of the later verdict of Rémy de Gourmont that he was 'the most advanced person in England'[25], it is hard to imagine a young man more embedded in his time – indeed, a more Victorian young man – than Havelock Ellis.

Our second couple – Eleanor Marx and Edward Aveling – have a more modern feel. By contrast with Ellis and Schreiner, both desperately, earnestly, searching for a moral code to fill that void which in an earlier generation had been satisfactorily occupied by conventional religion, Eleanor, at least, was at one with her upbringing. That, of course, had hardly been conventional, though one of history's odder surprises is the store set by the Marx family upon conventional trappings to give their three daughters a good start in life – odd considering their penuriousness and the work upon which the paterfamilias was engaged. But even this contradiction seemed to weigh less upon Eleanor, the beloved youngest child, known to family and friends (but never to Aveling) as 'Tussy', than upon her two older sisters, both of whom, once they were married, kept comparatively elaborate establishments.

Eleanor, being the youngest, had never consciously had to endure that time of dreadful misery when the Marxes were living in two rooms in Soho, not knowing how they were to get financially from one day to the next, watching helplessly while babies fell ill and died. By the time she was a small child, Friedrich Engels, her father's lifelong friend and supporter, had established himself as a Manchester manufacturer and his subventions had set the family up on a comparatively even keel, allowing them to move to a small house (and later a larger one) of their own. By this time the family consisted of Karl Marx, his wife Jenny, née Jenny von Westphalen, who had been his childhood sweetheart, and three daughters: Jenny, Laura, and, much the youngest, Tussy, full of brilliance and vivacity. Alone of Marx's daughters she inherited not simply his political commitment, but his political sense and intellect, so that towards the end of his life he could say of her (as she wrote to Olive Schreiner, then and for some time her most intimate friend), 'Jenny is most like me, but Tussy (my dear old home name) *is* me.'[26] However, there was one important sense in which this was clearly not true. Eleanor was not a man. That this influenced his treatment of her, as it influenced the world's treatment of her, was perhaps inevitable. She was her father's friend, his helper, his confidante, but never, as a son surely would have been and as her abilities entitled her to be, his colleague. She never railed at this – to have criticized her adored, revered and idolized father would scarcely have been possible for her. Perhaps she never thought about it in those terms. Olive Schreiner made her Lyndall say, 'This is a pretty ring, worth fifty pounds at least. I will give it to the first man who tells me he would like to be a woman. There might be one on Robben Island who would win it, perhaps, but I doubt it even there. It is delightful to be a woman; but every man thanks the Lord devoutly that he isn't one.'[27] Eleanor exemplified the reasons why this was so, then and throughout her life.

Eleanor's family life was in many ways a singularly happy one. But as she grew up there was one great exception to this rule, and this concerned her relations with men – or, as Marx saw it, the question of her choice of a husband. From bitter personal experience, Marx knew that being married to a revolutionary was no life for a woman. As he wrote to Paul Lafargue, then hoping to marry his daughter Laura, 'You know that I have sacrificed my whole fortune to the revolutionary struggle. I do not regret it. On the contrary. Had I my career to start again, I should do the same. But I would not marry. As far as lies in my power I intend to save my daughter from the reefs on which her mother's life has been wrecked.'[28]

The difficulty was that, just as one's tastes tend to be formed within the family (even if only as a model of what to react against), so one's choice of a mate is necessarily restricted to people one meets; a circle itself dictated, in the case of girls a century ago, by the family. The natural result of this was that the Marx girls met few men who were not revolutionaries. Both Marx's elder daughters married such young men: Jenny's husband was Charles Longuet, Laura's, Paul Lafargue, both of whom were French and had found themselves in London after the fall of the Paris Commune, which was how they met the Marxes. The girls' parents could not but notice that, despite high ideals, their daughters' domestic lot did not seem a particularly satisfactory one in either case. Both the sons-in-law were often broke and often absent, leaving their wives to the demoralizing routine of penny-pinching domestic drudgery – a pattern with which Marx was only too personally familiar. Perhaps this determined him that his beloved Tussy should not suffer the same fate. At any rate, when at the age of seventeen she fell in love with yet another French revolutionary, Hippolyte-Prosper-Olivier Lissagaray, a dashing veteran of the Commune, her parents put their foot down and forbade the engagement. This treatment, apparently so unfair, devastated Eleanor. The engagement secretly continued, the pair meeting when and where they could – an unsatisfactory situation of which the family officially were not, but in fact inevitably were, aware. It was not until 1882, when she was twenty-seven, after her mother's death and not long before her father's, that this engagement was broken off. Eleanor was in the Isle of Wight at the time, where she and Marx had gone in the hope that the mild climate would help Marx, who was suffering from various diseases of the chest (it did not) and where Eleanor herself was suffering something very like a nervous breakdown. She felt her life was slipping away, she had done nothing and she must make a fresh start before it was too late. She wrote to her sister Jenny: 'It seems selfish to worry you with my affairs, when you must assuredly have worry enough of your own. Still more selfish does it seem that I think at all about myself – instead of thinking only of our dear Mohr. ['Mohr' – the Moor, a reference to his dark colouring, was yet another of the family's many pet-names for Marx.] How I love him no-one can know and yet – we must each of us, after all, live our own life – and much and hard as I have tried I could not crush out my desire to *try something*. [Eleanor was referring here to her longstanding ambition to be an actress: she had just arranged to become the pupil of Mrs Vezin, an ex-actress with an excellent reputation as a teacher.] The chance of independence is very sweet. But if all this has been troubling me it is not all. There has been *much else*. For a long time I have tried to make up my mind to break off my engagement. I *could* not bring myself to do it – he has been very good, and gentle, and patient, with me – but I have done it now. Not only that the burden had become too heavy – I had other reasons (I can't write them – it would take so long, but when I see you I will tell you) – and so at last I screwed my courage to the sticking place. And now, dear, I have a *great* favour to ask you – namely that you will if possible see Lissa sometimes, and treat him just as an old friend. Remember *he* is blameless in this.'[29]

Eleanor's acting ambitions were soon swamped by family disasters. In January 1883, Jenny died, worn out by the effort of looking after four young children mostly unaided in the French provinces; in March the distraught Marx, whose favourite daughter she had been, followed her. Eleanor wrote to Laura (who had by then lost three children of her own): 'This sorting of [Marx's] papers will be terrible work. I hardly know how it is to be got through. I must give certain days in the week to it *entirely*. Of course I cannot sit down and do *only* that. I must keep up my lessons, and get all the work I can. I know Engels is goodness itself and that I shall always have all I want, but I think you will understand that I am more anxious than ever now to earn my own living.'[30] (Laura, on the contrary, was plagued by no such scruples about asking Engels for money, which she and Paul did constantly.)

Eleanor's main source of income at this time was literary hackwork. She ghost-wrote, for a fraction of the fee, reviews which appeared under someone else's name, and did scientific précis for publishers. To this end she, like her father before her, spent a lot of her time in the British Museum Reading Room.

The Reading Room had quickly been established as an excellent informal club by that generation of refugee radicals who flooded into London after the abortive revolutions of 1848 – of whom Karl Marx was of course one of the most prominent. It was warm and well-lit, there was an endless supply of books which could be read at well-appointed desks supplied with blotters, ink and paper, it was central, the opening hours were long and – most important of all – it was free. For Eleanor's generation there was also another advantage. The Reading Room was the only club in London which admitted members of both sexes, the only distinction drawn being that ladies were not allowed to read the contents of the cabinet of *curiosa* (a prohibition which outraged Eleanor when she found the *Kama Sutra* was forbidden her). For the young radicals, then, the Reading Room soon established itself as a place where one would probably meet old friends and might well make new ones.

One of the people Eleanor met in the Reading Room at this time was Beatrice Potter, who was three years younger than herself and was later to become the formidable Fabian, Beatrice Webb. Beatrice kept a regular diary, and recorded in it a vivid picture of Eleanor at this time. As so often in those days the talk turned on religion: Eleanor was helping with the radical journal *Progress* in the enforced absence of its usual editor, G. W. Foote, then in prison for blasphemy. Beatrice, inclined to religion herself, could not bring herself to approve of Eleanor, who assured her that ' "*We* think the Christian religion an *immoral illusion* and wish to use *any* argument to persuade the people that it is false . . . We want to make them disregard the mythical next world and live for *this world* and *insist on having* what will make it pleasant to them." '

'It was useless to disagree with her,' Beatrice recorded. 'She refused to recognize the beauty of the Christian religion. She read the Gospels as the gospels of damnation. Thought that Christ, if he had existed, was a weak-headed individual with a good deal of sweetness of character but quite lacking in heroism. "Did he not at the last moment pray that the cup might pass from him?" When I asked her what the socialist programme was she very sensibly remarked that I might as well ask her to give me in a short formula the whole theory of mechanics. Socialist programme was a deduction from social science which was the most complicated of all sciences. I replied that from the very little I knew about political economy (the only social science we English understood) the social scientists seemed to limit themselves to *describing forces*, they were more or less necessarians. She did not contradict this. I do not know whether it is true or not. In person she is comely, dressed in a slovenly picturesque way with curly black hair flying about in all directions. Fine eyes full of life and sympathy, otherwise ugly features and expression, and complexion showing signs of an unhealthy excited life, kept up with stimulants and tempered by narcotics. Lives alone, is much connected with Bradlaugh set, evidently peculiar views on love etc., and I should think has somewhat "natural" relations with men. Should fear that the chances were against her remaining long within the pale of "respectable" society. Asked me to come and see her. Exactly the life and character I should like to study. Unfortunately one cannot mix with human beings without becoming more or less *connected* with them,' concluded Miss Potter decisively.[31]

In fact, nothing could have been more proper and less 'natural' than Eleanor's relations with men until this time. (Whether she was a sexual innocent is another matter. Havelock Ellis says she told Olive Schreiner there had been 'a sudden sexual initiation, when she happened to be lying on the sofa at home, effected by a prominent foreign follower of her father'[32] – though who this was, Ellis does not say.) But for nearly all her adult life she had been engaged to Lissagaray, and her long engagement to him would certainly have precluded her forming a relationship with any other man. Recently she had struck up a friendship with the young Bernard Shaw, also a Reading Room habitué, who (he told his biographer, Hesketh Pearson, many years later) was much attracted to her. But before he could establish himself on a basis of anything more than friendship, he was supplanted in Eleanor's affections. Maybe one of the 'other reasons' which she mentions in her letter to Jenny announcing the end of the engagement was this other man – Dr Edward Aveling.

Much paper has been spoiled (to borrow Dr Johnson's phrase) in an effort to puzzle out the reason why Eleanor Marx picked on Edward Aveling, of all people, to share her life with. She was loved and admired by everyone who knew her; he was detested and despised almost as universally. He reminded Bernard Shaw of a lizard; while H. M. Hyndman, the leader of the Social Democratic Federation, trying to be charitable, wrote that ' "Nobody can be so bad as Aveling looks" was a remark which translated itself into action in my case. In spite of the most unpleasant rumours about his personal character, alike in regard to money and sexual relations, I put compulsion on myself and forced myself to believe that . . . his forbidding face could not in truth be an index to his real character.'[33] Most of his acquaintance, however, had no such reservations. More than one refused to work with him; many went out of their way to avoid meeting him. Anyone who trusted him where money or women were concerned was virtually certain to find that trust betrayed. Bernard Shaw, who did not dislike him and who had a considerable respect for him politically, nevertheless gave what is generally agreed to be an exact portrait of him as the appalling Dubedat in *The Doctor's Dilemma*. This was the man whom Eleanor would have chosen to marry, if she could; but she could not, for the very good reason that he was married already.

Edward Bibbins Aveling was born in 1849, one of the large family of a Nonconformist clergyman in Stoke Newington, North London. He was a brilliant boy, and fell easily into an academic career. His chosen field was natural science, specializing in physiology. He was particularly fascinated by the work of Darwin, and was generally acknowledged to be an outstanding teacher in this field. This of course meshed naturally with the fire-eating atheism he later professed; at the age of twenty-three, however, he was married by his father in a Congregational church to Miss Bell Frank, who lived down the road. The marriage did not last long. Accounts of its end vary. Edward's was that they parted 'by mutual agreement', but he told Engels that she had run off with a clergyman.[34] His brother Frederick, however, reported that 'He married Bell Frank for her money (300 a year). She could only get half. He soon made her do that. When not able to get any more out of her, he left her.'[35] In fact, as Yvonne Kapp, Eleanor's biographer, discovered, she had, like her sisters, been left £1,000 by her father, which she received at the age of twenty-one or upon marriage. This dowry would have been the money available to Edward.[36]

At the time of the marriage Bell must have felt she had made an admirable choice. Edward was embarked upon a most promising career. He had published his first book, *Botanical Tables*, in 1874, the year after his marriage. In 1875 he was appointed a lecturer at the London Hospital, in 1876 obtained a D.Sc. at University College, London, and was elected a Fellow of the Linnean Society, and in 1877 published another book, *Physiological Tables*. In 1878 he was made a Fellow of University College, and in 1879 applied for the Chair of Comparative Anatomy at King's College, London, withdrawing when he found that the list of rules required him to belong to the Church of England.

By this time he had become a militant atheist, associated with Charles Bradlaugh and Annie Besant, the famous and flamboyant

leaders of the secularist cause; indeed, it was not long before he was
Annie Besant's lover. Secularism rather than socialism was then his
main interest. However, after his meeting with Eleanor he naturally
got to know more about socialism, of which he soon became an ardent
adherent. Mrs Besant was outraged. In December 1883 she wrote in
the *National Reformer*, the paper she ran with Bradlaugh: 'My name
is being used by a Miss Eleanor Marx . . . to give authority to a gross
and scandalous libel on Dr Edward Aveling. . . . Warning should
be given of strangers who try to creep into our movement with the
object of treacherously sowing discord therein.' To which Eleanor
responded, 'The reason for this – "lady's" animosity is not far to
seek. The one clear thinker and scientific student whose popularity
in the Secularist Party almost equals Mr Bradlaugh's – Dr Edward
Aveling, has joined the ranks of the Socialists, & Mrs Besant does
me the honour to make me responsible for this. I am very proud of
Dr Aveling's friendship for myself, but I hope I need not tell you that
his conversion to Socialism is due to a study of my Father's book and
not to me.'37

Clearly, despite his detractors, and however justified they might
be, there was something fascinating about Aveling, at least as far as
the opposite sex was concerned. His power over women seems to have
been little short of hypnotic. Hyndman wonderingly remarked on it:
'Aveling was one of those men who have an attraction for women quite
inexplicable to the male sex. Like Wilkes, ugly and even repulsive to
some extent, as he looked, he needed but half an hour's start of the
handsomest man in London.'38 The secret was perhaps not so very
mysterious. The combination of a powerful intellect with an intense
and no doubt flattering concentration upon the object of desire is a
potent one. Add to this that in Eleanor's case – and that of Mrs
Besant was not so very different – the number of men whom she
could seriously consider was limited, since politics was so important
to her that there could be no question of her taking seriously a man
who did not to a very large degree share her commitment. And it
was not only her political views that Aveling shared, or was coming
increasingly to share: her other great passion, the theatre, was also
shared by him. Like her, he would have liked to go on the stage,
but failing that, enjoyed amateur theatricals and recitations. They
were both keenly interested in the new drama; and Edward was

something of a playwright (though, as it turned out, not much of one).

But, more important perhaps than all of this, Eleanor was simply besotted with him. Later in life she told a young friend, 'My father used to say that I was more like a boy than a girl. It was Edward who really brought out the feminine in me. I was irresistibly drawn to him.'[39] As 1884 drew on, her letters were ever more thickly bespattered with references to 'Dr Aveling'. That spring they decided to set up house together, and by July they had found some suitable rooms in Great Russell Street, opposite the British Museum. The agreement was duly signed and the furniture moved in by 19 July; and at five in the morning of 24 July, happy in the knowledge that all arrangements had been made, Eleanor and Edward left London for Derbyshire.

2

Eleanor and Edward, staying at the Nelson Arms, were having an unaccustomed break from money worries. Both now devoted their best energies to political work. Edward no longer held his London Hospital lectureship and scraped a living where he could from coaching (for which he was always in demand) and odd lectures, looking forward, as he would continue to do for the rest of his life, to the day when a success on the West End stage would set him up financially. Eleanor earned small amounts doing typing and odd literary jobs, but work was scarce, and ill-paid when she could get it. Moreover, as far as supporting the household went, Edward, even when he had some money, contributed very little. His freedom with other people's money was legendary. According to Shaw, 'On the same day he would borrow sixpence from the poorest man within his reach on pretence of having forgotten his purse, and three hundred pounds from the richest to free himself from debts that he never paid. . . . Girl students would scrape money together to pay him in advance his fee for twelve lessons. The more fortunate ones got nothing worse for their money than letters of apology for breaking the lesson engagements. The others were seduced and had their microscopes appropriated.'[40]

However, Engels, with his usual generosity, had given them £50 towards their honeymoon, so now all they had to do was enjoy it. On 22 July 1884, Engels wrote to Laura: 'Of course, . . . [we] have been fully aware of what was going on for a considerable time and had a good laugh at these poor innocents who thought all the time that we had no eyes, and who did not approach the *quart d'heure de Rabelais* [the moment of confession] without a certain funk. However we soon got them over that. In fact had Tussy asked my advice before she leaped, I might have considered it my duty to expatiate upon the various possible and unavoidable consequences of this step, but when it was all settled, the best thing for them was to have it out at once before other people could take advantage of its being kept in the dark . . . I hope they will continue as happy as they seem now; I like Edward very much [Engels, almost uniquely, had and retained a high regard for Aveling] and think it will be a good thing for him to come more into contact with other people besides the literary and lecturing circle in which he moved; he has a good foundation of solid studies and felt himself out of place amongst the extremely superficial lot amongst whom fate had thrown him.'[41] To Eduard Bernstein, a fellow German socialist, he wrote: 'My London is a little Paris' – which Bernstein took (somewhat primly) to mean that 'A somewhat free conception of life had perhaps permeated certain circles of London society.'[42]

If this were so, it was certainly not that carefree abandonment of bourgeois shackles conjured up by Engels's phrase, but something much more self-conscious. Havelock Ellis, for instance, wrote: 'I do not recall hearing of Aveling's previous marriage at the time. I think we regarded the free union which was open and public as based on principle.'[43]

Principle: that was a key word for Ellis and his fellow idealists. It was (as we shall see) to dog his own marriage to Edith Lees. All their lives were constantly measured against principle, in no sphere more than that of marrying (or not marrying) and setting up house. When the Fabians Edward Pease and Marjorie Davidson became engaged, for example, such questions were at the forefront of their minds. 'We want to know what is the right thing to do and how to do it,' wrote Marjorie to Shaw. 'All suggestions from the elect are thankfully received.' Some time later she was more specific: 'We want to know what is the ideal Socialist home – I don't think we ought to have servants, but that is an open question.'[44]

Eleanor had her principles – none more so – but they were not quite those of Ellis, nor yet of Miss Davidson. Household help, even in those days, on the Aveling finances was out of the question; fine points as to its morality therefore never had to be confronted. As to the question of marriage or its absence, she was far from being a principled exponent of 'natural relations'. On the contrary, she bitterly regretted not being married, and made no bones about it. The solid bourgeois principles of the Marx family were not so easily shed. Her assumption was always that the only reason Edward did not marry her was because he could not, and that should his wife's death ever set him free he would naturally do so. His family was less sanguine: his brother Frederick told her 'long before Bell died, that at Bell's death Edward would not marry her'.[45] As it was, Bell was very much alive and Eleanor had to make the best of a bad job. From London and Derbyshire she wrote (as Engels had advised) to her friends, informing them of the situation before malicious gossips should spread the news for her. 'I need not say that this resolution has been no easy one for me to arrive at,' she told Laura. 'But I think it is for the best. I should be *very* anxious to hear from you. Do not misjudge us – he is very good – and you must not think too badly of either of us.'[46]

To her oldest and closest friend, Dollie Radford, she wrote: 'My very dear Dollie, I had half intended to tell you this morning what my "plans" I spoke of are – but somehow it is easier to write – and it is perhaps fairer to you, because you can think over what I am going to tell you. Well then this is it – I am going to live with Edward Aveling as his wife. You know he is married, and that I cannot be his wife *legally*, but it will be a *true* marriage to me – just as much as if a dozen registrars had officiated . . . E. had not *seen* his wife for many, many years when I met him, and that he was not unjustified in leaving her you will best understand when I tell you that Mr Engels, my father's oldest friend, and Helen [Helene Demuth, the old Marx family housekeeper, now keeping house for Engels] who has been as a mother to us, approve of what I am about to do – and are *perfectly* satisfied. I do not want to talk about this *yet*, for the simple reason that I want to be with Edward before we make the matter public. In three weeks we are going away for some little time – I only need rest – and then, of course, everyone will know – indeed we intend to let everyone we care about know. When we return we shall set up housekeeping together, and if love, a perfect sympathy in taste and work and a striving for the same ends can make people happy, we shall be so. – I have already told a few very dear friends, and so I want you to make up your minds as to what you will do. I shall *quite* understand if you think the position one you cannot accept, and shall think of you both with no less affection if we do not any longer count you among our immediate friends.' And to Mrs Hubert Bland (the novelist E. Nesbit), another friend from socialist circles, she wrote: 'I feel it is only right that before I avail myself of your very kind invitation I should make my present position quite clear to you. The reason why I have not been to see you – and it required a great deal of self-sacrifice to keep away – and why I have not pressed you to come to me was simply that I would not do so till I could tell you frankly and honestly about the step that I have just taken . . . I need not say it was not lightly taken or that I have overlooked the difficulties of the position. But on this question I have always felt very strongly, and I could not now in fact shrink from doing what I have always said and what I distinctly feel to be right. I also feel that you and others may think differently' – scruples which in the case of the Blands, whose own married life was notoriously irregular, were somewhat ironic. And there were other letters in this vein.[47]

Eleanor need not have worried, on this account at least. 'Everyone *almost* has been *far* kinder than I ever expected,' she told Laura. From now on she was generally known as Mrs Aveling, and signed herself 'Eleanor Marx Aveling'. As she so constantly reiterated, she certainly considered herself married; one may even surmise that the fact of not being legally married, of being united to Aveling 'only' by principles – as though principles were not always, in the case of people like Eleanor, stronger and more important than mere law – tied her to him even more strongly than marriage lines would have done.

Olive Schreiner set off for Derbyshire unperturbed by worries of this kind. Olive, as we have seen, had grown up quite outside Eleanor's world of accepted social conventions. Cut adrift from her family emotionally at the age of ten and forced to support herself since she was fifteen, she had, unlike her friend, no experience of either the pleasures or the constraints of family life, except as viewed from the outside. Her experience of life had been something almost unimaginable to the sheltered daughters of Europe. By the time she was seventeen she had been engaged, to a Mr Julius Gau, and traumatically disengaged, and had then departed for an encampment at a place called New Rush (later Kimberley) in the newly discovered diamond fields, where her second brother Theo was hoping, as everyone there hoped, to find a big stone and get rich quick. Here Olive and her sister Ettie kept house, or rather tent, while the men dug their claims. In April 1873, just after her eighteenth birthday, when she had been at New Rush just four months, Olive wrote to her eldest sister Catherine that 'we have just had a reed enclosure put up all round our encampment which will shelter us nicely from the cold winds and dust . . . Theo has not been finding much lately and diamonds are still very low in price but we hope they may soon rise as so many people are leaving for the Gold Fields; every day waggons start for them . . . I have just been out in the Town to see a large diamond of 159 carats which was found yesterday by a Mr Hully. He hopes to get at least £4000 for it as it is a beautiful stone. I wonder when our turn for a big one will come, soon I hope. If Theo gets a *very large* one he has promised to send me to America to study at one of the large colleges that they have there for ladies. It is the great wish of my life and I hope that it is destined to be realized one of these days.'[48] But it was not; two years later she was writing to the same sister from another governessing post: 'I have quite given up all idea of going to America. Getting a salary of thirty pounds a year I might save till I was eighty before I had got enough to take me there.'[49]

No; anything Olive wanted she was going to have to find for herself, and that included intellectual stimulation. Since she was a very little child she had been in the habit of making up stories, and now she began writing them down. By April 1878 she was writing to Mrs Erilda Cawood, whose children she later taught and whose lifelong friend she remained, 'You say you wish it had been my own engagement I wrote to tell you of. You will never hear of that. The power of loving has burnt itself out in me; not in the widest sense, for I don't think I ever cared for so many people as I do now. But no one will ever absorb me and make me lose myself utterly, and unless someone did I should never marry. In fact I am married now, to my books! I love them better every day, and find them more satisfying. I would not change lots with anyone in the world, and my old sorrows look very foolish to me now.'[50]

In a sense this letter represents the key to Olive's life. It was the moment of bliss, the magical time to which she always later sought vainly to return, living in a place she loved and working happily and successfully at her books. This would always mean much more to her than any relationship with any man. Not that there was ever any lack of men in Olive's life: the combination of her shining intellect, her vivacity and her small, plump, pretty person was understandably attractive (especially so when allied to the degree of fame, or notoriety, which she was to experience after the publication of *The Story of an African Farm*).

The letter also shows why the Woman Question loomed very large in Olive's life, larger than in her friend Eleanor's. For Eleanor, brought up at the epicentre of the socialist movement, the fate of women was unjust, certainly, but its redressing was simply one part of that great redressing which would happen when the wider aims of socialism were achieved. She could never feel very much sympathy with the principal embodiment of women's protest in British political life, namely, the suffragette movement, which simply wished slightly to extend the vote – from property-owning males to property-owning males and females as well. Universal adult suffrage would take care of all that, and as women took their place in the wider struggle, so it would take care of them.

But for Olive, forced to work out her own principles from the beginning, the whole thing was on a much less theoretical level. She could never forget – how could she? – the difference the mere chance of being born a woman had made to her life. If she had been a man, how easy, or at any rate how much easier, her life would have been! She was brilliantly clever and, as she later showed, a consummate natural politician. Her younger brother Will, who was much less clever than she was, still made it to the Prime Ministership of Cape Province. But as a woman she was given no education, she could never go into politics – she couldn't even vote. Yet there were so many things she wanted to say and do! One possibility was to find a suitable man and work through him. (At one point, as we shall see, Cecil Rhodes seemed to be a likely candidate for this role.) But such men were not commonly found in the backveldt. So she would have to find her own way of saying what she wanted said, and getting what she wanted done. And the only way to do that was to act like a man – to live and work on her own terms. But she was not a man. She wanted to travel, and did travel – but because she was a woman, travelling alone was not easy. Money was short, but it was hard for a woman, even one as intelligent as Olive, to earn money in any acceptable way. Because, being a girl, she had been given no education, she could not be a doctor. She did not particularly want to marry, but neither did she particularly want to be celibate. But quite apart from the dangers to reputation and health if she took lovers – not to speak of pregnancy – there were difficulties even in receiving men friends. She necessarily lived in lodgings while she was on her travels, which meant she necessarily had to deal with landladies; and this in turn meant that she had little privacy, while her freedom as to whom she might or might not receive in her room was much curtailed. 'This afternoon Rider Haggard and Philip Marston called,' she wrote on one occasion to Ellis, when she was living in London after their return from Derbyshire. 'I had such a dreadful time. In the middle of the visit my landlady burst open the door in a rage . . . After they were gone the two women turned on me and stormed. They asked me if I had so many men always coming after me. Then they said they were much insulted that I hadn't asked them to come in and introduce them. I began to cry.'[51]

And these were merely social calls; any such difficulties would be compounded when it came to spending a whole week together with Ellis. For whatever their relation was, it was very soon clear that it was not merely social.

Olive, by the time she met Ellis, had had a not inconsiderable amount of sexual experience. It is possible that she had been seduced by or (more likely, considering her personality) willingly had sex with the mysterious Julius Gau. Certainly he retained a hold upon her imagination for many years; when she heard once that he might be coming to England, many years after their last meeting, she was tempted to go to Southampton to see if she could catch a glimpse of him coming off the boat. Later, while she was staying with her brother Fred in the Isle of Wight, there seems to have been a lover. She told Ellis that he had promised to come and spend a week with her during the holidays, but had never turned up; she had 'feared to go out of the house lest *he* should come when she was away'. She said, 'I would like *him* to tread on me and stamp me fine into powder.'[52] Here, perhaps, is some clue as to why she burst into tears on first meeting Ellis in the flesh. Clearly Olive liked being dominated, and Ellis, as was instantly apparent on meeting him, was the least dominating man in the world. Although he was tall and well-built his voice was high and thin, and his manner, as everyone who met him testified, very gentle; he himself remarks more than once on the passivity of his temperament. It was a terrible disappointment to her, the more so as they had by the time they met discovered that their view of life and interests were remarkably similar – 'My view of Socialism is exactly yours. I sympathize with it, but when I see the works and aims of the men who are working for it in London, my heart sinks,' she wrote.[53] Ellis was at that time secretary of a group called the Fellowship of the New Life, which held that the only way to socialism was through the betterment of individuals within themselves, and that political action was secondary to this and useless without it. The fledgling Fabian Society broke away from this group on account of what it considered this mistaken order of priorities, feeling that nothing would be achieved without political action. As Shaw put it, they intended 'the one to sit among the dandelions, the other to organise the docks'.

But Olive, like Ellis, was more interested in probing the moral causes of the present unsatisfactory state of things than in mundanely organizing for change. And it was not only on an intellectual plane that Olive's expectations were being built up, but also sexually. Almost all their letters at this time discussed sexual matters, mostly around the topic of Ellis's then great hero, James Hinton.

The ever more open and widespread discussion of sex, as Michel Foucault has pointed out, was one of the great cultural and political phenomena of the nineteenth century. At one level it represented the advance of the notion of the importance of the individual: Foucault talks about the *'deployment of sexuality'* which imposed itself upon, and helped to reduce the power of, the traditional *'deployment of alliance'* in Western society. 'The "right" to life, to one's body, to health, to happiness, to the satisfaction of needs, and beyond all the oppressions or "alienations," the "right" to rediscover what one is and all that one can be, this "right" – which the classical juridical system was utterly incapable of comprehending – was the political response to all [the] new procedures of power.'[54]

These rights were precisely what most concerned Olive and Ellis –

and, in his own bizarre way, Hinton. Part of the revelation Ellis had experienced through reading Hinton in Australia was the realization of how he personally could best go about helping people achieve these rights – in his case, by helping them to accept and recognize their sexual selves and those of others. Qualifying as a doctor was a mere necessary step along this road, which for him thereafter had the status of a quasi-divine vocation. For both Ellis and Olive the personal and the political were deeply intertwined, and their early letters are about this and about those authors who most closely express these feelings: namely Hinton and the newly-discovered – because only newly translated into English – Norwegian, Ibsen. 'Have you read a little work called *Nora* [later *A Doll's House*] by Ibsen, translated from the Swedish [*sic*] by Frances Lord? It is a most wonderful little work . . . It shows some sides of a woman's nature that are not often spoken of, and that some people do not believe exist – but they do,'[55] wrote Olive to Ellis at the very start of their friendship. Ellis had his reservations about it, as Olive had feared he might. 'With regard to *Nora*, I think Ibsen *does* see the other side of the question, but in a book which is a work of art, and not a mere philosophical dissertation, it is not *possible* to show all the sides,' she protested ten days later.[56] Ibsen was to become something of a totem for this group, a spokesman for their ideals much as Hinton was for Ellis. Judging by the date of Olive's first reference to him, it was she whose attention was first drawn to Frances Lord's translation – perhaps because it was clear from *African Farm* that she would be in sympathy with what he was saying. She then introduced his work to Eleanor, who in turn brought it to Shaw's attention, with far-reaching effects on his dramatic work. The Avelings and Shaw organized several readings of Ibsen plays at this time when they were quite unknown in England.

For Olive's part, after an early enthusiasm for Hinton, she cooled towards him somewhat. 'I have loved the man himself. In his feeling for women he *is* like Jesus but like few other men,' she wrote apropos of Hinton's declaration that 'Jesus was the Saviour of men, but I am the Saviour of women, and I don't envy him a bit.' That was on 8 April.[57] But by 21 May she was not so sure about him. 'I have so much to say about Hinton and Hinton's views (I have some questions to ask too) that I shan't try and say it to-day. . . . Hinton says much . . . that I have thought and felt but *never* seen expressed before; but, I think, I see what he does not see, and where his theory utterly breaks down. Did he apply the same measures to man and to woman? Would he have been satisfied if his wife had had six "spiritual husbands"?' she pertinently enquired,[58] referring to one of Hinton's most controversial teachings, namely, that it was not wrong – was, indeed, a thoroughly good thing – for a man to make the most of natural pleasures by sleeping with women who were not his wife. This was a teaching which both Hinton and his son Howard followed, with sometimes scandalous consequences; and there is indeed no record of either Mrs James or Mrs Howard Hinton ever having done likewise – both, on the contrary, showing a marked preference for solid respectability.

Talking about such things constantly, as they did, clarified their feelings. But of course it did more than that. Talking about sex with someone to whom you are attracted is exciting, as well as, or because of, being a more or less indirect statement. (Foucault makes the point that the West, never having had any equivalent to the East's *ars erotica*, was at this time developing a *scientia sexualis*, a discourse about sex which was not only informative but also a sort of erotic art in itself: 'The learned volumes, written and read; the consultations and examinations; the anguish of answering questions and the delights of having one's words interpreted; all the stories told to oneself and others, so much curiosity, so many confidences offered in the face of scandal, sustained – but not without trembling a little – by the obligation of truth; the profusion of secret fantasies and the dearly paid right to whisper them to whoever is able to hear them; in short, the formidable "pleasure of analysis" . . . which the West has cleverly been fostering for several centuries: all this constitutes something like the errant fragments of an erotic art that is secretly transmitted by confession and the science of sex.'[59] Ellis, of course, was to become one of the leaders in the development of this new science.) By the time they met Olive, at any rate, was tuned to a pitch of high sexual excitement, which the person of Ellis could not but let down. ('On my side,' he recalled, 'there was neither depression nor exaltation.'[60]) 'Don't you think there must *always* be some sense of pain in learning to know more of people whom you have known only through their books?' she wrote him at about this time.[61]

The sense of let-down passed, however, and soon Olive and Ellis were going everywhere together. Olive took rooms in Fitzroy Square, not far from where the Avelings were then living. Ellis had already met Eleanor at the Progressive Association, yet another society for social betterment whose programme of lectures he helped arrange. 'Our meetings were held at the Islington Hall (where also, I believe, the Parnellite members of Parliament habitually met in secret conclave), whither I would every Sunday faithfully make the dreary journey from my home in the south of London. Before the meeting we would distribute handbills and notices in the neighbouring streets, and during the meeting my place was at a table near the door to answer inquiries and enroll new members. It was here that, one Sunday evening, perhaps early in 1884, I first met Eleanor Marx. She had dropped in for a short time but could not stay. I can still see her, with the radiant face and the expansive figure, seated on the edge of my secretarial table, though I recall nothing that was said.'[62]

Olive, and sometimes Ellis as well, spent occasional evenings with Eleanor and Edward, who no doubt urged them to come down and meet them in Derbyshire, where they were going to spend several weeks in the summer. Olive, already neurotically incapable of staying in any one place for more than a few weeks in her unending search for that nirvana where her asthma would leave her and she would be able to work, must have agreed, although Ellis, who had to take some exams in July, would only be able to join her there for a few days. From Buckinghamshire, where she had taken a cottage, she wrote: 'This place doesn't suit me at all. I want to find a place that is not low and damp. If I go to Derbyshire I think I shall feel glorious, like I used to in the Karroo. . . . If I go to Derbyshire, and you felt you cared to come into the country a bit, would that be too far for you to come?'[63]

3

Perhaps Havelock Ellis was the person who most enjoyed the Derbyshire honeymoon. Olive dazzled him. 'She was in some respects the most wonderful woman of her time, as well as its chief woman-artist in language, and that such a woman should be the first woman in the world I was to know by intimate revelation was an overwhelming fact. It might well have disturbed my balance, and for a while I was almost intoxicated by the experience,'[64] he wrote in his autobiography, with an inexactitude typical of that arch, unclear and generally unsatisfactory document.

'Intimate revelation' – but *what actually happened*? It is a question which has intrigued biographers of both Ellis and Schreiner – a not unreasonable question given his later professional concern with such topics. The general conclusion seems to be, nothing much, then or ever.

Clearly this was not by Olive's wish. She was not a frightened innocent, she was attracted to Ellis mentally but also physically, they talked and wrote continually about sex, and she made it perfectly clear what she wanted. In the letters she wrote him from Bole Hill, while she was waiting for him to come, the sex talk becomes even more direct. There is no more hiding behind Hinton. She tells him how her sexual feelings are strongest at the time of her period, and how she is at her best mentally towards the end of this time and just after – Eleanor feels the same. Does Ellis ever observe 'the interaction of your manly upon your mental nature. I should like to know the man's side of the question . . . Look at the effects of celibacy on monks and hermits etc.!'[65] She was nervous of letting herself become too involved. 'Yet, when I get a letter, even like your little matter-of-fact note this morning, I feel: "But this thing is yourself." In that you are myself I love you and am near to you; in that you are a man I am afraid of you and shrink from you . . . I think of you like a tall angel, as you looked at the Progressive meeting.'[66]

She looked forward to his arrival, but there were difficulties. One concerned where they should stay. Bole Hill itself was lovely: 'This is a beautiful place and a delightful clean little cottage of four rooms on the side of a hill overlooking the little tiny town of Wirksworth. It is perhaps not so pretty as some parts of Derbyshire may be, but to me who have longed for my old hill life, it is delightful. One feels nearer God here.'[67] Unfortunately, God was not the only near neighbour. There were also the Avelings; and while Olive had come to Bole Hill partly to be near her friend Eleanor, this also meant being near Edward, whom she was coming more and more to dislike. It is hard to know whether this was purely personal or on account of the bad effect he seemed to Olive to be having on Eleanor – probably the two could not be separated. Eleanor and Olive were intimate friends; they loved and respected each other, and Olive could not bear to see the way in which Eleanor, at what should have been the joyous start of her new quasi-marriage, was already sunk in misery – or so it seemed to Olive. 'Dr Aveling and Miss Marx have just come to see me. She is now to be called Mrs Aveling,' she wrote on 24 July. 'I was glad to see her face. I love her. But she looks so miserable.' By 2 August, these observations had solidified into a growing dislike for Aveling: 'I have so many plans about your coming, and don't know which will be best. You see at Bole Hill it is nice, and in some ways I want so much to be there, but the Avelings being at Middleton makes it all different. I am beginning to have such a *horror* of Aveling, other-self. To say I dislike him doesn't express it at all, I have a fear, a horror of him when I am near. Every time I see him this shrinking grows stronger. Now you see, when I am at Bole Hill they come *every day* to see me. We shouldn't be much alone, and we have so many things to talk about. . . . It may be the last time we are together, certainly for months, perhaps for years. I have to stick to my book till the winter (and I don't know that I shall have it ready by November). [This was *From Man to Man*, which she never finished to her satisfaction: it was published posthumously.] Then I shall have to go to the South of France or at nearest to Ventnor, and if we are at Wirksworth the Avelings will be always with us. I love her, but *he* makes me so unhappy. He is so selfish, but that doesn't account for the feeling of dread . . . I had it when I first saw him. I fought it down for Eleanor's sake, but here it is stronger than ever.'[68]

As it turned out, Olive and Ellis spent far more time alone together than in company with the Avelings, and although they did leave Bole Hill after a week, the Avelings had by that time left for London. ('I have an "intuition" that they are in trouble,' Olive noted dolefully.[69] 'I heard later,' Ellis remembered, 'that Aveling, who had lived freely at the inn and ordered drinks without stint, had quietly decamped without settling the bill.'[70]) Ellis's journal of this interlude records a first quiet week at Bole Hill, for all but the first night of which he had the room next to Olive's at her cottage, the landlady of which was a Mrs Walker. Then Mrs Walker declared that lodging both of them was too much trouble, and they moved on, spent a night in Bakewell and another week at Cromford, near Matlock. The introspection which characterizes their letters went remorselessly on in the pages of the journal, which he kept and in which she added her own comments.

'Last night we were both sad and cried,' he records in Cromford.
'Olive felt as if it was wrong to be near me. She said that she thought
that "some day you will *really* care for someone, and then you will
think this impure." I think that that chiefly made me feel so miserable
because it was not understanding. But that was the only time . . . This
morning I was near to her and I feel happier and I know she feels near
to me. It was morbid [a favourite word of Ellis's] to be like that last
night. We are going to work today. That will be better.' They ate a
great deal of Derbyshire cream, which made Olive so sick on the day
Ellis was supposed to return to London that he put off his departure
for a day to be with her. 'I kissed away her tears and left her in bed
in that front bedroom of Mrs Walker's at Bole Hill. She came to the
window and we sent kisses to each other as long as I could see her as
I walked away. That indistinct white-clad figure at the window is the
vision that remains in my mind. It is like the last vision before she left
London – the white figure in the dark leaning over the foot of the bed
with outstretched arms – only this time there was less passion, more
tenderness on Olive's part; I had not so much to *tear* myself away. It
is not quite so sad as the parting in the back room in Fitzroy Street.
I have been *very* happy. I am quite satisfied. It is strange that such
little things can sometimes make us feel so satisfied and happy.'[71]

Was Olive, too, satisfied and happy? Physically, this seems unlikely.
The tone of the journal, which is scarcely a record of passionate abandon, is confirmed by Ellis's elliptical comment in his autobiography
(which was written many years later): 'As I left her one evening to
return home she raised her face up to me as we shook hands. [This was
while they were still in London.] I hesitated to realise the significance
of the gesture, and we parted. But on my next visit, when the moment
to part arrived, the gesture was more significantly repeated: she put
her arms round me and from that moment our relationship became
one of intimate and affectionate friendship. I hasten to add that it
scarcely passed beyond that stage.

'It is necessary to be precise. She possessed a powerfully and
physically passionate temperament which craved an answering impulse
and might even under other circumstances – for of this I could have no
personal experience – be capable of carrying her beyond the creed of
right and wrong which she herself fiercely held and preached. . . .
For a brief period at this early stage of our relationship there passed

before her the possibility of a relationship with me such as her own temperament demanded. But she swiftly realised that I was not fitted to play the part in such a relationship which her elementary primitive nature craved. I on my side recognised that she realised this and knew that the thought of marriage between us, which for one brief instant floated before my eyes, must be put aside. . . . We were not what can be technically, or even ordinarily, called lovers.'[72] In other words, Olive wanted the kind of relationship which is normal between lovers, especially at the exciting start of the affair, while he, for one reason or another, did not want this. Possibly he did not desire Olive strongly enough. This is what he implies: the passage just quoted follows almost immediately after one in which he describes his temperamental slowness either to form or act upon impulses, so that his peak of feeling (by implication) may be reached after his partner's is spent. As far as their emotional relationship goes, the record of their correspondence seems to indicate that this is indeed what happened. Olive made the running at first – if she had not done so, as she doubtless realized, nothing at all would have happened. As it was, not very much (in sexual terms) did, although they did, for about a year, maintain a very close emotional intimacy: Olive liked to call Ellis her 'other self'. 'It seems to me such a wonderful and sweet thing that you should have come into my life,' she wrote in September from Derbyshire, after he had returned to London.[73] And a little later, in November, 'My boy, my own, for so many years I have longed to meet a mind that should understand me, that should take away from the loneliness of my life. Now I have found it.'[74]

Just after that they had another mildly physical interlude at St Leonard's, on the south coast, where she was now staying. He noted in his journal: 'Yesterday evening we read together some of her old journals etc. I was very happy. I had never felt so near her. She had never felt so near me. . . . Just before leaving this afternoon I made her feel very sweet – it was a sudden impulse which I had never felt towards anyone before. Ever since she left London a month ago I have felt more or less sad in many ways just as I used to before 1879 in Australia. It has given me pain to think much of Olive. It would be good for me to see her oftener; that helps to produce – not less love – but a kind of more healthy indifference. I mean an absence of morbid hypersensitiveness.'[75]

Referring to what seems to be that same weekend in his autobiography he records, in his bizarre, impersonal way, 'I see her in her rooms at Hastings where I had come to spend the week-end with her, bringing at her desire my student's microscope, for she wished to observe living spermatozoa, which there was no trouble in obtaining to place under the cover glass for her inspection, and I see her interest in their vigorous motility.'[76] Were they so intimate that he could happily masturbate in front of her?

At any rate, the vigour of the sperm provided an undeniable contrast with the passivity of their provider. It was a situation which might satisfy him but could never be enough for the 'elemental, primitive' Olive. Two years later, while he loved her as much as ever and still dreamed of marrying her, she wrote to him, contrasting his nature with her own: 'When I want to go to Trafalgar Square and fight the enemies of Freedom of the hour wildly and get my head broken, *you* say I am a fool, and you are *right*. . . . The man who sits quietly in his study, writing and working out a great scientific truth, while his little petty state is going to pieces, is greater, more human, more moral than one who, like myself, would rush out wildly and fight. *You* of all people I ever met . . . are a man of the study and nothing else. You are perfectly dead on the other side, *that* is your weakness and your strength. That is why you will do great and useful work in the world. The world is *crashing* about you, and you sit grubbing out whether an old English dramatist put two dots over his *i*. Your dearest friends are being dragged to prison, theories you have been interested in are being practically tested, cruel and wicked wrong is being done to innocent little children – and you look with astonishment and disapproval at another when you come to see them and they are not untouched by it! . . . Your very medical work you only undertake under compulsion and necessity; give you £200 a year and you would curl yourself up in abstract study and thought for the rest of your life.' Olive ended the letter, 'I know that there is a little to be said in favour of the practical side of my nature, but the side of my nature that is like yours is the most valuable side.'[77] But the afterthought is unconvincing. This is an aggressive personal attack, and what she is attacking is that part of Ellis which she found, literally, so unsatisfactory, or unsatisfying. 'If I marry,' she was later to tell her friend Edward Carpenter, 'it'll be . . . a man compared to whom I shall be a sort of saint!!! A sort of small Napoleon! . . . *Not* the man of thought and fine-drawn feelings like . . . Ellis . . . but the wish to marry comes towards the man of *action*, the philistine, with me.'[78]

This self-knowledge was one facet of that almost obsessive self-absorption which was the pivot of Olive's life. It is easy to see how this arose from the grim necessity of her childhood: there had never been anyone else prepared to take such an interest in her. Unlike most women, Olive always did what she perceived to be necessary for *herself* at any one time. Such an attitude is of course not unusual in men – indeed, it is true of all the men we shall meet in the course of this book. But most women's lives, determined rather than self-determining, do not admit of it. Why this should be so was and remains the nub of the Woman Question. Allied as it was in Olive to tremendous ability and a determination, then and still unusual in women, to realize her professional ambitions – which were, as she saw it, the most important part of herself – it perhaps accounts for the undoubted fascination she exercised over not only the men but also over many of the women she met. In the end her ambitions were mostly unfulfilled, and her life was not a very happy one; but it was obvious to the end that she was quite different from other women.

This difference was already apparent very early in her life. It is evidenced by an extraordinary letter written to her by her friend Mrs Cawood in 1879, when Olive was twenty-four. Olive had just left the Cawood household, where she had for a while been acting as governess to the many Cawood children. 'My dear Olive,' wrote Mrs Cawood, 'I have the less reluctance to write as I do now; because I think, from what you know of me, you are quite prepared for what I have to say. I no longer love you, and cannot act hypocritically. If you needed friends, I could not have allowed my heart to turn against you. You are rich in intellectual, influential friends. And I am quite sure you only valued my acquaintance because you thought I loved you. And I have *loved* you, at times with an almost idolatrous love. I have sometimes felt it in my heart to say, Olive Schreiner, I love you so, that for your sake I could become anything. That is why God in his goodness and wisdom used you as a means to show me what an awful soul-destroying thing freethinking is. You know, I have often told you I can only learn through my affections.

'I must tell you I am not alone in what I now feel. Richard and

I have both, while pointing out to the children that they owe you gratitude, told them that you are God's enemy and that they cannot love God and you at the same time. I tell you this, so that you shall be spared the pain and humiliation of expecting more from them, than they have been taught to give.'[79]

Olive replied to this terrible letter with great courage and restraint. 'We cannot help love's going, any more than we can help its coming,' she assured Mrs Cawood.[80] (In fact the two were reconciled and remained friends throughout their lives.) But it seems clear from the letter that the free-thinking was only an excuse. What Mrs Cawood really feared – for this letter is filled with fear – was perhaps the emotional thrall in which she felt Olive held her. She sensed Olive's irresistible magnetism and was terribly, unbearably envious of her, even though to all appearances, and certainly to herself, Olive, a penniless, isolated governess, must have seemed the most unenviable of women.

Part of what Mrs Cawood felt so sharply was undoubtedly also the contrast between her own ordinariness and Olive's extraordinariness. But other women much more extraordinary than Mrs Cawood were also irresistibly drawn to Olive. One of them was Eleanor Marx. In 1885, nearly a year after the joint honeymoon, she wrote what was almost a love-letter to Olive, in a moment of deep depression – one of many – when Aveling had left her alone in order to dine out.

My Olive, I wonder if I bore you with my stupid letters – as I wonder if, one of these days, you will get horribly tired of me altogether. This is no 'figure of speech'. I really *do* wonder, or rather fear. I have such a terror of losing your love. I have such a strong feeling, borne of a pretty large experience, that to care over much for a thing is to make sure of losing it. I think of you, and one or two other real friends, in an agony of fear and doubt. Silly perhaps, but so it is, and I can't pretend to you to be better, or stronger, than I am. I keep wanting to hear you *say* you love me just a little. You do not know, Olive, how my whole nature craves for love. And since my parents died I have had so little *real* – i.e. pure, unselfish love. If you had ever been in our home, if you had ever seen my father and mother, known what *he* was to me, you would understand better both my yearning for love, given and received, and my intense need of sympathy. Of my father I was so sure! For long miserable years there was a shadow between us – I must tell you the whole story some day (if it will not be too much worry for you) – yet our love was always the same, and despite everything, our faith and trust in each other. My mother and I loved each other passionately, but she did not know me as my father did. One of the bitterest of many bitter sorrows in my life is that my mother died thinking, despite all our love, that I had been hard and cruel, and never guessing that to save her and father sorrow I had sacrificed the best, freshest years of my life. But father, though he did not *know* till just before the end, felt he must trust me – our natures were so exactly alike! . . . except that I shall never be good and unselfish, as he was. I am *not* good – never shall be, though I try, harder than even you can think, to be so. There is too much of the devil in me. It is the consciousness that I am not good that makes me fear often that when you know me more you will tire of me. . . . If I dared to I should have gone off to you this evening. Edward is dining with Quilter and went off in the highest of spirits because several ladies are to be there (and it just occurs to me you may be one! How odd that would be!) and I am alone, and while in some sense I am relieved to be alone, it is also very terrible; I can't help thinking and remembering, and then the solitude is more than I can bear. I would give anything just now to be near you. You can always help me and give me *rest* – and I am so tired, Olive. The *constant* strain of appearing the same when nothing *is* the same, the constant effort not to break down, becomes intolerable. How natures like Edward's . . . are to be envied, who in an hour completely forget anything. If you had seen him, for example, today, going about like a happy child with never a sorrow or sin in his life, you would have marvelled. Yet apart even from all the other troubles, we have mere money troubles enough to worry an ordinary man or woman into the grave. I often don't know where to turn or what to do. It is almost impossible for me now to get work that is even decently paid for, and Edward gets little enough. And while I feel utterly desperate he is perfectly unconcerned! It is a continual source of wonder to me. I do not grow used to it, but always feel equally astounded at his absolute incapacity to feel anything – unless he is personally incommoded by it – for twenty-four consecutive hours. . . . We, into whose hearts joy and sorrow sink more deeply, are better off after all. With all the pain and sorrow – and not even you, my Olive, know quite how unhappy I am, it is better to have these stronger feelings than to have practically no feelings at all. . . . Write me a line in case I do not see you to-morrow or the next day. Just one line – say you love me. That will be such a joy, it will help me get through the long, miserable days, and longer, more miserable nights, with less heavy a heart.[81]

Various things emerge from this long, sad outpouring. One is the importance of Eleanor's relation to her father (she seems to have exaggerated the strength of the bond between her and her mother). It is hard to imagine any man measuring up satisfactorily to such an ideal. This is perhaps the price daughters pay who have known the delight of a close bond with an outstanding father. It was certainly true of another such woman in Eleanor's close circle of friends, May Morris, William Morris's daughter. But of course Edward Aveling was, by any standards, an unhappy choice. It is clear that Eleanor no longer had any illusions about the nature of her chosen partner. This was perhaps the low point in Eleanor's life with Aveling (until the very lowest point, which came at the end). Shaw, in his diary, recorded, 'Rumour of split between the Avelings'.[82] That was the signal for Shaw, who had been maintaining a close friendship with Mrs Aveling in the security of her being safely attached to someone else, to sheer off; thus setting the pattern for a habit of triangular friendship, or 'Sunday husbanding', among his married friends which was to endure until his own marriage in 1898. There were to be many dissatisfied wives who fancied themselves as undyingly appreciated by as they were appreciative of the witty Irishman, only to be dropped as soon as things threatened to turn serious. (Next on the list after Eleanor was to be that very Mrs Bland, later known as the children's novelist E. Nesbit, whose approval Eleanor had been so eager to secure for her union with Aveling; Shaw was also interested at this time in Annie Besant and May Morris.) But in Eleanor's case Shaw need not have worried. Eleanor could never seriously consider leaving Edward. Marriage in her book was for life, whatever the legal status:

once she had committed herself, that was that. There was a way out, and that way she would finally take. Ellis, to whom Olive passed Eleanor's letter just quoted, recalled an unsuccessful suicide attempt when she took an overdose of opium, when 'by administering much strong coffee and making her walk up and down the room the effects of the poison were worked off. I never knew what special event in her domestic life it was which led to this attempt. Her friends were grieved; they were scarcely surprised.'[83]

It is impossible to imagine Olive, self-centred as she was, allowing her life to be ruined and herself to be used in this way, and perhaps it was this, together with the ideals and outlook which they so strongly shared, which constituted Olive's attraction for Eleanor. For such an attraction there clearly was. Yvonne Kapp, Eleanor's biographer, assumes that Olive's real inclinations were lesbian, and that the secret lay there. But although she had close friendships with some women and was deeply concerned with the position of women in the world, her letters are thickly scattered with phrases showing how little she liked women in general, and they abound with evidence of a strong heterosexual drive.

For both these women, though, their work was as important to them as any personal relationship (Eleanor's work being not the miserable hacking for which she was paid such a pittance, but her political work among the newly organizing trades unions and the various national and international socialist parties). Had either of them had children, their priorities might have been more divided. As things stood, this shared sense of what was important, so rare among women then, no doubt bound them closely together; a closeness amplified by the sense of priorities they also shared with regard to sex and marriage. There were so few women who shared their particular outlook and experiences, and with whom the kind of friendship which bound them together was possible. Certainly, as Olive was to find out only too soon, it was not possible to maintain such a friendship with a man, however hard she might try.

Eleanor's early fears that the irregularity of her arrangement with Aveling would lead to social estrangement turned out to be unfounded. But, as Ellis (and many other people) remarked, the union 'tended to separate her from her friends. They were, for the most part, not conventional enough to be repelled by the informal nature of the union, but they were disinclined to associate with Aveling.'[84] As for Ellis himself, nobody could have seemed more different from the appalling Edward. Olive, at the end of one of the many letters she wrote him at this time, both claiming him and pushing him away, wrote, 'Take care of that sweet old body that I can love so. There's a long, beautiful life and much love waiting for my boy somewhere, far away.'[85]

OLIVE SCHREINER AND THE NEW MEN

Somewhere; but not with Olive. Their relationship had never been balanced. At the start, it was Olive who had wanted Havelock more than he wanted her. 'I envy you sometimes because you have drunk deeply of the cups that I have, for the most part, been satisfied with sipping. But I know that I am satisfied,' he wrote early in their acquaintance.[1] It was the same at the end of the Derbyshire excursion: he did feel, but not so strongly as she. 'I feel as you do about a physical feeling towards each other. At least I think so,' he wrote after he had returned to London, but while she still remained in Derbyshire. 'I should have felt more as you do, if you had felt less so.'[2] But as 1884 wore on, Olive began to draw back. Was this really love that she felt for her 'own boy Harry'? 'I *assumed* that your impulse to come over to me was strong enough to make it right for you – whether it was passionate or not (I did not ask myself whether it was that or not),' he wrote uneasily. 'You used to say so often that the form of love without the feeling was the one impurity that I took for granted that you cared enough to make it right for you.'[3] And soon he began to feel that he had lost her: 'I never *feel* that you love me now. I say all sorts of things to myself intellectually, and I know how horrible I am to feel so, but my heart feels just as hungry and as aching as ever. Once I used to think you loved me too much. Now I never do.'[4] But the more he felt Olive did not love him, the more he found he loved and needed her. 'It doesn't trouble your serenity what ever I do but the *least* thing you do or say is everything to me';[5] 'Don't forsake me more than you can help, leave me a little bit of your heart.'[6]

Things had indeed changed, and the agent of their change, as once before in Havelock Ellis's life, was (though this time indirectly) James

Hinton. Hastings, where Olive was living during the last months of 1884, is not very far from Brighton; and at Brighton lived Caroline Haddon, Hinton's sister-in-law, who kept a girls' boarding school there. Olive had been introduced to Miss Haddon by Ellis; and now it was through Miss Haddon that she met Elisabeth Cobb.

Mrs Cobb was ten years older than Olive, and the picture of Victorian respectability. She was married to a merchant banker, and lived with him and their six children in the outer London suburb of Stanmore. But beneath this sternly respectable exterior the inner Mrs Cobb preserved her own aspirations, which were those not of a matriarch but of a free-thinking intellectual. And while the dutiful matriarch remained the devoted wife of the rich Henry Cobb, who hankered after a Parliamentary seat in the Liberal persuasion, the daring intellectual had found her ideal man: a young man by the name of Karl Pearson, who had just been appointed to the Chair of Applied Mathematics at University College, London.

Pearson came from a family of Yorkshire Quakers. He was a dazzlingly intelligent and very serious – indeed, it would seem almost completely humourless – young man. (He was two years younger than Olive: in 1885, when they first met, she was thirty, he was twenty-eight, while Mrs Cobb was then forty-one.) He had read and deeply admired the writings of Karl Marx, in whose honour (as well as in honour of German culture in general, of which he was a devotee) he had changed the spelling of his first name, and spent much of his free time in London lecturing to radical and revolutionary groups. However, as perhaps befitted a Professor of Mathematics, he inclined more towards theory than practice. His name (like that of Havelock Ellis, as it happened) was later to be associated with the study of eugenics; but at this time his interests, and those of his particular friends, were mainly concerned with the knotty question of the relations, actual and ideal, between the sexes, and in particular – as was almost inevitable – with the Woman Question. This group of friends, who included a lawyer, Robert Parker, later to become Lord Parker of Waddington, and two unmarried sisters of Mrs Cobb, Maria and Letitia Sharpe, felt in this connection that it was 'a great loss that men and women should discuss together all subjects except those most vitally important to both sexes alike'[7] and determined to found a group which *would*, precisely, discuss such topics. It was

to be called the Men and Women's Club, and was to consist of not
more than twenty hand-picked members among whom tricky topics
could be discussed with freedom and without embarrassment. At the
time Olive met Mrs Cobb, the latter was scouting around for suitable
prospective members for this select body.

It was not long before Olive and Mrs Cobb were meeting and
exchanging letters fairly regularly, and it was immediately clear that
Olive was just the kind of member the new discussion club needed.
Not only would she be quite a catch on account of her celebrity; her
interests were clearly centred on just the area that concerned Pearson,
Mrs Cobb and their friends, and, what was more, she was evidently
unembarrassable. By the time they had known each other a couple of
months, Olive was making the most intimate inquiries of Mrs Cobb,
for instance about the frequency with which she had sexual intercourse
– all on a purely scientific basis, naturally. 'I often think that a thing
quite as necessary as that women and men should understand and
know more of each other, is that women should know really and
understand more of each other, and each woman not be so much
shut up to generalising from her own single experience. When you
try to argue with men about many things they will turn round and
say, "Ah yes, that is all very well, but you are speaking for yourself,
most women do not feel or think so," etc. And one doesn't know
what to reply, does one?'[8]

To write such letters, ask such questions, came perfectly naturally
to Olive. They were the kinds of things she was used to discussing all
the time with such friends as Havelock Ellis and Eleanor Marx; why
not with Elisabeth Cobb, a married woman, a feminist, an advanced
thinker? But Mrs Cobb was not quite what she seemed.

What Olive was clearly hoping, as the tone of her letters shows, was
that she would be able to establish here another confidential friendship
between women, such as she had with Eleanor Marx. Not as close,
perhaps – Olive and Eleanor were united by similarities of age and
outlook which Mrs Cobb could not share – but similarly without
false modesty, and genuinely confidential. The relief and pleasure to
be gained from such a friendship, as Olive and Eleanor both found,
was enormous.

The first prerequisite of this sort of intimacy is that the friends'
first loyalty, at least in such matters as concern themselves and their

confidences, is to each other. This, in Olive's view, did not occur very frequently among women. She did not much like women; her correspondence is studded with references to this dislike of women generally and middle-class women in particular – she thought they were 'wicked and mean and jealous'.[9] But to this generalization, as to all such generalizations, there were exceptions. Olive was always hoping that her relations with Elisabeth Cobb would prove to be such an exception. She tried to treat Mrs Cobb as though this were indeed so – but without ever being quite sure that it *was* so. There was always an ambivalence. This ambivalence was in fact perfectly justified. Mrs Cobb's first concern, even within the terms of their friendship, was never with Olive, but with Karl Pearson.

By the time she met Olive, Mrs Cobb had known Pearson for some years, and – as her letters to him make clear – she was obsessed with him. Her life as a suburban matron did not fulfil her; she wanted something more than her husband or children were able or willing to supply. In Pearson, brilliant, outspoken, young, good-looking, unattached, she saw the embodiment of her ideal. Naturally this was never made explicit. But she could not deny herself the pleasure of writing him letters – voluminous letters full of gossip and personalities as well as generalized high-flown sentiment and intellectualizing. And of course the formation of the new discussion club gave a new impetus to this correspondence, in which Olive figured prominently.

For Mrs Cobb this new friendship had particular advantages, the main one being that it was a legitimate source of spicy gossip with which to regale Karl Pearson. She had her reservations about Olive, and did not hesitate to convey these to Pearson. When Olive asked her about sexual intercourse, for example, she certainly responded; but she also wrote to Pearson remarking (in a phrase reminiscent of Beatrice Potter's view of Eleanor Marx) that Olive 'has much more varied experience of men than most women, I doubt if she believes in marriage at all'.[10]

Despite, or perhaps because of this slight sense of titillation, Pearson expressed his wish to meet the interesting Miss Schreiner. Mrs Cobb was delighted to arrange a meeting, but not before she had made her own feelings on the subject quite clear. 'Of course you are to meet Miss Schreiner some day, but how to do it as you wished "as one of the common herd", puzzles me! I have not wholly made up my mind about her. I think perhaps she is wanting in culture . . . I can hardly believe we are as similar in thoughts and feeling as I find we appear to be.'[11] This was in February 1885; Mrs Cobb managed to spin things out so that Olive and Pearson did not actually meet until June. Pearson evidently sent her a report as to what had transpired, and she was soon at her writing desk again: 'I was wondering so much what would have been your impression of my excitable little friend. I think you are greatly right. The artist is very strong in her, she *looks at* things rather than lives them. I am not sure I could say there is a want of earnestness and want of depth in her, and yet I feel she is rather vivid and rapid and sparkling, than calm and solid. And yet there is strength in her . . . And she is very kind . . . I was glad you should see such a new type of womankind . . . I think Miss Schreiner is doing just now as you say, taking honey where she finds it. Though it may be from able and thinking people, yet it is taken as honey. A good many people are showing her thoughts beneath the surface, and it excites her much.'[12] It was precisely the kind of effusion which Olive most loathed, and predicated exactly the kind of relationship between Pearson and Mrs Cobb, as far as she was concerned, which would most have mortified her. If there was one thing Olive hated more than anything else, it was the thought that her private life was an object of discussion for other people.

But, of course she was not aware of all this, and when she was invited to join the Men and Women's Club, happily accepted. The club's records show that she was present at its first committee meeting, on 14 July 1885, together with Pearson, Robert Parker and Maria Sharpe, who took on the job of the club secretaryship. At this meeting it was agreed that Miss Schreiner would read a paper at the first autumn meeting of the club, and that she would ask Dr Donkin to read a physiological paper at the second meeting.[13]

Dr Horatio Bryan Donkin, to give him his full name, was Olive's contribution to the club, as far as membership went. He had been introduced to her by Eleanor Marx, who knew him because he had been the Marx family doctor. But despite his radical ideas and associations, he was also extremely fashionable and successful; his rooms were in Upper Berkeley Street, Mayfair, and he was on the committee of the Savile Club. He was also at this time in love with Olive. She knew this, and knew too that she could never reciprocate his feelings; nevertheless, she enjoyed his company and continued to see him, even though she was aware that this was probably unfair to him.

It is easy to see why Olive was so attracted to the Men and Women's Club. Its concerns were those which had, as we have seen, most deeply shaped and affected her own life; they were at the centre of *The Story of an African Farm* and of the book on which she was now chiefly engaged, *From Man to Man*. Moreover, the club's serious, philosophical and (it was hoped) no-holds-barred approach was very much Olive's own. The idea was to have ten members of each sex (although in fact there was usually an imbalance in favour of women). There would be weekly meetings at which members would take it in turns to present relevant papers. Nothing could have been more attractive to Olive. She was always much attracted to philosophical discussions, as much for their own sake because they clarified her mind as for anything they might lead to in the immediate future. In this she was unlike Eleanor Marx, who had literally no time for such things unless they led to practical action. Eleanor was in fact invited to join the club by Dr Donkin, at Pearson's behest, early in 1886, but she declined. 'It is a very different matter to advocate certain things in theory, and to have the courage to put one's theories into practice,' she wrote, alluding tactfully to her semi-married status. 'Probably many of the good ladies in the club would be much shocked at my becoming a member of it.' In addition, and perhaps even more to the point, she felt she must devote her time to 'the highest and most important work she could do' – fighting for socialism. Club members were much put out by this refusal. With regard to the notion that they might be shocked by her social circumstances, Miss Annie Eastty felt that Eleanor had done them an injustice, while Maria Sharpe was 'extremely resentful'. As for Eleanor's choosing to devote herself to practical political action rather than discussion, Miss Sharpe felt that this left her 'no more open to reason than the various propagandists against whose admission we almost framed a resolution'.[14] Olive, however, was not surprised nor put out. 'I should have written to remonstrate with K.P. on the matter, but knew she would decline,' she told Maria Sharpe. '. . . I am sure that all of us men and women would be proud to have her if she would spare time to join, and that we all honour and respect her for having had the courage of her opinions; but while personally looking up to her and admiring her for her fearless conduct (even if we disagree with her theory) I should not have felt at all sure that some man or woman might not have felt that they suffered in being connected with one whom the outside world holds to have broken the most important of its conventional rules.'[15] The last thing Olive wanted was to expose Eleanor to unnecessary humiliation at the hands of people like these.

Eleanor's point about preferring to use her time for active political work evidently stirred some latent feelings of guilt in Pearson, who had done a certain amount of this sort of work – but not in Olive. She wrote to K.P. (as he was generally known) some months later on this topic: 'You say we need a Jesus Christ, that we leave the work of preaching on the streets to the Hyndmans [H. M. Hyndman, the leader of the Social Democratic Federation, a self-declared Marxist at that time much scorned by the Marx family] and Avelings! We do need a Christ; but the Christ of one age is not like to that of another. As for preaching in the streets, or indeed preaching and lecturing anywhere, it is pretty well dead as a power to move men with. The press has taken the place of the preacher. . . . Let me take my own experience, if I may. An untaught girl, working ten hours a day, having no time for thought or writing, but a few in the middle of the night, writes a book like *An African Farm*; a book wanting in many respects, and altogether young and *crude*, and *full of faults*; a book that was written altogether for myself, when there seemed no possible chance that I should ever come to England to publish it. Yet, I have got scores, almost hundreds of letters about it from all classes of people, from an Earl's son to a dressmaker in Bond Street, and from a coalheaver to a poet. . . . Now if a work so *childish* and full of *faults*, simply by right of a certain truth to nature that is in it can have so great a power, what of a *great* work of art? No, K.P., we will leave Hyndman and Aveling and do our own work.'[16]

But exactly what was that work? This was precisely what the members of the Men and Women's Club were meeting to discuss. Pearson kicked off the proceedings with a paper on 'The Woman's Question' which, considering his radical reputation and the impetus which had led to the formation of the club, was surprisingly conservative. (This was certainly Havelock Ellis's view of Pearson at this time, though this was presumably not uncoloured by personal considerations. 'I want to bring as many good and modernising influences on him as possible,' he wrote to Olive.[17]) Before Pearson gave the paper he modestly disclaimed any importance for it: it was 'a man's – and *one man's* view', and its sole aim was to start the club off at a level of the most fearless, most frank discussion, in an attempt to set the tone for what would follow. But, coming from the club's intellectual leader, it was inevitably taken seriously; and it could hardly have been what many of the members were expecting to hear from this particular source. For example, on the question of votes for women, he wrote: 'Granted that women's emancipation is desirable, still I am not sure whether even its ardent advocates have fully realised the fact that her enfranchisement and universal suffrage would at one stroke *theoretically* place the entire power of government in her hands, for she possesses a majority of half a million upwards in this country.'[18] Did this mean that K.P. felt that it was all right for women to have the vote so long as there was no risk of their ever wielding any real power? If this were the case, it would follow on naturally from his views that 'Woman's past and present subjection probably depends to as great an extent on her presumed intellectual as on her presumed physical inferiority. We must face the problem of her being naturally man's intellectual inferior; her prerogative function of child-bearing may possibly involve this.'[19] And these were the views of a radical particularly concerned with the Woman Question! What could the women members of the club, in particular, make of such stuff?

Some of them, naturally enough, were outraged. Emma Brooke, who had been one of the first women undergraduates at Cambridge and was now a member of the Fabian Society, wrote a long paper in reply – 'Notes on a Man's View of the Woman's Question'. Miss Brooke was particularly appalled by Pearson's views on the inevitably central place of child-bearing in women's lives – not surprisingly, being herself a childless unmarried woman of considerable intellectual powers. The essence of Pearson's views on this subject was contained in the aphorism 'Race-evolution has implanted in Women a desire for children, as it has implanted in man a desire for women': an idea which was evidently in the air at the time, since Freud made it, a little later, central to his own theories of male and female sexuality. Miss Brooke took especial exception to this and went on to put Pearson right in no uncertain terms. She refuted his views as to the differentiation of sexual desire between the sexes and the overriding importance of children in any woman's life with some heat. 'The assumption of this strong Desire in Women for Children – so strong that it can only be compared to the mighty impulse of men towards women – is a *most* important one; because if such an imperial Desire exists there is an end to the Sex-question; what remains is a population-question,' she tartly observed.[20] Olive, while she could see many good things in the paper, made an even more sweeping objection. 'The omission [from the paper] was "*Man*". Your whole paper reads as though the object of the club were to discuss woman, her objects, her needs, her mental and physical nature, and man only insofar as he throws light upon her question. This is entirely wrong.'[21]

Such reactions are not surprising. But not all the women members had the intellectual self-confidence of Emma Brooke and Olive Schreiner. For all her pretensions to advanced thought, even Mrs Cobb could not, when it came to the point, quite swallow the notion that women should perhaps not automatically defer to men intellectually. 'I can't shake off the feeling men are the leaders of women . . . I am afraid you will care little for this, you will say it only comes from – for all your goodness towards us – a *woman*, and an emotionalist,' she wrote nervously to Pearson.[22] For Pearson was a rationalist who had reduced all his friends, especially his female friends, to a terror of undermining their arguments, and their standing with himself, by displaying emotion where reason should rank supreme.

2

'I've been so troubled and despairing about the woman question,' Olive had written to Ellis the previous November. In saying this she was making a statement not only about politics and society but about her own life, for the two were not separate. Olive was not simply a campaigner working for a cause; her life *was* that cause, its difficulties were, as we have already seen, in a very real way her own. As Ellis put it, 'Life has been cruel to you. You pay that price for the good things you have. They are strictly related.'[23]

The notion that she felt troubled and despairing about her life was something which those who saw her in society, surrounded by admiration and loving friends, laughing and witty, might have found hard to credit. On the face of it there seemed little reason for Olive to feel discouraged on either a personal or a political level. She had, surely, proved that the world was open even to a lone woman, if she were only talented and courageous enough? But Olive did not see her life in this way. Surrounded by friends, she felt terribly alone; in the midst of apparent success she saw only what she was failing to achieve – a fact to which her body, racked continuously by the asthma which increasingly debilitated her, testified even when her face did not. (Almost all Ellis's hundreds of letters to her enquire anxiously as to her health, which always seems to be bad. He prescribed various drugs for her, including large quantities of potassium bromide, quinine and morphine; it is doubtful whether they helped her as much as they harmed her.) 'The life of a woman like myself is a very solitary one,' she wrote to Pearson. 'You have had a succession of friendships that have answered to the successive stages of your mental growth. When I came to England a few years ago I had once, only, spoken to a person who knew the names of such books as I loved.'[24]

Such a sense of solitude, implanted over the most impressionable years of a life, is not easily shaken off. And of course it had had its effects. Olive, as we have already noted, had had very much to construct her own approach to life. The kind of family existence within which a young person simply absorbs certain principles and attitudes, either to repeat or to reject, had not been available to her. The one lasting effect of her missionary background had been to implant a stern sense of principle; only, she had had to evolve her own set of principles, and by these she lived. They were the basis of her life. They were what she spent her time writing, or trying to write, books about. They were, for example, expressed in the character of Lyndall in *African Farm*, who preferred to die rather than contract a marriage for external reasons, such as to provide a father for her baby and a home for herself.

Naturally these principles deeply affected the whole area of Olive's relations with men. And the milieu in which she now found herself was particularly sympathetic to the notion of living strictly according to one's principles. The myriad societies and groupuscules which flourished among the radicals of the late nineteenth century reflected, indeed, a positive obsession with principle: to each man his own ruling principle, whether it be militant vegetarianism, universal suffrage or free love. We have already seen that Havelock Ellis assumed that Eleanor and Aveling were unmarried on principle; this simply reflected an assumption in those circles that every move one made was, in some sense, a statement of principle. This habit of thought came particularly easily to Olive, reinforcing as it did her tendency to set herself stern goals and standards, which, of course, she invariably failed to attain. (This is one explanation for the paucity of her published work after her spectacular and early début. There were also other reasons – to which we shall return.) This obsessiveness, which found physical expression in her asthma, meant that, even had her principles not been what they were, she would never have taken life or people easily.

By 1885 she had constructed an emotional edifice wherein she could reject Havelock Ellis on principle, while retaining his special friendship. 'Oh, Havelock, when I have even £200 of my own, so that once again I can have that feeling of perfect freedom and independence,' she wrote in March. 'If it were you or any other man it would be the same. I can't live on dependence. Ah, freedom, freedom, freedom, that is the first great want of humanity.'[25] It was, of course, easier for her to construct this sort of relationship with Ellis than for him to accept it, since she was no longer sexually attracted to him as he was to her; he at this time was wishing that he might become a 'small organ' of her body, so that he might be able to be with her always. But when she rejected him sexually in the name of principle, it was difficult for him to argue with her.

By the end of that year a very similar situation had arisen with Donkin. Olive saw him frequently, although she knew that he was in love with her while she could not return his feeling. In January 1886, he proposed to her, and while she must have seen this coming, the actual event threw her into a panic. 'I can hardly bear to think even of any more strain. I must try and forget there are such things as moral questions,' she wrote to Ellis. '. . . I am too broken down – not miserable only but worn out – to be able to write really a letter to anyone . . . More and more I feel that marriage is not and cannot be a right thing for a nature like mine. If I am to live I must be free, and under existing circumstances I feel more and more that no kind of sex relationship can be good and pure but marriage. [Donkin] is so tender and sweet and reverent to me. My heart aches when I think that I can never marry him. When I find a man as much stronger than I am as I

am than a child, then I will marry him, no one before. I do not mean
physically strong, I mean mentally, morally, emotionally, practically.
I do not think there is such a man.'[26] The point was, of course, that
she didn't want to marry Donkin and didn't want to have sex with
either him or Ellis. Sweet subservience was sexually repellent to her,
however admirable her adorer. To Pearson she wrote at this time, 'All
I know is that I am not a marrying woman; when it comes to the point
my blood curdles and my heart is like stone.'[27]

Rejecting marriage, rejecting sex outside marriage, was there any
kind of relationship with a man which Olive might consider acceptable? There was: it was the kind of relationship she hoped for with
Karl Pearson.

The picture we have of Olive's relations with Pearson, and the
role he played in the Men and Women's Club generally, is a rather
one-sided one. He kept her letters to him, but none of his to her
survive, although she frequently refers to them. Nevertheless, an
impression of him emerges, both from the attitudes Olive and others
consciously tried to strike with him – and, even more telling, from
those they – especially the women – tried not to strike.

Essentially, Pearson emerges as rather a stern figure. He was when
Olive knew him at the start of what was to be, as it certainly promised
to be, an illustrious academic career. Pearson's interests were very
wide-ranging. He had already, by the age of twenty-eight, trained as
a lawyer, conducted a number of studies in medieval German social
history, and become a Professor of Applied Mathematics. He was
deeply interested in biology and philosophy; he is remembered for his
advocacy of eugenics, which combined his biological and mathematical
interests, and for his pioneering work on statistical method. He drove
himself hard and took himself and the world very seriously – a point
not lost on Olive. 'I have long conversations with you and I do the
talking for you too, and you are always then a "prig", I make you
say such priggish things,' she wrote to him.[28] He was altogether an
admirable young man, and rather an intimidating one.

From the start Olive enjoyed his company, and it seems pretty clear
that he must have enjoyed hers. She found him an invigorating partner
in argument, and one whom she need not be afraid of shocking by her
outspokenness. For his part, he remembered her to the end of his life
as having had the greatest mind of any woman he had met.

It seems clear that he never worked out quite how to deal with the unprecedented phenomenon that was Olive Schreiner. In 1889, some months before his marriage, he wrote to his fiancée about the difficulties he had encountered: 'Believe me, I have found it, especially in the years gone by, so hard to do without women's friendship and yet seen that, however cautious and self-controlled one might be oneself, there was danger, perhaps evil, produced which one would do anything to avoid. It was just such an experience which led me to tell Olive Schreiner, at the beginning of our friendship, that it should and could only be the free open friendship of man to man.'[29]

If this was really Pearson's opening gambit, then it very much suggests that he realized from the start that, as far as Olive was concerned, a purely comradely footing would be hard to maintain. Whether she herself was aware of this at that time is another matter. The notion of being on 'man to man' terms with a man was not unfamiliar to her: she had, as it happens, observed to Havelock Ellis at least once that she wished they were not of different sexes, so that the question of love and sexual relations need not continually obtrude into their friendship. It was a feeling Ellis did not reciprocate. When it came to her friendship with Pearson, it is clear that she tried her hardest to keep to the 'man to man' compact, signing herself on more than one occasion 'Your man-friend'. She wanted Pearson's friendship more than she had ever wanted any other man's, and if those were his terms, she was prepared to accept them. In view of the intellectual equality such terms predicated between them, she probably even welcomed them. When, in one of the last letters she was to write him, she said, 'Seeing you, speaking to you, hearing from you, has been mental stimulation and strength to me. Emotionally you have been an exceeding great joy to me because of the intellectual strength you have given me'[30] – she was telling the exact truth – though not all of it.

As far as social and political matters went they were interested in the same things. Olive's comradely letters give the sense of a continuing conversation. They concern the topics discussed at the Men and Women's Club, which were the topics crucial to her being.

Many of them discuss prostitution, a central issue in the Woman Question, and one of particular interest to Olive. It was, at the time the Men and Women's Club was beginning, a topic of particular interest on account of W. T. Stead's personal investigations of child prostitution, which he published in that summer of 1885 over several issues of his paper, the *Pall Mall Gazette*, under the lurid title 'The Maiden Tribute of Modern Babylon'. Stead's investigations, which peculiarly suited his bizarre personal combination of evangelical religiosity, megalomania and popular journalistic genius, were intended to change the law concerning the age of consent, which he wanted raised from thirteen to sixteen. In this he succeeded; he also succeeded in concentrating public attention upon the whole question of prostitution. Olive's attention needed no such urging: prostitution was always to concern her in an especially personal way. The novel on which she was then (and for the rest of her life) working, *From Man to Man*, was about prostitution, both within marriage (as when a woman stays in a loveless marriage simply for financial security) and in the more usual sense. She saw as central to the whole Woman Question the issue of economic independence and the escape from what she termed 'parasitism', and the enormous numbers of prostitutes in the late nineteenth century, particularly obvious in large cities such as London, as an inevitable result of women's powerless economic position. Living as precariously as she did, knowing the sensuality of her own nature, Olive was only too aware of the knife-edge that separated a life such as her own from a life like theirs.

'My dear Mr Pearson,' she wrote not long after they had first met in that summer of 1885, '. . . When I came home I carried on our conversation for an hour or more walking up and down my room [a habit that her landladies understandably abominated.] . . . Sometimes when I have been walking in Gray's Inn Road and seen one of those terrible old women that are so common there, the sense of agonised *oneness* with her that I have felt that she was *myself* only under different circumstances, has stricken me almost mad.'[31]

Later that same year she experienced only too personally the ubiquity of prostitution, and also the deeply unequal distinction society drew when it came to apportioning guilt as between the man and the woman. On 31 December 1885 the *Daily News* published a letter from her. She had been spending the evening with friends, and at the end of it Donkin escorted her home in a cab. She was then living in Blandford Square just behind Marylebone Station.

We alighted from the cab, the man having drawn up at the wrong number. We walked slowly up and down for a few moments continuing our discussion. A policeman passed us and said good evening in a somewhat insulting manner. He then turned shortly, and said – "What's this; what's up here, what's up here; I won't have this. What are you doing here" – or words to exactly that effect.

My friend said that the house before which I stood was the one in which I lived. He said he didn't believe it: what was I doing out at that time of night, etc. (about twelve o'clock) and he would ring the bell.

We said that he might do so. My friend offered him his card, and remarked with self-restraint and politeness that he was astonished at his interfering with two persons who were in no way breaking the public peace. He said, "I've nothing to do with you, I don't want to interfere with you. It's her I've to do with." He had appeared to ring the bell but too lightly for anyone to have heard it.

We moved a few steps further. He said I had better stand still where I was otherwise he would take me off to the station . . .

I asked my friend for his pencil and a piece of paper that I might take his number. He said, "Want my number, do yer? *I'll walk yer off to the station.*" He touched the bell lightly again and then came down the steps and said in a skulking whisper, that if I would give him my address he would go away. It was evident that he wanted money. I asked him to ring the bell again loudly and he would be answered and learn my address. He touched the knocker lightly; but as someone was expecting me, the door was at once opened. We asked him if he were satisfied: he slunk down the steps with the look of disappointed greed.[32]

After this, Olive began to take a special interest in individual prostitutes, trying to get to know them, and sometimes inviting them out to spend days with her in the country.

As the year 1886 progressed, Olive wrote Pearson a great many long letters. As in her correspondence with Ellis they frequently discussed sex, but the tone was quite different. With Ellis (who was after all a medical man) the letters had been physically very intimate. With Pearson, the discussion was pitched on an altogether more intellectual plane. 'The most ideally perfect friendship between a man and a woman that I know of is one where the man in addition to sympathy with the woman's whole intellectual nature, feels that she is to him also sexually perfect,' she wrote in April from a convent where she was living for a while in Kilburn, one of London's north-western suburbs. (She spent a good deal of this summer in convents, either this one in Kilburn or, later on, another in Harrow, out in the country on the edge of London. She found that the simple life suited her, and that the nuns offered her a respite both from landladies and from the unwelcome attentions of men such as the importunate Donkin.) Significantly, she went on: 'If I so loved a man that I felt he were the only human being it would have been possible for me to love wifehood under; yet it would never touch my friendship for him, I should never even feel a wish that he should know it. "And if I love thee, what is that to thee?", *that* is the passion that grows out of friendship.'[33]

Other letters dealt with more factual matters – such as her brother Will's passionate love for his new-born baby, which Olive held out as a refutation of Pearson's thesis that the parental instinct was strong only in women. Or she might describe to him how she had spent a day in the country with a prostitute she had persuaded to come out and visit her. But whatever the particular topic, the letters always came back (as was only natural between fellow committee-members of the Men and Women's Club) to the question of relations, and particularly sexual relations, between men and women.

However, although these letters all reflect Olive's intellectual delight at having found such an ideal sparring-partner, on a more personal level the tone is rather awkward, as in a postscript to a letter in which she anxiously enquires whether he is, as she had heard, ill. '(K.P. *Idiots these women are*) – but I'm not a woman, I'm a man, and you are to regard me as such.'[34] Which could not but underline the fact that Olive was *not* a man, and could not forget it.

With Havelock, Olive had been able – had been on her honour, indeed – to hold nothing back: to put down everything she might think, however fleetingly, that might regard the two of them; he would do the same. The result was inevitably slightly mawkish from time to time, but there was nothing forced or artificial about it. By contrast, in the letters to Pearson, even when they discuss the most intimate topics, Olive was always most careful to stand back and make sure she was adopting the correct tone. If she failed to do so, what might he not think of her? 'I send the enclosed that you may forever feel remorse at the thought that you have falsely accused a most innocent person of the sin of emotionality,' she wrote to him in July 1886, from the convent in Harrow where she was spending the summer. 'If you had curled up like a porcupine when you were nine years old and never uncurled for twelve years, and never made an indication that you were not of the consistency of stones, brick-bats, and other persistently insensitive materials, you would feel it a terrible aspersion in your old age to be accused of that deathly crime.'[35]

Emotional or not, she wrote to Pearson almost every other day from the convent in the summer of 1886, enormously long letters, about herself, about him, about life, work and art, but always coming back, in the most impersonal way, to the central topic – women and sex. Olive had visions of Pearson devoting the next several years of his life to a study of the Woman Question – 'I think your work for the next nine or ten years is the woman question. After that may come socialism, philosophy, God knows what, but now, to-day, turn your mind away from all other things except for pleasure and rest.'[36] Certainly, that summer, she herself seems to have thought about little else. She was working on *From Man to Man*, and asked if she might dedicate it to Pearson – 'If I thought that perhaps I could inscribe the book to you, I think it would just give the spring I want. (*K.P.*: "Watches that can't go by themselves had better stand still.")'[37] She often added these little touches of dialogue to her letters, lightening the tone and giving, perhaps, some idea of the delightful conversations that went on between them.

Then, in the autumn, she moved back from Harrow to London, and found herself once more caught up with the Hintons.

The Men and Women's Club, as was perhaps almost inevitable given its predilections and Olive's and Elisabeth Cobb's acquaintance with Caroline Haddon, had already had a brush with the Hintonians. Olive had invited Miss Haddon, rather against Pearson's will, to an early meeting, and she had been so delighted with the Club that she had paid it the highest compliment in her power and called it 'Hintonian'. Pearson, predictably, was appalled. A spirit more antipathetic to the mystical Dr Hinton and his slightly seedy cult of polygamy and nudism ('I don't know anything about Hinton's daughter Ada being undressed with her father and brother. I don't quite know that I could ask. It is quite *possible*. The nakedness of women is a point he insists on a great deal. He puts it rather one-sidedly; he doesn't say much about men going naked,' Ellis wrote to Olive during one of their interminable discussions of Hinton and Hintonism[38]) than that of the priggish Karl Pearson would indeed be hard to imagine. Just what did Hintonism entail? As far as could be made out it implied a woolly mysticism liberally seasoned with rumours of free love. Pearson now set himself to search for solid proof of what Hintonism really meant.

The upright Emma Brooke was only too glad to enlighten him on the subject. Once as a girl she had been thrown by some covertly Hintonian friends into the company of the lecherous doctor. He had been inordinately familiar, preached to her about 'others' needs' and the virtues of self-sacrifice, and followed this by repeated attempts to corner her alone in a deserted part of the garden in order that she might sacrifice herself to his needs. She retailed this episode to Pearson in the most lurid detail. What appeared to have shocked her most was the fact that her friends had thought she was silly rather than that Hinton had behaved badly.[39]

Pearson was triumphant. Here was the proof he had sought of Hinton's complete worthlessness. The man had been nothing but a charlatan bent on forcing innocent girls to his will. Even Olive, herself (as we have seen) no partisan of Hinton's, was rather shocked at the violence of his attack and tried to calm him down. 'I have been thinking about Hinton,' she wrote two weeks after Emma Brooke's letter had been received. 'WE, I, must not be too bitter against him. *I am sure that he was mad*. Mrs Barnes has thrown a good deal of light on his character to me. She says he often told her that if when he was forty he had "quietly taken a mistress as other men do, nothing of all this would have happened." He used to sit Miss Haddon naked on his knees and play with her; his theory was that a man's wish for a woman's body was right, and must be gratified. My loathing for Hinton grew so strong that it is painful to mention him, but I want to be just to him.' There was a postscript: 'I must have a talk with you about Hinton. You are going too far to one side. You are *just* in the state I was in about Hinton a year ago when I read his "Thoughts

on Home". Miss Haddon has just called.' Enclosed with this letter was
a note: 'One must be very careful of what one says because of Miss
Haddon and her school. We must not crush other human lives. It is the
men Hintonians I feel so bitter against.'[40] To Havelock Ellis she wrote,
'I'm going to stick up for Miss Haddon like old boots. Compared to
those white-washed sepulchres, the Hintonians are simply saints.'[41]

She did not disclose the identity of the sepulchres; but now they
had a chance to display their dubious qualities once again, because in
October of 1886 the preliminary hearings were held in the prosecution
of James Hinton's son Howard for bigamy. His wife had found out that
he had seduced another woman by whom he had two children. Howard
was committed for trial, first at Bow Street, then at the Old Bailey. It
seems that Olive may have known about this situation for some time;
at any rate, she took the part of Maud Weldon, the 'other woman'. The
case much excited members of the Men and Women's Club, several of
whom knew the participants, and all of whom were much concerned
to dissociate advanced thinking from free love. Indeed, Howard does
seem to have behaved abominably: his wife had known Miss Weldon's
children for a long time before she found out who their father was.
Elisabeth Cobb clucked about these shocking goings-on in long letters
to Karl Pearson; meanwhile Olive busied herself trying to give some
support, both moral and substantial, to the wretched victims of the
affair.

It was the Hinton trial that brought the real feeling of distrust
between Olive and Elisabeth Cobb out into the open. While Olive
thoroughly disapproved of Howard Hinton's stupid and cowardly
behaviour, she felt the most important thing was to help, so far as
she could, the unfortunate women who were suffering on his account
– his mother, his wife and his mistress, who, quite apart from the
disgrace, saw destitution staring them in the face. She tried vainly to
get mathematical teaching jobs for the hapless Howard, evidently with
little success. Mrs Cobb meanwhile was avidly discussing whether or
not Howard's behaviour did or did not prove that James Hinton *must*
have practised free love, so that upbringing and example were now
having their unfortunate and inevitable effect. 'Would one feel so
despairing of the meanness and smallness of women? if there was not
something in one's own soul that answered back to it?'[42] Olive asked
Pearson after a meeting with Mrs Cobb during which this topic was

aired. There is certainly a vindictive note in Mrs Cobb's final reaction to the affair, after the Old Bailey trial: 'There was practically no trial, or investigation, or report,' she complained to Pearson, 'and Mr George Lewis . . . "managed it well" to have no exposure, or sentence. One hardly feels it was fair, it seems as if it would have been better if James Hinton's name had come in, and people who think about him had understood more.'[43]

Olive's letters now were more excited in tone; after the quiet summer life at Harrow, autumn in London presented an endless stream of demands. There was the Hinton trial; there were editors always asking her for articles and stories; there was Donkin, still hopelessly pressing his suit. 'It is not my reason that has failed in my friendship with Donkin. I was first selfish in letting him come to see me when I knew he loved me; and then sorry. (It is strange that the most wrong things I have done in my life I have done from pity),' she wrote in October.[44] She talked to Pearson a lot about Donkin and her worries on his behalf. She also talked to Donkin about Pearson, and slipped coy sentences to this effect into her letters to Pearson.

The comradely, often humorous calm of the earlier letters was now quite gone; Olive was forever having to pull herself back from the brink of the personal and the emotional, which she knew were anathema to the cool Professor. But she did not succeed, and he, in place of the detached intellectual pleasures of the 'man to man' friendship he had specified, now found himself at the centre of an emotional storm which was only intensified by Olive's desperate efforts to maintain that nothing out of the ordinary was happening. Perhaps it was the knowledge that Pearson was emotionally out of her reach that attracted her as much as the abject love of Ellis and Donkin repelled her, until the constant contact with what she knew was ultimately forbidden drove her, literally, out of her mind.

The other participant in the drama was Elisabeth Cobb, who figured more and more frequently as an object of irritation. What Olive could not bear was the thought, now more and more present and irritating to her, that she might be an object of discussion between this lady and Pearson – which of course she had been from the very start of their friendship; discussing Olive was one of the ways in which Mrs Cobb could establish the intimate and confidential nature of her relations with Pearson.

So Olive, in November, chided Pearson for having passed on to Mrs Cobb what Olive told him about Howard Hinton, and for talking about Olive and Donkin; and told him to pass this letter on to Mrs Cobb. Then, later the same day, she wrote, 'I should not have sent you that letter last night. It was brutal, very brutal of me . . . Burn my letter to Mrs Cobb if you like; . . . Please do not let us talk on the subject to each other; what ever you did or said *I should be satisfied.*'[45] Soon followed another letter on the same subject: 'The gentlest impulse in your heart to Mrs Cobb is the manliest. Follow it. I will not write again. Work. I will work.' That was on 10 December. But next day she could not forbear to write yet again: 'Dear Mr Pearson, I did not tell you in yesterday's note that I wrote on Thursday asking Mrs Cobb no more to write to me or to come and see me. Perhaps I ought to have done so, but I knew you would hear it from herself.

'I am unable to understand Mrs Cobb.

'If you feel that this step makes a change in our relations necessary or necessitates my leaving the club, speak frankly. Yours, O.S.'[46]

What did Pearson make of all this? There is no indication. Most likely he hoped that if he lay low it would all go away. Mrs Cobb meanwhile wrote him long letters protesting her friendship for Olive and declaring herself baffled by her behaviour. Certainly there could no longer be any doubt about the state Olive was in. 'My Man-friend, write to me,' she implored the very next day, 12 December. 'Find fault with me, please, if I am doing wrong; oh, my soul is so little, so little. Can't your larger one for a moment put out a hand to me? O.S.

'My Man-friend, some days when your spiritual life is burning low and dim I will put out my hand and help you if you will help me now.'[47]

It could not go on. Earlier in the summer Olive had described to Pearson the weakness in herself which she had come most to dread: 'I am very strong, I can stand quite alone, my reason and my will govern all my actions; but at any time I am liable to find my emotion gathered in strength and flinging me to the ground. All my life I knew I had this to dread but I never lost control of myself but for a few moments. Three or four years ago I broke down utterly, floating like a cork on the water with will, reason, all powerless. It is a very terrible form of weakness.'[48] This was the breakdown which Havelock Ellis deduced had been brought on by her break with the man by whom she fantasized about being 'stamped to powder'. Now the same thing happened again. On 13 December, not Olive, but Donkin, wrote to Pearson in the most unequivocal terms: 'I wished to see you and to ask you to go and see Miss Schreiner at once. I should not have telegraphed to you had I not deemed it a matter of the greatest urgency . . . I found her in the morning in a state of complete temporary madness – and having [lost?] her normal control, I gathered from her words what I have known of myself for long; that she loves you. . . . Now it is not for me to give you counsel, but let me say this as one man to another on a subject on which I at least feel strongly. If you love her as she loves you – or at all – I don't want to ask you any questions: go to her *and soon* and whatever your feelings may be, speak – don't write.'49

Poor Donkin! What more thankless task could a lover imagine than to be forced to nurse his beloved through an illness caused by her unrequited love for another? He was at his wits' end: terrified to leave Olive in case she should do herself an injury, aware of no other friends who might share his burden; in great emotional pain; and, on top of all this, in receipt of nothing but abuse from all parties. On 14 December Olive evidently received a letter from Pearson: in spite of Donkin's urging he had not been able to nerve himself to face her in person.

Thank you for your letter [she wrote]. It is the most valuable and helpful I ever got from you. Thank you for your directness in it.

What you say must be based on something Dr Donkin wrote. I think I can see how he came to write it. I am sure his motive was pure and good. He came in on Monday morning and found me much worse with your letter in my hand. . . . He came to a conclusion of his own I imagine and rushed away, and later on in the day he told me he had thought it would do me good to see you and had written. I could not question him as to what he had written, or be angry, this state of feeling is sensitive, but it hurt me more than I can tell you that he should have asked you. Donkin can't understand with his simple beautiful child-nature. If he told you I loved you with sex-love it was only a mistake on his part. You will forgive him. I do. . . . For me, when I look into the depths of my own heart I see a feeling that is deeper than the feeling I have had for any human being; but it is not *sex*-love. I do not love you as a soul loves itself. You will say "O.S., you are deceiving yourself, that is sex-love." *I deny it.*

Do you know what draws me closer to you than to any human being? It is that your mind works in the *same way* as mine. . . . This is the case with no other human being. I cared as much for you almost before I had seen you, when Mr Ellis showed me a thing you had written, as I do today.[50]

On 14 December Donkin wrote to Pearson again. He had found Olive in a state of great distress looking for a messenger to take a parcel to Pearson, within which the letter just quoted was enclosed. He seems to have commissioned Mrs Cobb to take the parcel; she had visited Olive that morning. Donkin was evidently angry that Pearson had not come in person but merely written, and had mentioned in his letter that Donkin had told him of Olive's state, and told him to write. This got back to Pearson, who was angry in his turn at the implication that there was anything dishonourable in his action. But the distracted Donkin would perhaps have been even more furious had he known what Mrs Cobb (whom, perhaps influenced by Olive, he did not like) was really doing in this affair. For on 14 December Mrs Cobb, too, wrote to Pearson, about a visit she was to make to Olive's lodgings next day: 'I will wait at Blandford Square [where Olive then lived] whether Olive will see me or not, till 12 o'clock, and if you are able, you can telegraph me to say how soon after that you could see me – the only place of meeting I can suggest is the Central Hall at Euston . . . I find, on thinking it over, I cannot speak to her in the least of your feeling and I do not think it would be right I should attempt it – all I can do is try if it is not possible for me to make her calmer and to try to take away some misunderstanding there seems to be in her mind as regards myself.' Indeed, had Mrs Cobb presented herself as the intermediary between Olive and Pearson, she would probably have driven Olive to total despair: it was one of the two things she most dreaded, this confidential pair talking her over – the other being that (as she was evidently convinced) Mrs Cobb was misrepresenting her to Pearson in some unspecified way; hinting that

Olive was unworthily in love with him, perhaps? And perhaps this was not so far-fetched. 'Thinking it over,' Mrs Cobb concluded, 'I find that I did not exactly understand from you that there was *no* reciprocal feeling on your side – if it is possible there may be, *why* should you struggle against it?'[51] Next day, after seeing him at a meeting of the Men and Women's Club in the evening (where he had apologized for being understandably distracted), she continued this discussion: 'It grieved me to hear you say . . . that friendship between women and men was impossible . . . My sisters have always felt Olive Schreiner thought too much the purely animal feeling *must* sway, and could not be resisted.'[52] Evidently Mrs Cobb felt, with Pearson, that such feelings were in some way unworthy and ought to be resisted.

On 17 December Olive left for Paris, accompanied by Mrs Browne, her landlady, en route for Switzerland. It was to be a year and a half before she returned to England.

3

The Olive who played so eagerly at sex in Derbyshire and the Olive who fled off to Switzerland two and a half years later, abjuring any interest in sex whatever, were two very different people. It was in a way a regression from the outlook Havelock Ellis was to spend his life preaching – that sex was a normal and healthy part of any happy life – to the prudish Victorian cant summed up in Mrs Cobb's disapproving reference to 'purely animal feeling'. Olive's feelings at this time were expressed in one of her 'Dreams' or allegories, 'The Sunlight Lay Across My Bed', in which she has a vision of God who gives her a tour of the different heavens. In the course of this tour He explains that 'In the least Heaven sex reigns supreme; in the higher it is not noticed; but in the highest it does not exist.'[53] Having lost the friendship she most valued on account of false imputations of sexual feeling, she was determined to prove not only that she was now an asexual being, but that life was much better that way. 'All that my sexual nature had to give I gave years ago, and it is *agony* now when men call on me for what my nature has not to give,' she informed Havelock Ellis from Switzerland in February. 'That Karl should have misunderstood my love for him cuts deep. I don't think you can understand it. I've loved Karl better than anyone else in the world ever since I was at Portsea Place [her lodgings when she was first introduced to him] but it's just the absence of sex feeling that has drawn me. I can't bear sexual relationships any more even in a kiss. I have tried hard to feel sexual to you and Donkin and you don't know how it sometimes hurts me. You don't know how much I've had a kind of Hintonian feeling (not idea!) that I ought to sacrifice myself and my feelings in this way.' But her postscript makes it clear that she is certainly capable of sexual jealousy with regard to her asexual idol: 'What do you mean by suggesting such a thing as that Pearson ever had a sexual relation with Mrs Cobb? Pearson has never loved Mrs Cobb and I do not think her love for him was sexual. The kind of love he makes women feel for him is that of Dante for Beatrice.'[54] But in fact it was the potent *combination* of intellectual and physical attraction which had made Olive fall so intensely in love with Pearson. He, for his part, was probably gratified by this passion (as who could fail to be?) and doubtless did little to discourage it; indeed, Olive being the kind of woman she was – hypersensitively unwilling to expose herself to relationships which might end badly for her – it seems more likely that he actively encouraged it, at least for a while. In the end, of course, Olive terrified him. Perhaps the sudden recognition that, beneath all the words, she was in fact in love with him was accompanied by an appalled realization that this was not at all what he had had in mind, and that he did not reciprocate her desire. That this is indeed what he did feel is indicated by the fact that in a letter he wrote to his secretary about Olive towards the end of his life (and which was later destroyed) he discussed what should be a man's behaviour to a woman who has a sexual passion for him which he does not reciprocate.[55] But by then it was too late: she was in love with him, body and soul. He ignored this for as long as he could and then tried to deflect it, and excuse his own behaviour, by erecting boundaries between 'sex-love' and other kinds of love which Olive, in her desperate desire to intellectualize her feelings so that she could control them, was eager to fortify. 'Sex-feeling has an aberrant effect on the intellect,' she had assured Pearson. 'With the brain-worker who has anything to give the world marriage is a peculiarly difficult question, it may benefit the general health and so lengthen life, but what if while it makes the flame burn longer it makes it burn *duller!*'[56] Her flame had burnt so strongly that, for the present, it had burnt her entirely out.

Whether Olive really believed her own protestations as to the nature of her feeling for Pearson it is impossible to say. In a letter to her friend Edward Carpenter at this time she wrote, 'I am ashamed of the letters I wrote you the other day, but I've been very weak and ill, with no power of self-repression left'[57] – which argues that she generally spent a good deal of effort concealing what she really thought and felt, from herself as well as others. At any rate, few of her friends were convinced, either that she had no feelings of sexual desire for Pearson, or by the argument that this lack of desire transmuted friendship to a higher plane. Charlotte Wilson, an anarchistically-inclined Fabian friend of Olive's, wrote an angry letter to Pearson some time later saying that she felt both of them, but especially Olive, had been much damaged by the successful attempt to destroy the emotional side of their natures, and were lesser people as a consequence of it.[58] Certainly Mrs Wilson had no such qualms about repressing her animal nature: married to a stockbroker, she was rumoured to be the lover of the Russian anarchist Prince Kropotkin.

The truth was that Olive, at this stage of her life, was torn between two powerful and (it seemed to her) conflicting necessities: to satisfy her sexual and emotional nature, and to achieve acceptance in the man's world of work and the intellect. It was the nature of this conflict which lay at the centre of that question, the everlasting Woman Question, which obsessed her. The Pearson débâcle had finally convinced her of something she had long suspected – that it was not possible for a woman to combine the two. '*He* made her feel like a prostitute,' Ellis had noted about the lover who had so excited and appalled her a few years earlier;[59] and this was the very opposite of what she experienced in that wonderful intellectual comradeship with Karl Pearson which she had now – by falling in love – lost. Was there any hope for a woman like her of leading a full and happy life? Perhaps this is why she felt (as she told Pearson) that 'legal marriage is an immorality in the highest members of the race (not in the lower), [and] that it is their duty to lead in this matter, not only in speculation but in action'.[60] The kind of relationship she aspired to was that of Mary Wollstonecraft with William Godwin, free, equal and entirely voluntary. Of course this was not a sexless partnership, and the passionate Mary can hardly be imagined as extolling such. Olive would have liked to be able to be on such a footing with Karl Pearson, but things had not turned out that way, and his particular combination of immaturity and priggishness laid all the burden of guilt upon Olive. 'I am so humiliated for my sex that a woman has so broken down before you,' wrote the odious Mrs Cobb to Pearson following Olive's precipitate departure.[61] But what Elisabeth saw as humiliation could also be seen as dignified renunciation, which of course was what Olive wanted.

So there was nothing for it now but to work. That was where her true identity lay. But here Olive encountered a real difficulty. She thought incessantly about her work; she defined herself in terms of it, and the world too, because of the success of *The Story of an African Farm*, defined her in those terms. But *she could not do it* – or only with the greatest difficulty.

After Olive died, Edmund Gosse, in a review of her husband's biography of her, mused on the strange inability of one so obviously gifted to produce another novel to set beside *African Farm*. (Two other novels, *Undine* and *From Man to Man*, were published posthumously, and are not good books.) Gosse concluded that some people have only one novel in them, and, having written that, can write no more, and that Olive evidently fell into this category. This may have been true; certainly Olive did not try any more novels other than these three which had all been begun years ago, even before she first came to England. But perhaps a clue to the puzzle may be obtained if we ask another question. Instead of why could she never write another novel, perhaps the relevant question might be: if she had been a man, would she have tried to define herself as a novelist? To which, looking at Olive's predilections and character, the answer would almost certainly have to be no.

A novel can be almost anything its author wants it to be: it is one of the most flexible of art-forms. This is one reason for its enduring popularity, among authors as well as readers. When Olive started to write *The Story of an African Farm* it is highly unlikely that she indulged in great heart-searchings about what she was trying to do. She was very young, and she didn't have much free time; all she knew was that she had to write this story, and she wrote it. Writing a book is hard work, and only a real compulsion could have driven her to sit up as she did night after night working at it. This sense of urgency – that this was a book which had to be written – is one of the reasons it succeeds. There are of course others. The writing is vivid and flowing; the author writes like this because this is how she sees life, not because this is how people write books. The world she describes lives in every detail; the reader can picture it intimately, even though Tant' Sannie's farm is a strange and alien place. And the people live, though some of them are sketched a little crudely and not all their adventures are convincing.

The book was of course a work of imagination. But, like many first novels, it was also largely autobiographical. The places were drawn from life, and so were many of the characters. Of the least believable of them, Bonaparte Blenkins, Olive told Ellis (in the first letter she ever wrote him), 'He is drawn closely after life, but in hard straight lines without shading, and is not artistic, nor idealized enough.'[62] Lyndall and Waldo both expressed aspects of herself; Waldo's old father was drawn very much from Olive's own father; even the enigmatic Stranger was drawn from someone she had once met who had given her a book (Herbert Spencer's *First Principles*) which had a profound effect on her, and who had passed out of her life. (Her family, it may be noted in passing, disliked the book – perhaps because of its very truth to life as well as its uncomfortable message.) It is a strange and compelling book, and it establishes Olive Schreiner as a writer of the highest quality. But whether it establishes her as an imaginative writer is another question. Undoubtedly the parts of the book which succeed least well are the flights of literary fancy (the Hunter's allegory, Lyndall's deathbed scene) which, ironically, Olive liked best. The best are those, such as the Boer wedding and the scenes of daily life on the farm, which are clearly pictures of life as the author knew it. The same is true of her other novel, *From Man to Man*. The only part of the book which succeeds is the prelude, 'A Child's Day', which is clearly drawn from life – Olive's own.

What were Olive's intentions in writing these books? One was, naturally, to tell stories. Of *African Farm* she wrote to Ellis, 'It was just one of the many stories I had been making ever since I was five years old.'[63] But that was not the only intention. These were books with a message, a message about what women's lives were really like. 'You know, Henry,' she wrote to Ellis just before they went to Derbyshire, 'all these months when I have been in such suffering, and have had that yearning to do something for others that I feel when I am in pain, I have always built upon the fact *From Man to Man* will help other people, it will help to make men more tender to women, because they will understand them better; it will help to make some women more tender to others; it will comfort some women by showing them that others have felt as they do.'[64] To Pearson she expanded this idea of the novel as a vehicle. 'One man might set Europe in a blaze still, but he must do it in a new way. If spoken and delivered speeches, say Mr Gladstone's or Hyndman's, have power it is not because they were spoken, but because they were repeated in all "the papers". . . . The press is manifestly becoming the governing and ruling power. It matters comparatively little (of course it does matter somewhat) whether we send donkeys or sane men to parliament. It matters everything in the political world what "the papers say" and who rules them. Even more clearly the novel has taken the place of other forms of art in carrying to the *heart* of the people the truths (or untruths) of the Age.'[65]

For Olive, as time went on, the 'truths of the Age' came to matter more and more – certainly more than the fact of being a novelist. *From Man to Man* undoubtedly suffers from being made a vehicle for such truths. The characters suffer from being message-bearers. They are not believable, they talk in clichés, and it is hard to care about what happens to them. They have strange, stilted voices that bear little if any relation to real life. Is it possible, for example, to imagine any man, ever, speaking to any woman as Olive's John-Ferdinand does to Rebekah about her sister Bertie (later to fall into prostitution)? 'When as a youth I asked you to marry me I was drawn to you by your intellect, your strange intensity and delicate physical refinement and beauty, and your devotion to your duties. My feeling for her is wholly different. For the first time I understand now how men have made a god of woman – the eternal virgin mother! – If I am all the world to her, Rebekah, she is more than all the world to me.'[66] But John-Ferdinand does not marry Bertie because he finds out that she was tricked into losing her virginity when she was fifteen, a fact which as a matter of course makes respectable marriage impossible and condemns her out of hand to prostitution. She is lured downhill by a character known only as The Jew, and is lost thereafter.

Writing *From Man to Man*, as it was expanded to contain more
and more messages, was – as Olive's correspondence testifies – an
uphill struggle. Not unnaturally she began to search for other ways in
which to convey what she wanted to say. Most of her published work
at this time consisted of allegories – short symbolic scenes written in
consciously poetic language. She was writing an introduction to Mary
Wollstonecraft's *Vindication of the Rights of Woman*, and commented:
'It has cost me already about four times as much labour as *African
Farm* did, but in one sense immeasurably more so because I have
gathered into it the result of my whole life's work. . . . There is
no side of the sex question, women's intellectual equality (or as I
hold, inequality with man), marriage, prostitution, in which one
has not to speak. My present work is bringing down the immense
mass of material I have into a condensed form. Sometimes I find by
throwing a thing into the form of an allegory I can condense five
or six pages into one, with no loss, but a great gain to clearness.'[67]
Such an allegory was the hunter's dream in *African Farm*; another,
'The Buddhist Priest's Wife', she considered her best work. But she
later abandoned even allegory as a vehicle. Her *Woman and Labour*,
published in 1911, is a straight factual and theoretical discussion of
the Woman Question – the 'sex book' she had been working on for
so many years.

So here she was, marooned in Switzerland, about to embark on years
of apparently aimless wandering around Europe ('The Wandering
Jew', she signed herself once in a letter to Pearson) – there being
no particular reason other than that it seemed a pleasant place and
might help her asthma for choosing one town or country rather than
another; a powerful mind denied, because of the peculiarities of her
position, the company of other such minds; far from family, friends,
home – wherever *that* was. No wonder she clung on desperately to
the thought of her work: work defined, more and more, as getting
the message across and, if possible, changing the world.

There was, of course, a far more direct way of achieving this than
by writing allegories, or even political tracts, and that was to go into
politics directly. This was what Eleanor Marx was doing, in the
thick of the fray, helping to organize the budding trade unions,
co-ordinating strikes, leading marches, speaking to meetings. But
that was not a possible course for Olive, as she had signalled when

she chose to join the Men and Women's Club and spend her time discussing rather than doing. She was with them, of course – 'Isn't the strike splendid?' she wrote to Edward Carpenter from London, where she was temporarily perched, about the great Dock Strike in 1889 in which casual labour won the right to unionize. 'You ought to see the East End now. The strange, earnest look on the people's faces, that sort of wide-eyed look. You look straight into their faces and their eyes look back at you; they are possessed with a large idea. It's very wonderful.'[68] (Oscar Wilde, who moved in radical artistic circles, observed: 'Olive Schreiner is staying in the East End because that is the only place where people do not wear masks upon their faces, but I have told her that I live in the West End because nothing in life interests me but the mask.'[69]) But organizing dock-workers in person was not Olive's life. And though it contained so many of her friends, England was not her country.

That, of course, was South Africa, and increasingly she was tempted to return. She finally did so in the autumn of 1889, ostensibly to see her brother Will and play with his two little babies, but really for wider reasons. She had had enough of a rootless life. The time had come for her to take her place in the community of which she was inescapably a part. She sailed for the Cape in October 1889, and finally put Karl Pearson behind her.

In 1890 Karl Pearson married Maria Sharpe, Mrs Cobb's sister – from Elisabeth's point of view, the most satisfactory possible solution. But it was less satisfactory for poor Maria. *Her* view of the marriage is set out in a sad letter written to Elisabeth by Pearson, but never sent, in 1927, when he was seventy and she eighty-three. By then Pearson had become famous throughout the world, not so much for his ideas as for the methods he devised for investigating them. As J. B. S. Haldane, who was then the holder of Pearson's chair at University College, London, put it in a speech given to celebrate Pearson's centenary: 'I believe that his theory of heredity was incorrect in some fundamental respects. So was Columbus' theory of geography. He set out for China and discovered America. But he is not regarded as a failure for this reason. When I turn to Pearson's great series of papers on the mathematical theory of evolution, published in the last years of the nineteenth century, I find that the theories of evolution now most generally accepted are very far from his own. *But* I find that in the search for a self-consistent theory of evolution he devised methods which are not only indispensable in any discussion of evolution, they are essential in every serious application of statistics to any problem whatever.'[70]

At the time he wrote this letter Pearson was already celebrated for this work. His wide-ranging interests had gained him an enormous array of friends. He was loved by his students, and had been to all appearances happily married for thirty-seven years. He should have been a contented man; but he was not.

> As I look back on it now, [he wrote to his 'dear Bessie'] I think life has been largely a failure. I have sacrificed everything – Maria would add wife and children included – to the idea of establishing a new tool in science which would give certainty where all was obscurity and hypothesis before . . . Now that I am old the younger men, especially in America, Russia and Japan, are rushing in and devastating all the paths I have tried to hew through the jungle. Thirty years hence a curve or a symbol will be called 'Pearson's' and nothing more remembered of that toil of the years. It is not so much the waste of mine but of others' lives, in particular Mia's. She has been a splendid wife, if you mean by that, that she has ever worked for her husband's purposes. But she has done it from her inbred sense of duty, and not from something else. I have never really won her, and in recent years, although she would have done everything she could for me, I realised that her first love was her children. Marrying as we did after what had happened previously [was he referring to Olive?] I ought to have realised that I had still to win her, but I spent my life over my work and she sacrificed her life in looking with slender means after home and children. What she has been feeling all these years comes out now, when she is less clear in mind and has less control of herself. That very night after you came she said to me: 'You must not let other people say that you have killed me.' I don't suppose 'other' people would say so, but I know what she meant that I was to say so to myself . . . I do not blame Mia for this want of trust. I blame myself for never having really won her confidence. Only I cannot let

you of all people believe that our marriage has been an ideal
one. It wanted delicacy of handling to make it so, and I have
given too little time and thought to it . . . Now that the end is
drawing nigh she discloses against her will, what has been the
undercurrent all these long years, and I can do nothing.[71]

In view of this sad summation, it is perhaps instructive to look
back at a note Pearson sent to Maria Sharpe, then Secretary of the
Men and Women's Club, on 14 December 1886 – the very evening
of Olive's breakdown. 'There is an independence of spirit about the
woman earning her own livelihood by contributing to the social labour
stock, which I never find in the woman whose claim to independence
consists in fulfilment of the "home duties" for a husband,' he wrote
then.[72] But when it came to the point, as so often happens, theory
was not so easy to reconcile with practice. The New Man and the
New Woman were both submerged in the facts of Victorian domestic
life, and both were the worse for it.

4

But when she got to South Africa what should she do? That was the
question.

Olive's position at this time very much recalls that of another
radical and politically-minded woman earlier in the decade: Beatrice
Potter. Beatrice, in the early 1880s, found herself in a most frustrating
situation. A woman of penetrating intellect and abundant energy,
conscious of wishing to do great things in the world, she could see
no way in which she could both satisfy these ambitions and retain
her social position. Several of her many sisters had married men who
were involved in politics, but of course women were debarred from
entering politics directly, as Beatrice doubtless would have done had
she been a man. Then, in 1884 – at just about the same time that Olive
was getting to know Havelock Ellis – Beatrice, who was then in her
mid-twenties (she was three years younger than Olive) was faced with
a great temptation. She was introduced to the great Liberal politician
Joseph Chamberlain, then a widower, and fell deeply in love with him.
It was clear that he, too, was much attracted to her. Should she marry
him? She knew she had only to say the word, and she would be the

wife of one of the most influential men in British politics. She would be at the centre of things.

But should she accept him? Beatrice agonized over her decision. The temptation was enormous – but would her conscience let her do it?

Let me look facts clearly in the face and take counsel with myself [she wrote in her diary on 22 April 1884]. Ambition and superstition began the feeling. A desire to play a part in the world, and a belief that as the wife of a great man I should play a bigger part than as a spinster or an ordinary married woman. Let me analyse the part I should play. He has taken his line for better or for worse in politics; he has an overpowering ambition, he will not hesitate much as to the means of gaining his ends. He has told me distinctly that he will not bear his opinion being 'controverted' or his action criticized. He desires a woman who is personally attracted to him, who will sympathize and encourage him, be a continual rest to him, giving him the uncompromising admiration which the world withholds. His temperament and his character are intensely attractive to me. I feel I could relieve the gloom, could understand the mixed motive and the difficulties of a nature in which genuine enthusiasm and personal ambition are so curiously interwoven. The outward circumstances of the life of a politician's wife would be distasteful to me or, rather, they would be supremely demoralizing, unless they were accepted as the means to an end in which I myself believed. And here is really the kernel of the question. Do I believe in the drift of his political views and do I believe that the means employed are *honest*? If I do not believe that this line of political action is right, if I do not believe that the end is pursued without deviating from the first moral principles, and were yet to sign both aims and means with my signature, I should be selling my soul and should deserve misery . . . Once married, I should of course subordinate my views to my husband's, should, as regards his own profession, accept implicitly his views of right and wrong. But I cannot shirk the responsibility of using my judgment before I acknowledge his authority. . . . I should *not* influence him. He has shown me that distinctly. He has been straightforward all through, has told me distinctly his requirements. When I have been absolutely honest with him he has turned away. That is not what he wants and *I know it*. It is only when I have simulated *la femme complaisante*, turned the conversation from principles to personalities, that he has desired me. . . . And I have not only no devotion to [his] aims, but have to twist my reason in order to *tolerate them*.[73]

Beatrice, of course, did not marry Chamberlain – at what cost to herself, only her diary knew. She was for the next several years tortured by the consciousness of her love for him. But her devotion to the political life did not waver, and indeed led her into the marriage she did eventually contract, with Sidney Webb. Her analysis of her own nature proved to have been correct: the bliss of shared principles and a perfect communion of minds overcame even the physical repulsion with which Beatrice at first viewed Sidney.

Now Olive, in South Africa, faced a similar set of temptations. On 16 March 1890 she wrote to Ellis: 'I am going to meet Cecil Rhodes, the only great man and man of genius South Africa possesses, the owner of most of the Kimberley diamond mines and the head of the African exploration company. If he backs me up at all I shall be able to carry out my plan.'[74] She had already glimpsed Rhodes on board ship, and had liked him very much.[75]

Cecil Rhodes was at that time riding the South African economic wave. The 1870s and 1880s had seen great discoveries of gold and diamonds on the Rand in the Transvaal, which was a Boer republic. The great aim of the British, whose main South African possession was the Cape Colony, was to displace the Boers and get the mineral wealth for themselves. This was the impetus behind Rhodes's British-South-Africa Company – the Chartered Company to which Olive refers – and it was to be enacted unofficially in the Jameson Raid at the end of 1895, which was repelled, and officially and decisively in the Boer War four years later.

The particular plan Olive had in mind was to visit Matabele and Mashonaland; but there was no doubt that, if she could get Cecil Rhodes on her side, she would feel able to implement almost any plan she wanted. To W. T. Stead, the editor of the *Pall Mall Gazette*, and now of the *Review of Reviews*, whose campaign against child prostitution in 1885 had led to great scandal and changes in the law, and who was an old supporter of hers, Olive wrote in July: 'the only big man we have here is Rhodes, and the only big thing the Chartered Company. I feel a curious and almost painfully intense interest in the man and his career. I am so afraid of his making a mistake, as he would do, I think, if he accepted the Prime Ministership of the Colony, as there is some talk of his doing.'[76] In fact, he became Prime Minister the very next month, and Olive wrote to Stead: 'Rhodes's Prime Ministership is answering splendidly, beyond all expectations.' Stead needed no urging to support Rhodes. The two had first met the previous year, when Rhodes had won Stead over to his capitalist/imperialist dream; in return, it was Stead, in the pages of the *Review of Reviews*, who was largely responsible for lifting Rhodes from obscurity.

In November 1890, Olive did meet Rhodes. By then she was not living in Cape Town any more, as she had done on her first arrival in South Africa, but in a little Karroo town, Matjesfontein. 'This is a wide long plain with rocky mountains running down both sides. There are one or two little kopjes on it . . . There are no farms or homesteads; the only place is this. It consists of the railway station, Logan's house, and a row of outbuildings or cottages of which mine will be one. There is not a tree in the veld, nor a bush in the mountains as far as the eye can reach. The water is brought from a long way off in iron pipes. Even near the house there is not a tree or bush except a few little blue-gum saplings . . . *The* event of the day is when twice in the twenty-four hours the railway train sweeps by. Once in the morning the Cape train on its way up to the Diamond Fields and Gold-Fields stops about 9 o'clock and the people get out to have breakfast here, and they leave our mails. Again, about six in the evening, the train from the Diamond Fields passes and stops for half an hour.'[77] Here on the platform Rhodes and Olive would sometimes meet and talk, as they also did from time to time at Cape Town when Olive went there to stay with her brother Will. It seems clear that they were much attracted to one another, and there were rumours that they were to be married. Naturally this gave rise to much interest and gossip, to Olive's disgust. In January 1892, Olive wrote to a friend in Cape Town to apologize for having refused to see another woman friend: 'I know my nature is much too sensitive but I thought she *might* wish to come and discuss Mr Rhodes and his character and affairs with me, as Mrs Sivewright and other people always try to do, and I get so weary of personalities; always that, nothing else, between women. They don't want to discuss a man's public character, his policy (and even *that*, with regard to people I know, I am not particularly fond of discussing!!) but they want to discuss all the smallest little personal things about them and that makes life unideal.'[78] And to her brother Will at the same time: 'In case any one *were* to mention my name and Rhodes in your presence or to you, you might say *that I have not spoken to him for 10 months*, and that we are not in any way friends, beyond that I admire his genius . . . I would of course never have anything to do with him again after it had been said I wished to make him marry me. One's self-respect demands that; and all beauty is gone from our relation for me.'[79] This convoluted code of sexual honour was perhaps one of the legacies of the Pearson affair, which had left Olive with a view of possible relations between men and women in which women were seemingly almost powerless to take the emotional initiative in a relationship. She expressed this clearly in 'The Buddhist Priest's Wife', a story which she wrote in 1890–91, at the time of her involvement with Rhodes: 'If a man loves a woman, he has a right to try to make her love him because he can do it openly, directly, without bending,' remarks the woman in the story, who is clearly a self-portrait. 'There need be no subtlety, no indirectness. With a woman it's not so; she can take no love that is not laid openly, simply, at her feet. Nature ordains that she should never show what she feels; the woman who had told a man she loved him would have put between them a barrier once and for ever that could not be crossed; and if she subtly drew him towards her, using the woman's means – silence, finesse, the dropped handkerchief, the surprise visit, the gentle assertion she had not thought to see him when she had come a long way to meet him, then she would be damned; she would hold the love, but she would have desecrated it by subtlety; it would have no value. Therefore she must always go with her arms folded sexually; only the love which lays itself down at her feet and implores of her to accept it is love she can ever rightly take up.'[80]

In fact things were more complicated than that: it was not so much Olive's outraged feelings as Rhodes's politics that had destroyed their friendship. She had started out with high hopes of him. 'He was represented to me as a millionaire who was going to devote his life to the freeing of the Irish peasant from the landlord, to the education and development of the Native races of South Africa, and to the benefit of all poor and down-trodden people generally,' Olive wrote to her mother in an attempt to explain her position vis-à-vis Rhodes after the Jameson Raid (Olive's mother, like most of her family, supported Jameson, whom Olive, however, fiercely denounced). 'As painted to me he seemed the ideal of human greatness and one of my great wishes was to meet him . . . It was the beginning of the disappointment. As long as he and I talked of books and scenery we were very happy, but, when he began on politics and social questions, I found out to my astonishment that he had been misrepresented to me; especially when we got to the Native Question, we ended by having a big fight, and Rhodes got very angry. All our subsequent meetings were of the same kind. I think Rhodes liked me for the same reasons that I liked him, because of his *life* and energy, but we *never* met once without a royal fight . . . I have felt so terribly about him, when he was acting in a course that seemed to me most disastrously wrong – I have gone out of the House of Parliament when he was speaking and written a note, and hired a boy to take it over, imploring him to abstain from damning his own soul as it seemed to me he was doing. With all his genius, with all his beautiful, wonderful gifts, to see it going so! [This was probably on the occasion of debates on the so-called 'strop bill', designed to legalize the flogging, for certain misdemeanours, of African servants. It was known to disapproving liberal opinion as the 'Every Man Wallops His Own Nigger' Bill. Rhodes, who needed the support of a Boer farmers' party, the Afrikaner Bond, to keep him in power, voted for this bill, much to Olive's horror, in 1890, when it was defeated. It came up again in 1891 and was finally made law in 1892.]

'A little time after this I gave up all political hope of Rhodes. . . . There came a day when Rhodes and Sivewright were on the Matjesfontein railway station; we had a talk, and my disappointment at Rhodes's action was so great that when both he and Sivewright came forward to shake hands, I turned on my heel and went to my house. Some days after, Rhodes came as usual to see me. I heard him knocking at the door but did not open it. Some time after, I went to Town and he invited me to dinner but I declined. He then gave . . . his closest friend . . . a message to me, asking what was the matter. I told [the friend] to tell him that in political matters I was absolutely opposed to him, and was going to fight him on every point. He twice invited me to his house again, but I refused both invitations. I have never seen him to speak to since.'[81]

Politically, in fact, Olive had discovered that she was diametrically opposed to practically every principle Rhodes stood for. Her decision to drop him was not as hard as Beatrice Potter's to drop Joseph Chamberlain in similar circumstances, because although Olive was attracted to Rhodes, she was not in love with him as Beatrice was with Chamberlain. But she faced the same problem that Beatrice had faced: how, as a lone and voteless woman, was she to make her political mark? For politics, in the fullest sense of that word (and not just issue politics of the kind in which it was easier for a woman to participate personally rather than vicariously), were what interested both Olive Schreiner and Beatrice Potter.

Olive's friend and Beatrice's acquaintance, Eleanor Marx, had faced no such conflict. Her work was anyway outside the mainstream politics of the day, so that the fact of having or not having a vote was pretty much irrelevant to her: she would not have been tempted to use it under the existing circumstances, and as for Parliament, her inclination was to overthrow it rather than join it. Living with Aveling, who shared her views, naturally strengthened her, but he was not essential to her political activity, which at this time consisted largely of trades union organization. But the situation of Olive Schreiner and Beatrice Potter was less clear-cut. Beatrice solved her problem on that day in July 1892, when she noted, 'Exit Beatrice Potter. Enter Beatrice Webb, or rather (Mrs) Sidney Webb, for I lose alas! both names.'[82] Her political future as a working unit with Sidney lay clear before her. But at that time Olive saw no such solution for herself. Her younger brother Will, for whom she had great respect and affection, was planning to enter politics with Rhodes, who wanted him to be his Attorney General. Olive encouraged him in this, 'but only if you could stand perfectly erect – so we shall not see it, I fear. He is great and sincere himself; there is not a spot of hypocrisy in Rhodes; he never calls his diplomacy principle.'[83] While Will supported Rhodes Olive could not work directly through him since they disagreed on too many issues – principally with regard to the treatment of black Africans. All she could do was try to bring him round to her point of view. This did happen, but not until after the Jameson Raid. Will then became Prime Minister of the Cape Colony, which office he held at the outbreak of the Boer War. But meanwhile she had to bide her time.

What next? Given Olive's age – she would be forty in 1895 – there was one obvious preoccupation. 'I am busy taking care of a woman who is going to have a little child next month. Having a child always seems to me the one compensation the Gods give woman for being a woman. The only thing that makes me sad in thinking I shall have to live all my life alone is the thought I shall never have a child,' she wrote W. T. Stead in 1892.[84] Gossip, however, kept marrying her off: to Seymour Fort, a well-known local figure to whom her engagement was announced in the *Kimberley Times*; to an unspecified 'leading French politician', an item in all the Paris papers in the spring of 1892. Then, at the end of the year, while she was staying at Ganna Hoek, her girlhood paradise, she met Samuel Cron Cronwright, generally known as Cron.

'He's a beautiful fellow who draws me greatly, he's something like Waldo [one of the characters in *African Farm*] but fiercer and stronger,' she wrote to Edward Carpenter.[85] From the first it was clear that she was attracted to him physically, and in other ways. 'Of the wonderful activity and force in you there is no doubt – of the life! . . . Most men lack the force for great things. You have the force, the thing which no man can ever produce by his own will; all the things you lack are the things you can supply,' she wrote him four months later.[86] Then she sailed for England, where she spent the summer of 1893 debating whether or not she should get married.

One clue to Olive's life is to remember that *she wished she was a man*. She never made any secret of this. She thought, probably rightly, that her life would have been a better and happier one had she been a man. To take only one instance, if her brother Will, who was much less gifted than she was, could attain high political office, what might she not have done had she been able to act politically in her own right instead of continually having to find the devious way round to her goal? But in default of this, she acted throughout her life as far as possible in the same way as if she had been a man. Thus, in her relationships with men, and in spite of the constricting limitations she imposed upon herself after the débâcle with Karl Pearson, she took the initiative and dictated the course – a most unusual state of events.

This was true with Havelock Ellis, with Cecil Rhodes, and with the unfortunate Dr Donkin. The Pearson affair threw her partly because she was, unusually for her, unable to follow this course in it; perhaps part of Karl Pearson's attractiveness for her was a sense that she could not do so; we know that she craved, usually in vain, a man who would be stronger than she was. The fact that she could not cope with such a man when he presented himself had nothing to do with the case, any more than such cravings have to do with logic.

But these were all formidable men, Olive's intellectual equals. Cronwright did not fall into this category. How could he? He was eight years younger than Olive; quite apart from any disparity in natural gifts, she had seen the world, while he had seen nothing. As far as he was concerned she was a glamorous figure, the most famous woman in South Africa. He must have been flattered to have made such a conquest, while politically he clearly found her inspiring. For her part, the whole affair is clarified if we simply transmute the roles and think of Olive as the husband. After so many years of failing to find a suitable man to be her husband and helpmeet, after despairing of ever marrying and having children, it is hardly surprising that Olive, like many active and energetic women, had come to the conclusion that what she needed was a wife.

'I'm sometimes afraid that the desire to have a child weighs very heavily with me in making me willing to marry . . . This friend of mine wants me so much to have a child and that's one great bond between,' she confided to Edward Carpenter during the summer in England.[87] Another was sex. Cron had a lot of what in a woman would be known as sex appeal. He was very attractive – Olive often referred approvingly to his physique. As for his politics, Olive would shape those.

By the time she returned to South Africa Olive had decided that she would get married. Very appropriately, Cron agreed that he would take Olive's name instead of the more usual transfer. On 24 February 1894, he became Mr Cronwright-Schreiner. His future was clear: it was expressed in a sonnet sent him by Will on the wedding-day:

Life has begun – take up thy work – advance!
Thou'lt have an influence now than which no spell

Could e'er more power have given. – And soon,
   perchance
The Senate of thy native land will hear
Thy voice for Progress pleading calm and clear.[88]

The marriage seemed to start well enough. The newlyweds went to
live at Cron's farm, Krantz Plaats, near Ganna Hoek where Olive
had been so well and happy as a girl. She wrote ecstatic letters to all
her friends. But her body did not seem to bear them out. She at once
got terrible asthma, though this was the climate she had always cited
as being ideal for her condition. Obviously they – or she – would
have to leave Krantz Plaats. Equally obviously such a move would
be no good for Cron, who was just beginning to make a go of his
farm. Undaunted by this, he went to Kimberley, to see if he could
find a suitable property; she wrote, 'It would be more bitter to me
than you dream to be separated from you even for a few years; but
unless I felt I was paying for your other farm and that there was no
doubt you were bettered by the move materially, I could not bear it;
I would rather go away alone, much.'[89] The compulsion to move on,
always to try a new, better place, had returned with the asthma, in
full force. Perhaps what Olive really meant was that she would rather,
after all, be alone. Nevertheless, by August they were both settled
in Kimberley; and by the end of August she was pregnant. For the
next nine months her letters are filled with news of her progress and
of the ideal happiness of her marriage. The asthma disappeared and
the little house in Kimberley was pronounced perfect in every way.
Olive had never been so contented.

The baby was born on 30 April 1895. On May 1, it died.

Olive never ceased to mourn for her baby. For any woman such an
event must be shattering; for Olive, even more so than for many others.
She had craved this child so long and so ardently. The desire for it
had been one of her main reasons for getting married. The thought
of it had quite changed her vision of what life might be. She clung
to Cron, who valiantly played his part. He even kept her pregnant:
over the next eighteen months, Olive had three miscarriages. But
even more important now was his role as Olive's voice in active
politics. Politically they saw eye to eye – inevitably, for although his
sympathies had been liberal in the first place, it was Olive who had

overseen his detailed political formation. Cron could play an active role in canvassing and speaking in the liberal cause as she could not – though her growing influence was well-known. In August 1895, a leader in the *South African Telegraph* entitled 'The Eternal Petticoat' strongly deprecated, in general terms but clearly with Olive in mind, the female influence in politics.[90] And indeed, with Will's growing importance in South African politics – he finally accepted the premiership in October 1898 – and her intimate knowledge of Rhodes and his *modus operandi*, Olive's was a voice that could not be dismissed.

The years 1895–1900, which were the happiest of Olive and Cron's married life, were also of course violent and dramatic years in South African politics, leading up as they did through the ill-starred Jameson Raid, which took place over the New Year 1895–6, to the Boer War, in which the British Government, having disowned the Raid, completed Jameson's and Rhodes's work for them. To read Olive's correspondence for this period is to become aware of the never-ending political intrigue and activity in which she was involved. She knew most of the main protagonists well, and knew too how they should be manipulated. Had she been a man, and so able to take an overt part in political life, her course would have been more straightforward, though possibly no more successful. As things were, she had to make the best use of the political instruments – i.e., sympathetically-disposed men – to hand.

Chief among these was her brother, Will Schreiner. He was her favourite, certainly her closest friend, among her siblings; an amiable lawyer who had married into a leading Cape political family and later gone into politics himself. (Will's wife was a Boer, but the Schreiners, despite their name, were not: their father, Gottlob Schreiner, had been German, and their mother was English.)

Until the Jameson Raid Will Schreiner had been, like the rest of Olive's family, a supporter of Rhodes. But the Raid showed that anyone of even mildly liberal views could no longer support Rhodes, and Olive prophesied correctly that Will would now, with Boer support, make his own political way. She did not think he was cut out for politics – 'You know, Will, you have more the qualities of a great and successful administrator than those that go to make a politician,' she told him in 1893. 'You have none of the vices that are almost indispensable to the successful politician, and your virtues are not virtues that will tell.'[91] Olive, however, had exactly the acute political sense Will lacked; her letters to him are filled with shrewd advice and the telling insights of the born politician.

About Rhodes, her old adversary whom she so much admired, Olive had mixed feelings of political disgust and personal sympathy. To W. T. Stead she wrote, 'For Rhodes himself one feels intense pity, as one does for the little Corsican, when one thinks of him eating his supper alone in the little inn the night after the Battle. Rhodes will never rise again in South Africa. His career here is ended; and the terrible thing to us who have admired his talent and personality is to have to say, "IT IS WELL SO!"'[92]

Whether Rhodes was or was not finished, it was during these years that Olive's career – the political career that had always been her true bent – can be said most to have flourished. She turned her literary talent to it, publishing a bitter short novel or allegory about the brutal activities of the Chartered Company, *Trooper Peter Halket of Mashonaland*, the effect of which Rhodes tried to minimize by putting it about that she had been paid £4,000 for it – a slander which infuriated the always-broke Olive. More presciently than most South African politicians, she saw that Rhodes was down, but not necessarily out. To John X. Merriman, a leading liberal, she wrote after the Raid: 'I am exceedingly depressed about political and public affairs in this country. To you who are more behind the scenes it may seem ridiculous, but I am continually haunted by the dread that Rhodes and his backers in high circles at home will yet plunge South Africa in war. It seems to me his last card. If he fails in that he is done for.'[93]

This being so, her great mission at this time was to turn English opinion away from support of Rhodes, and to this end she set to work on her old acquaintance W. T. Stead, the friend and supporter of Rhodes and his brand of imperialism. Immediately after the Raid, Stead did his very best to see his old friend exonerated and the Parliamentary Inquiry into the whole business dropped, and when that failed, to get all blame heaped upon Joseph Chamberlain, who was now Colonial Secretary. Olive wrote endless papers and articles for the English and South African press promoting the liberal view of the Raid, trying to show that the interests of big business and those of the British in South Africa were not necessarily identical, that the Boers were not tools of the Kaiser, and that nothing was to be gained from brutalizing and enslaving the black population. Up to the end she was intriguing frantically to avert the war, and still, despite everything, hoping for a child: as late as September 1899 she wrote to Mrs Isie Smuts, 'I am better though not yet quite strong after the miscarriage I had the last week at Johannesburg. I knew I should never go my time in all that sorrow and darkness . . . You see the better half of the English nation is moving for us now, but I fear for me it is too late.'94

And indeed Stead, at least, had moved. As the facts about the Jameson Raid emerged at the Commons Inquiry, he could no longer support either Chamberlain's South African policy or his old friend Rhodes. Much influenced by Olive's 'An English South-African's View of the Situation', he produced in September 1899 a pamphlet of his own, 'Shall I Slay My Brother Boer?' But it was too late: by then war was inevitable. A letter of Olive's to Will written at this time shows the kind of delicate game she was playing:

Dear Laddie,
I enclose a letter I have just got from Hobson, the Manchester Guardian representative (he's the man whose book on Modern Capitalism I once sent you, a splendid fellow).

You will see he is very anxious I should cable home. I am sending a short cable today, merely stating how enormous the evils of war would be, and backing John Morley's speech. [Morley had spoken in his constituency at Arbroath on 5 September, the first important British politician to warn against the drift to war.]

I should like to cable much more fully were I in Pretoria or Cape Town and therefore *fully in touch with the movement of the moment*. If you or Hofmeyr [leader of the Cape Boers] can suggest anything which it would be well I should cable I would find it helpful. Would a eulogistic mention of Butler [the British Commander-in-Chief, who had resigned and sailed for England on 22 August] be out of place? *You* can not well so praise him, as being ministers of the Crown your relation to Milner [the Governor and High Commissioner, a one-time protégé of Stead's] is very delicate, *mine different* . . .

There is only one point on which it seems to me that you and I are inclined to differ. I fancy that you hold that it would not be a bad thing if the flag of the Transvaal as an independent state went down, and by peaceful means it became a colony under the English crown. Now to myself, this means the death of South African freedom. *Ultimately* we have nothing to fight the capitalists with but the guns and forts of the Transvaal. Milner would have turned you all off long ago and put Rhodes and Co. in your places, but for that armed shadow in the background. . . .

I can't go into a consideration of all the arguments on which I base my view – no doubt you have gone over the whole ground as carefully as I have myself. I would like to know on what a thoughtful mind like yours bases its desire for Union. If the English government once gains control of the Transvaal in a military sense, it seems to me South Africa may and almost must fall entirely into the hands of the Capitalists.[95]

Olive had mocked Stead years before for his devotion to spiritualism. She recounted to him a dream she had had about Rhodes 'walking by with his big felt hat on, drawn down very low on his head, and an overcoat with the collar turned up, and his head sunk very low between his shoulders. I ran up to him and stood before him. He did not speak a word but he opened his overcoat; as he turned it back I saw his whole throat and chest covered with blood, and his face ghastly pale like a dead person's.'[96] The dream had been so vivid that when she met her brother Will and he said, 'I have something to tell you,' she had immediately assumed it was to say that Rhodes had fallen off his horse and been killed. But he had not. Now, however, with the war-clouds darkening, she wrote to Will: 'I have a curious deep feeling that I cannot explain, that Rhodes's blood-stained hand will never grasp that Johannesburg gold he has so sinned for. I see for that miserable man his doom approaching rapidly.'[97]

This time she was right: Rhodes died in Cape Town in 1902, before the conclusion of the war.

With the war, Olive's real life ended, and so did that of her marriage. It had been sustained by two things: the hope of a child and shared political endeavour. At forty-five there was no longer much hope of a child, and political hope and activity were also ended. When Cron returned to their old house in Johannesburg, he found the place looted, and her desk and papers, the manuscript of the 'sex book' on which Olive had been working for so many years, almost entirely burned and destroyed.

But the Woman Question that had so dominated her life was not to be so easily dismissed. 'Some months later in the war when confined in a little up-country hamlet . . . I was living in a little house, on the outskirts of the village, in a single room, with a stretcher and two packing-cases as furniture, and with my little dog for company . . . A high barbed-wire fence, guarded by armed natives, surrounded the village, through which it would have been death to try to escape. All day the pom-poms from the armoured trains, that paraded on the railway line nine miles distant, could be heard at intervals . . . When a conflict was fought near by, the dying and wounded were brought in; three men belonging to our village were led out for execution; death sentences were read in our little market-place; our prison was filled with our fellow-countrymen; and we did not know from hour to hour what the next would bring to any of us. Under these conditions I felt it necessary I should resolutely force my thought at times from the horror of the world around me, to dwell on some abstract question, and it was under these circumstances that [*Woman and Labour*] was written.'[98] *Woman and Labour*, published in 1911, was her last substantial book; as far as Olive was concerned, a token for that 'sex-book' on which she had been working for all her adult life.

For Olive, her marriage during these years was little more than a token. For Cronwright, too, it was a disappointment. He became a successful businessman; he offered Olive all the financial and domestic security she could need; but she remained unable to produce her great work, and they grew further apart as the years went by. In 1913 she left, alone, for Europe – a separation which acknowledged, with some relief on both sides, what was now the reality of their marriage. As she grew older Olive became increasingly trying to live with. Her asthma meant that she slept very little; she generally spent the night pacing from room to room, slamming doors behind her as she went – a habit not calculated to endear her to anyone who preferred to sleep. It was a habit which had grown up in South Africa, but it persisted in England, and because of it, she found herself an unwelcome guest even among her oldest friends. This in turn exacerbated her sense of isolation during the next few years, which she spent willy-nilly in London, caught as she was by the Great War. It was a hellish period – particularly so for a person with a German name and pacifist convictions. 'No-one wants me,' she wrote to Cron. 'I'm [in] no relation with the life or thought in England or Africa or anywhere else. What I do feel a little hard is that people should now turn on me – twenty-five years ago . . . they all approved and admired . . . I am only holding the same views now!'[99] Once again she was a displaced person, old now, and alone. Her brother Will, meanwhile, whose political hand she had held for so long, was comfortably placed as High Commissioner for the Union of South Africa in London.

In 1920 Cron sold his business and came to London that July to look for Olive, whom he had not seen for six years. He was shocked by what he found. 'She had aged greatly. Her bright hair was grey; her glorious eyes were almost closed and but little remained in the sick woman of that bursting elemental force which was so arresting and dominating in her tremendous personality. Her bright, vivid colour had gone; she looked small and dark and Jewish; her vibrating voice was so gentle.'[100]

They had some happy times together. Then, in August, Olive sailed for South Africa – alone. She died soon after.

5

Not the least part of Olive Schreiner's remarkableness was that she not only formulated principles by which she thought women ought to live, she tried to live by them herself. She did not bow to circumstances.

The Woman Question was her life, but, as she told Karl Pearson at the very start of their friendship, this did not exclude the Man Question. The New Woman sought the New Man. 'If anywhere on earth exists the perfect ideal of that which the modern woman desires to be – of a labouring and virile womanhood, free, strong, fearless and tender – it will probably be found imaged in the heart of the New Man,' she wrote in *Woman and Labour*, 'engendered there by his own highest needs and aspirations.'[101] To a certain extent her life was a search for this ideal personage.

Did she ever find him? Havelock Ellis, Karl Pearson, Cecil Rhodes were, in their very different ways, among the outstanding men of their day; but none of them fitted Olive's ideal, though Ellis consciously strove towards it – not always successfully. To judge from her letters, the person who came nearest to Olive's ideal was Edward Carpenter. Carpenter, who was some years older than Olive (he was born in 1844) was a proponent of fulfilment through the simple life. He had been a Cambridge mathematician, and had held a curacy as well as a college fellowship, but had rejected this easy life for university extension lecturing in the north of England where, after some years, he decided to settle on a smallholding where (helped by two friends) he could be self-sufficient. He was by now a vegetarian and enjoyed, as well as the manual labour of the smallholding, swimming, sunbathing and writing in the open air – activities taken up by Havelock Ellis and Bernard Shaw. He was also a Rational Dresser (he preferred loose, usually woollen garments) and – most important from Olive's point of view – a committed and vocal proponent of sexual freedom. He himself was homosexual, and at his smallholding lived an open, though discreet, life with a series of lovers. This courage and tolerance won him (as we shall see) a devoted following among some New Women. But of course his homosexuality allowed him to retain his halo without ever having to put it to the test of living with one of them.

And Cronwright? How did he fit into this pattern?

In many ways, he fitted the specifications remarkably well. In one of the most telling passages of *Woman and Labour*, Olive demolishes the theorist who asserts, ' "Let Woman be content to be the 'Divine Child-Bearer', and ask no more." ' She continues: 'And to-day, when the lofty theorist, who to-night stands before the drawing-room fire in spotless shirt-front and perfectly fitting clothes, and declaims upon the amplitude of woman's work in life as child-bearer, and the mighty value of that labour which exceeds all other, making it unnecessary for her to share man's grosser and lower toils: is it certain he always in practical life remembers his theory? When waking tomorrow morning, he finds that the elderly house drudge, who rises at dawn while he yet sleeps to make his tea and clean his boots, has brought his tea late and polished his boots ill; may he not even sharply condemn her, and assure her she will have to leave unless she works harder and rises earlier? Does he exclaim to her, "Divine child-bearer! Potential mother of the race! Why should you clean my boots or bring up my tea, while I lie warm in bed? Is it not enough you should have the holy and mysterious power of bringing the race to life? Let that content you. Henceforth I shall get up at dawn and make my own tea and clean my own boots, and pay you just the same!" '[102]

Should such a paragon ever have existed, Cronwright, whom she had formed intellectually and politically and who hero-worshipped her, was the man. After they were married, 'Olive had practically nothing to do except give the house-servant orders. I had run the house myself for many years and, as far as possible, continued to do so, largely in order to leave her free to do her literary work. She had not even to supervise the dairy, which I personally continued to run just as before.'[103] And in point of tenderness, especially while she was pregnant and after the loss of the baby, her letters testify continually to Cron's excellence.

No, it was not Cron who, when it came to the point, did not keep his side of the contract – but Olive. He was the perfect wife, as the perfect wife has most traditionally been defined. He gave her the ideal conditions for work; she could not work. She was prostrated by asthma and 'I do not think she did any writing of consequence on the farm,' he says. Indeed, it turned out that she could not do any writing of consequence on any farm, since farms need water and water brought on Olive's asthma. So, although Cron liked farming and was good at it, he agreed to move to Kimberley, where she felt better, and take articles in an attorney's office. On Olive's side, 'she said that if she had two years there, she would finish her two "big" novels, *From Man to Man* and *The Buddhist Priest's Wife*, which she calculated would bring in £30,000 and make us independent. Once more I had to decide against myself; I felt I simply could not pursue a course which would prevent her writing. . . . It mattered little to me personally whether she made much or little money by her writings; the problem was for her to do her work, which was in my estimation, of much greater importance than anything I could do.'[104]

But however ideal the conditions, the reasons Olive was never able to write were, as we have seen, not to do with the climate. The fact was that, when it came down to it, writing – or writing *only* – was not what she was cut out for. In her own way she was as much a woman of action as her friend Eleanor Marx. Capacity for action was one of the psychic attributes which most attracted her – that was the secret of Cecil Rhodes's attraction for her, and that was the reason why Havelock Ellis could never have held her, as she herself pointed out. Olive's peculiar psychology probably meant that contentment was impossible for her except perhaps with the lost child; and perhaps it was her own perception of this which made that loss so especially and terribly hard for her to bear. She both liked men and needed them sexually, and at the same time found it impossible to live with the kind of man whose tenderness might have made her happy. Perhaps it is a tribute to the optimism of the New Woman that she took so very long to reconcile herself to the bleak fact that, even among the New Men, there was in the end no man for her.

THE USES OF PRINCIPLE
1 : HAVELOCK AND EDITH

I

It was not until Olive returned to South Africa in 1889 that Havelock Ellis was able to accept what he had in fact long known – 'that we were never to be more than affectionate friends'.[1] Thus freed, he began a new and uncharacteristically active social and professional life; and in December 1891, married Edith Lees.

There are certain difficulties in telling the story of Havelock and Edith, the greatest of which is that there remains no direct account of her side of the affair. She kept no diary; few of her letters survive, and even if they did, it is doubtful if they would be very revealing, since her view of their marriage followed her husband's prescription almost until the end. The main source is Havelock's memoirs, *My Life*, which he wrote after her death in 1916. This book, although it contains many verbatim transcriptions of Edith's letters, is otherwise exceedingly unreliable as an account of what really took place in the marriage.

Edith was not a new acquaintance. Since 1887 she had been active in the Fellowship of the New Life, and although Havelock was no longer much connected with this group he usually went along for its country walks. On one of these he was introduced to Edith. On that occasion neither of them much took to the other. Havelock struck Edith as badly-dressed and feebly irreverent, while she did not attract him – he was particularly repelled by her large, rather protuberant pale blue eyes, a feature which he never grew to like.

During the course of the next couple of years they inevitably ran across each other from time to time, sharing as they did many of the same friends and interests. 'Thirty years ago two significant and yet apparently insignificant matters drove thinking women further towards their own emancipation,' Edith was to write in a pen-portrait of Olive. 'One was the publication of a book published under the name of Ralph Iron called *The Story of an African Farm*, and the other was the banging of the door in Ibsen's *Doll's House*. How well I remember, after the first performance of Ibsen's drama in London, with Janet Achurch as Nora, when a few of us collected outside the theatre breathless with excitement. Olive Schreiner was there, and Dolly Radford the poetess, Dr. Alice Corthorn, Honor Brooke (Stopford Brooke's eldest daughter), Mrs Holman Hunt and Eleanor Marx.'[2] This roll-call of New Women of course included many friends of Ellis, who was himself an enthusiastic Ibsenite and had attended the early Ibsen playreadings organized by the Avelings, Bernard Shaw and May Morris. In 1885 he invited Eleanor to translate *An Enemy of Society* (now generally known as *An Enemy of the People*) for a cheap English edition of Ibsen's plays which he was planning, a commission which she gratefully accepted. This appeared in 1888; the first public performance of *A Doll's House*, on the occasion mentioned by Edith, took place in 1889. Edith had at that time just become secretary of the Fellowship of the New Life. But, although they knew each other, there seemed no reason why she and Havelock should become better acquainted.

Then, in 1890, the spirit of James Hinton fatefully intervened yet again in the life of his most ardent disciple. In the summer of that year, Edith set out on a walking tour of Cornwall, accompanied by her friend and servant Ellen Taylor. They left Penzance, and on 13 August reached Lamorna, where Miss Agnes Jones lived, an acquaintance of Edith's who had been in correspondence with her regarding the Fellowship. Edith called to see her and was invited to stay the night.

Agnes Jones had been a great devotee of James Hinton, and one of those instrumental in financing Ellis's medical studies. She had at that time mistakenly taken his interest in Hinton to mean that he was interested in her, had fallen in love with him, and had been terribly jealous of Olive on that account. But that episode was now closed, and she and Havelock had resumed their friendship. He had finally qualified, and had just completed a week's work as locum for a Dr Bonar at Probus, near Truro. After that he planned to take a holiday, and Miss Jones had invited him to stay for ten days from 13 August. She mentioned this to Edith after Edith and Ellen had been shown their rooms, and Edith immediately wondered whether they should perhaps not stay after all. Havelock described this occasion in his memoirs: 'A man was coming (so, she used to tell me, she said) whom she disliked, and would prefer not to meet. Should they push on that same day to Land's End? It was Ellen who decided the matter. Her feet were already sore from much walking; she pleaded for a quiet rest in that comfortable house. Edith agreed, the more readily as it was not easy to reject the accepted invitation. A servant's sore feet changed the whole course of my life. Late that afternoon Edith saw a figure in a professional silk hat, bag in hand, and wearing (so at least she always asserted) a torn mackintosh, walk up the path to the house.'[3]

The meeting this time was quite different from that three years earlier. They found an almost immediate easy intimacy, and the next day Ellis and Miss Jones accompanied the two walkers along the coastguards' path towards Land's End. 'No fragment of the conversation remains, only the reminiscence of a pleasant feeling of association . . . The lithe and sturdy little figure passed on with knapsack on back, and the stout staff, as long as herself ("the little lady with the big stick," the people called her) she long afterwards used.' For a week the two rambled separately around Cornwall, then, unexpectedly and without arrangement, they met again in St Ives. Now they were able to talk alone, without Miss Jones or Ellen, who 'could be left to trudge in our wake. We exchanged views on marriage and they proved congenial. I can no longer remember what I said, but I know that in her mind some of the things then said always remained.'[4]

In September Havelock returned to London, where he and his sister Louie, after their mother's death, had taken a house in St Mary's Terrace, Paddington. Edith, too, was living in London. The Fellowship had decided to set up a house, 'Fellowship House', at 29 Doughty Street, of which Edith, as secretary, was organizer, and Ellen the domestic mainstay; the other main organizer was Ramsay MacDonald, later to become the first Labour Prime Minister, then just beginning his political life as private secretary to a Member of Parliament. He already had his eyes set on higher things – Edith told Ellis that he had just declared his intention of becoming Prime Minister some day – though his friends had less confidence in his future career than he did himself: 'When in some moment of misplaced irritation MacDonald once told Edith that she was trying to reach success by clinging to his coat-tails she received the accusation with mixed feelings; it had never occurred to her that this was a road to success.'⁵

Edith wrote a novel about this experiment, entitled *Attainment*, portraying the house and its inmates as the members of the Brotherhood of the Perfect Life. The work is fairly mediocre, but it has its moments, including one in which the members of the Brotherhood, universally incapable of housework, try to justify to themselves the fact that it will, inevitably, be done by Ann, the servant (a portrait of Edith's servant Ellen Taylor).

'It will be awfully nice to get rid of that badge of servitude, won't it, Ann . . .?' He pointed to Ann's cap and apron. Ann instinctively touched both as if in fear that they had already disappeared. She answered simply:

'I've never been in no capless place. I should feel a sloven without cap and apron.'

'But it implies you are a servant,' broke in Henry Staines emphatically, 'a mere means, a drudge for another's pleasure and profit. You must feel free and be free. In our house we shall all join in the work.'

'Oh, dear!' sighed Ann. 'I can't abide betwixt and between work. I was in a place once where the young ladies did a bit of housework in the mornings for their health, but the tidying up after them was a bigger job than the work itself. I got so fretted over it, the doctor ordered them golf instead.'

'It will all be very different in our scheme,' said Stott decidedly. 'We shall live so simply that there will scarcely be anything to do. Of course, you will be one of us, not only as a member but as one entitled to the same leisure as ourselves, and you will, of course, have your meals with us and be free in every way.' . . .

Ann's face was serious.

'What wages?' she asked at last. 'Because I'd rather do a bit more work and not have my wages lowered.'

Rachel bent forward and addressed the group.

'Surely that is one of our chief ideas, is it not?' she asked; 'that servile work, if undertaken willingly by any member, should be better paid, because of its disagreeableness, than skilled labour.'

'Certainly,' said Stott. . . . 'If – turning to Ann – 'you undertake the chief part of the rough work in the house we will willingly give you double the wages you are now receiving.'

Ann's eyes opened very wide . . . 'I'll work like a black,' she said, 'and work my fingers to the bone. I'm no great eater and I'm an early riser and don't never answer back.'[6]

It is a scene that recalls the stories told about the Fabian household of Sidney Olivier, who became Lord Olivier and High Commissioner of Jamaica. The Oliviers' servants, as befitted a good socialist household, ate together with the family, by all accounts to everyone's acute embarrassment. And indeed Sidney Olivier lived for a time in Fellowship House. 'Fellowship is Hell,' Edith would later declare, 'and lack of Fellowship is Heaven.'[7]

The Edith figure in the book is Rachel, an idealistic young girl who comes from Cornwall, where Edith spent a large part of her life. But in one very important respect Rachel differs from Edith. Rachel is the daughter of a country doctor who is in every way an ideal father figure, loving, tolerant, trusting and generous. This may have been the father Edith would have wanted; but he in no way resembled the one she actually had.

Edith's family came from Lancashire. Her great-grandfather had made a fortune; he was a miserly, tyrannical man, but (Ellis notes) 'very kind to animals'. He left £30,000 to charity and £20,000 to his grandson Samuel, Edith's father; his son Silas, Edith's grandfather, was 'a drunken collier who would chase his wife round the room with a carving knife'. Samuel Lees inherited many of the family characteristics, though not the ability to make money: he soon ran through his inheritance. 'He was,' writes Ellis, 'highly eccentric in some of his ways and habits, of angular disposition, nervous, hypochondriacal, fastidious, irritable, cruel, one of those tortured persons who cannot help torturing others. It was in this way that he tortured his daughter. . . . He tried to break her spirit by force and punishment, but the very opposite effect was produced . . . At the same time he aroused in her a deep resentment not only against himself but to some extent against all men, which persisted through the greater part of life.'[8] To compound Edith's miseries, her mother died giving birth to her, and her father remarried; the stepmother proved as unable as the father to love or even like the little girl.

Edith received a scrappy schooling, partly in a convent, partly in London. When she was twenty-one she started her own school, in Sydenham, south London. It was not a success, and after two or three years she was hopelessly in debt and in the midst of a nervous breakdown. From this distress two good friends rescued her. One was a Mrs Drake, a wealthy old lady who heard of Edith's troubles and eased her money worries. The other was Honor Brooke, the eldest daughter of a fashionable preacher, the Revd Stopford Brooke, who lived in Manchester Square in the heart of the West End and urged charity upon his wealthy congregation. Honor took Edith to Manchester Square, nursed her back to health, and directed her reviving energies towards social work in the slums (also described in *Attainment*). It was at the Brookes' house that Edith met Percival Chubb, the then secretary of the Fellowship of the New Life.

Edith was small but strong, with curly fair hair and an exceedingly beautiful speaking voice. She was two years younger than Ellis: when they met in Cornwall she was twenty-nine, he, thirty-one. After they returned to London, she took to calling by his house from time to time, and one day, suddenly and for no obvious reason, burst out with the news that she was in love with Percival Chubb, who, however, showed no signs of reciprocation and had now moved to America.

Havelock was somewhat nonplussed by this confidence. 'How I responded to that confidence I am unable to recall,' he wrote after Edith's death nearly thirty years later. 'But gradually a certain degree of intimacy developed, without any ardour of absorption . . . I scarcely think that then, or indeed ever, I showed much inquisitive eagerness to question her. When I first began to know Olive Schreiner I had carefully formed with her help a complete and orderly picture of her earlier life. I never at any time felt a similar impulse in regard to Edith.'[9]

Nevertheless, the pair began to see more of each other: an intimacy that grew the more readily since neither of them had any other particular attachments. They visited concerts, music-halls, any Ibsen performances, the occasional restaurant. Ellis, though poor, always enjoyed good food, an interest which Edith had never till then shared: she had always been too poor or too preoccupied with other things, and at the Fellowship House had been led to adopt a vegetarian diet consisting mainly of fruit and nuts. As time went on the position was to be reversed, and she was to care more for good food and wine than Ellis ever did.

With Olive, Ellis had talked and written about sex; with Edith, the talk was of marriage. They discussed its economics, and agreed that it was essential for the partners to be economically independent of each other as far as possible. They discussed its form, and agreed that although neither of them felt any need for a religious marriage ceremony, they were not attracted, either, by the idea of a free union such as that between Eleanor Marx and Edward Aveling – 'hardly . . . an enticing example to follow,' as Ellis put it.[10]

By the beginning of 1891 they were meeting and writing frequently, and Edith began to feel she should warn Havelock that she had a melancholic side to her nature which he had had as yet no occasion to see. 'She [warned] me repeatedly of her "moods and morbidities," of which yet indeed I had seen little. Then, and ever, she felt humbly about herself at heart, however arrogant and domineering she could be on the surface, far too proud to let the world guess her humility. In reply I assured her that I could bear with the morbid – having perhaps a trace of it in myself – better than with the commonplace.'[11]

By the middle of the year it was clear they were heading towards marriage, and once again Edith had worries which she felt she must make clear. They were both talking about 'marriage', but each seemed to have in mind a very different type of union. Edith wanted to be properly and totally married. 'She set forth her . . . inability to accept symbols in place of realities, or a part in place of the whole, and her own ideal of a complete and permanent union of body and soul.' In other words Edith, who all her life had been alone and buffeted by the world, wanted the assurance of a secure base, recognized by society as well as by themselves, before she would commit herself. Havelock, on the other hand, was not eager to rush into matrimony just yet: he wanted to see if the relationship would work first. 'I held that an intimate personal relationship need not necessarily be open to the world, that the State was only concerned with it when the question of children arose, and that the formality of marriage should consecrate an existing relationship rather than be set up irrevocably before it could ever be ascertained that a real relationship was possible.'[12] As to the nature of this ideal relationship he had been quite clear even before he met Olive; he described it to her in a letter early in their friendship, a description that embodies much of what he set out to achieve with Edith: 'You would keep the ideal of a man and a woman both intensely absorbed in, and devoted to, each other,' he wrote then. 'That was mine till a year or two ago. But it means so much torture – a striving after what cannot perhaps be attained and then a falling back – "a striving & a striving, an ending in nothing". I see now that the best kind of union between a man and a woman is a sort of camaraderie (temporary or permanent, better permanent) between two people who care about the same things, who are going the same way, and can walk arm in arm, and kiss and encourage each other on the way.' He added, almost as an afterthought, 'I would have the passion thrown in.'[13]

The thought of Olive understandably worried Edith. It was clear that Havelock had entertained – possibly still did entertain – feelings for her of a quite other quality than those between himself and Edith. For her he had felt a great passion; between Havelock and Edith, passion (even 'thrown in') was just what there was not. 'It was clearly not a union of unrestrainable passion,' he wrote. 'I, though I failed yet clearly to realise why, was conscious of no inevitably passionate sexual attraction to her, and she, also without yet clearly realising why, had never felt genuinely passionate sexual attraction for any man. . . . The union was thus fundamentally at the outset, what later it became consciously, a union of affectionate comradeship, in which the specific emotions of sex had the smallest part.'[14] In June this discontent came to a head, and Havelock was forced to confront it. The letter he wrote Edith was 'perhaps the most difficult and deliberate letter I ever addressed to her' – its singularity indicated by the fact that – unlike most of his other letters – it was carefully dated: 13 June 1891.

We have never needed any explanations before, and that has always seemed so beautiful to me, that we seemed to understand instinctively. And that is why I've never explained things that perhaps needed explaining. This is specially so about Olive. I have never known anyone who was so beautiful and wonderful, or with whom I could be so much myself, and it is true enough that for years to be married to her seemed to me the one thing in the world that I longed for, but that is years ago. We are sweet friends now, and always will be; but to speak in the way you do of a 'vital relationship' to her sounds to me very cruel. Because one has loved somebody who did not love one enough to make the deepest human relationship possible, is that a reason why one must always be left alone? I only explain this to show that I am really free in every sense – perhaps freer than you – and that I haven't been so unfair to you as you seem to think. . . .

Now I've got to explain what I feel about our relationship to each other – and that will be all! Perhaps the only thing that needs explaining is the absence of passionate feeling. I have always told you that I felt so restful and content with you, that the restless, tormenting passionate feeling wasn't there; and I have seen that you didn't feel passionate towards me, but have said over and over again that you didn't believe in passion. So we are quite equal, and why should we quarrel about it? Let us just be natural with each other – leaving the other feeling to grow up or not as it will . . .

We aren't so young that we need fear to face the naked facts of life simply and frankly. You know how much you are to me – exactly how much. Putting aside Olive, I have never loved anyone so deeply and truly, and with the kind of love that seemed to make everything possible and pure, and even my relationship to Olive has not seemed so beautiful and unalloyed as my relationship to you. It has seemed to me that we might perhaps go on becoming nearer and nearer, and dearer and dearer, to each other as time went on. . . . Even as it is we shall be dear comrades as long as we live. You have hurt me rather, but I don't mind because there mustn't be anything false, and our relationship is strong enough to bear a good deal of tugging. Havelock.[15]

After this the tensions between them relaxed; Edith would often write to him as 'My Husband' and sign herself 'Your Wifie'. Later in the summer Miss Jones lent them her house at Lamorna and they spent a week there together. 'Lamorna remains to me the memory of a Paradise I never entered again,' Havelock wrote.[16] They always looked back on that week as their honeymoon. Finally, on 19 December 1891, they were married at the Paddington Register Office: Havelock's witness was his sister Louie, Edith's, her friends Evelyn and Sybil Brooke. The wedding ring, according to their notions of strict financial equality, had been bought jointly at Hatton Garden. 'There was no wedding breakfast. Edith used to say that her only wedding breakfast was of porridge. For the afternoon, however, she had invited all her numerous friends in town to an At Home at the Fellowship House. It was necessary for me to appear at this function, but she mercifully arranged for me to arrive late, so that my discomfort might be of brief duration. Next morning we started for Paris.'[17]

2

One of the important matters that Edith and Havelock had discussed so exhaustively before the marriage was the question of whether or not they should have children. On this question Ellis records 'not the slightest dispute': they decided that parenthood was not for them, in spite of the fact that, then and always, Ellis saw motherhood as the apogee of woman's existence. In *Man and Woman*, the book for which he must have been collecting material throughout this period (it was published in 1894) he wrote in the conclusion: 'Nature has made women more like children in order that they may better understand and care for children, and in the gift of children Nature has given to women a massive and sustained physiological joy to which there is nothing in men's lives to correspond.'[18] Yet this joy was to be denied to Edith.

It is worth looking at this decision in some detail, because the reasons for it, overt and covert, tell us so much about the people concerned – or at least about Havelock: what Edith thought about it all we can only divine obliquely.

There were two practical reasons, they agreed, for not having children. One was economic. They each had a small income, Edith's private, Havelock's earned: in neither case enough to support a family, or indeed more than one person. The kind of lifestyle they envisaged, living part of the time separately, part together, each being economically independent of the other, was what they could reasonably expect to support if things continued in the same way financially. And certainly neither of them wished for anything else. Edith was neurotically independent – or rather, neurotically afraid of being dependent on any man, and so in a position to be ordered about by him. Havelock, meanwhile, had no wish to alter his working habits in order to make more money. This led on to the second reason, which was that children cause noise and disturbance unconducive to the contemplative life. Havelock did not wish to have to accommodate this.

But there were other, much deeper reasons. The first of these was medical.

We have already noted what a very Victorian figure Havelock Ellis was, despite his reputation for daring modernism. This was as true of his medical opinions as of everything else. He was a child of his time, and in this context the current of his time was Social Darwinism. Heredity was all, the fittest would rise to the top, and in an ideal world the least fit would be eradicated. In this way Social Darwinism led on naturally to the new science of eugenics, propounded by Francis Galton and enthusiastically taken up by Karl Pearson, with whom Ellis was at this time in frequent and friendly correspondence. Ellis was an enthusiastic Social Darwinist and was to become an equally enthusiastic proponent of eugenics. In 1890 he had published his second book, *The Criminal*, a study much influenced by Lombroso, with such chapter headings as: 'Cranial and Cerebral Characteristics of the Criminal', 'The Face of the Criminal', 'Criminal Physiognomy', 'Heredity', and so on. Its frontispiece was one of those famous blurred photographs obtained by superimposing different pictures of (in this case) criminals one on top of another until a general 'type' face was obtained.

Of course criminality was not the only characteristic thought to be handed down in this way. Another, it was firmly believed, was mental instability. The hereditary nature of mental disorder was one of the first principles of Victorian psychiatry, one of whose most distinguished proponents, Dr Hack Tuke, was a friend of Ellis's. (In fact recent advances in microbiology seem to confirm that such diseases as schizophrenia and clinical depression may be caused by an inherited gene.) Another such principle was the peculiar proneness of women to mental weakness, a proneness which was 'specifically and confidently linked to the biological crises of the female life-cycle – puberty, pregnancy, childbirth, menopause – during which the mind would be weakened and the symptoms of insanity might emerge'.[19] Not only this: once insanity was established it was considered ineradicable, liable to be handed down from mother to daughter ad infinitum. 'All Darwinian psychiatrists agreed that "the greater tendency of mothers to transmit insanity to their female children" was among the chief causes for the predominance of women among asylum patients.'[20] There was indeed such a predominance, but, as studies such as Elaine Showalter's demonstrate, this seems to have had more to do with a tendency to diagnose insanity in women who showed their discontent with their allotted role in life, and the allied tendency of these discontented women to become deeply depressed, than with anything else.

Against this background, the prognosis for Edith as a potential mother, in Ellis's view, seemed grim. Her father, grandfather and great-grandfather were eccentric and unstable, and she herself had had a nervous breakdown after the failure of her school. As so often, his account of what went on blandly glosses over what must have been some fairly extraordinary conversations. 'We were . . . able to discuss the matter with fair impartiality as a question of her health and ancestry, since my heredity was as nearly as possible perfect, and my health – with due allowance for an intellectual worker's nervous hyperaesthesia – would pass all ordinary tests,' he wrote. 'In resolving this difficulty we were both much influenced by the opinion of her Harley Street physician, Dr Birch.' Dr Birch took a close – possibly, Ellis hints, too close – interest in Edith: and on this point his opinion was clear-cut. 'That opinion was that she ought not to marry, but that if she should marry she certainly ought not to have children. At the same time he . . . told her that he believed she would never find her way to the lunatic asylum, but that if she were ever to enter it she would never come out again.' Ellis was also influenced by a remark made by James Hinton's daughter Margaret, who sometimes went to Bethlem Hospital to play the piano for the women patients. When Ellis asked her what they were like she replied 'Like that Miss Lees.'[21] Under these circumstances, both of them agreed that children were not to be considered.

Ellis makes a point of remarking that this decision had an adverse effect on their subsequent sex-life. 'She always disliked the idea of any kind of what seemed to her unnatural union, and that dislike soon became stronger and had a significant bearing on our relationship,' he records;²² and, 'she had experienced from the outset a dislike to the mechanical contraceptive preliminaries of intercourse.'²³

But all this begs a rather large question. The making of children involves two partners, and contraceptives are unnecessary unless full sexual congress takes place. And this was something that Havelock had never yet achieved – not even with Olive, with whom he was so passionately in love. Was it, then, likely that he would manage it with Edith, for whom he felt little physical desire? It is impossible to imagine that he never thought about this, though he did not record any such thoughts in his autobiography, which is the source of almost everything we know about his relations with Edith – which is, indeed, more or less a case history of his marriage, mostly written in the troubled time after her death. It was, of course, a test he never had to face: Dr Birch and Edith's tainted heredity got him off the hook. It is impossible to be sure, but it seems most improbable that Havelock ever had a full sexual relationship with Edith. If one dislikes mechanical contraceptive devices there are of course always other ways of having a sexual relationship while avoiding pregnancy. But Ellis is always evasive when it comes down to the detail of his own sexual relations. The frankness with which he writes in his *Studies in the Psychology of Sex* does not extend to his autobiography.

What it does contain, however, is a good deal of self-justification on the question of Edith's enforced childlessness, which seems to indicate that this was not a decision she would have reached had he not backed up her doctor's advice so enthusiastically. That she would very much have liked to have a child is indicated by a letter she wrote him a year after their first honeymoon week together at Lamorna: 'My love, do you know that by the day of the week this is the day a year ago when you and I went to our little house with the foxgloves and gave ourselves to ourselves? I look back and it seems years and years ago. I was shy and frightened and cried over my wee babe that was never to be, and you! – you made me think of how beautiful men could be.'²⁴ Presumably some form of sex took place then, though exactly what it was Ellis does not say. One of the things which had given him most pleasure with Olive was to lie together naked and cuddle. Olive had found this unsatisfying and, indeed, very frustrating, but perhaps it was more to the taste of the shy and inexperienced Edith.

The thought of the child she had failed to have remained in her mind. A few years later, perhaps thinking, as every woman and especially every childless woman must, that she was getting older and soon it would be too late, she proposed that they resume sexual relations (which had by then entirely ceased between them); but Ellis simply let the proposal 'drop without discussion, and she never brought it forward again. The whole matter seemed entirely to pass from our minds; so much remained that it seemed to leave no blank.'[25] To him perhaps not; but Edith reverted to the subject at least twice more. In 1909 she wrote a wistful letter to Edward Carpenter: 'A new and beautiful person has come like a bolt from the blue, into my life as my son to me. A starving artist of 21 . . . His kiss last night effaced all the barrenness. What matter who bore him? He is mine now.'[26] And in 1916, just before her death, Ellis mentions that she became attached to another such young man. But how could she insist on having a child against the massed forces of medical advice and eugenic principle, urged by the two men who knew her best and cared for her most? To persist with her own desire in face of all this would simply place her among the ranks of the hysterical and unreasonable. Besides, this was to be a model marriage, an exemplar of advanced thought. They must put into practice what they would preach to others.

So Edith forwent her child, a decision that of course affected the whole of the rest of her life – and Havelock's too; but none of the regrets were his, all were hers.

Once a woman has made a conscious decision not to have a child, the way she looks at the rest of her life is changed. Immediately, an enormous importance is attached to everything she does instead. To some degree the rest of her life has to justify this decision, which is after all momentous for any woman. If she has a career, it must be particularly successful and fulfilling. Where this is so there need be no regrets, though it is still hard entirely to dismiss thoughts of what might have been. Beatrice Webb, for instance, who was three years older than Edith, made several diary entries on the subject in 1901, when she was forty-three: 'Nearly nine years of married life leads me to bless the institution and my good fortune in entering it with such a partner. We are still on our honeymoon and every year makes our relationship more tender and complete. Rightly or wrongly we decided against having children; I was no longer young, he had been working from childhood, we were both of us unusually energetic. Our means, though ample for ourselves and our work, would not have allowed a family and continued expenditure on investigation and public life. But perhaps the finally conclusive reason was that I had laboriously and with many sacrifices transformed my intellect into an instrument for research. Child-bearing would destroy it, at any rate for a time, probably altogether. Sometimes I wonder whether I have been dutiful to the community in shirking motherhood, whether in point of fact I have not lost at once a safety valve for feeling and a valuable experience. But on the whole I do not regret the decision, still less does Sidney.' That was in January; in April she reverted to the same subject: 'Are the books we have written together worth (to the community) the babies we might have had?'[27]

Beatrice never really had any regrets; and indeed the difficulties of those women who tried to combine an active political life with the care of a young family seem to bear out her decision. Eleanor Marx's two elder sisters, Jenny and Laura, for example, suffered extremely through their children – firstly through the sheer boredom and frustration of domestic entrapment, later watching, agonized and helpless, while the little ones died. In 1882 Jenny, married to Charles Longuet and living at Argenteuil, near Paris, wrote to Laura: 'Those blessed babies, though really charming, good-tempered little fellows, put such a strain upon my nervous system by day and by night, that I often long for no matter what release from this ceaseless round of nursing, and think with a pang of Farringdon Street, where when I was not stifling with asthma, I could at least indulge in my morning daily, and on alighting run down the muddy Strand . . . which I miss more than I can say in this Argenteuil waste, where I hear and see nothing but the baker and butcher and cheesemonger and greengrocer. I do believe that even the dull routine of factory work is not more killing than are the endless duties of the *ménage* . . . Some women, I know . . . glory in this home drudgery – but we are not all made of the same stuff.'[28] Not that the Marx girls, brought up as they had been in a warmly affectionate family, would ever have dreamed of choosing *not* to have children; her lack of children was a source of never-ceasing sadness to Eleanor (and was probably attributable to Aveling, since there were never any rumours of his having fathered any despite his indiscriminate sexual habits).

But in none of these cases was the decision imposed on the woman by the man. It was either genuinely mutual, as in the case of the Webbs, or, as with the Marx daughters, the kind of decision that simply did not need to be taken: babies were something to be eagerly loved whatever the other consequences. And the point is that it *could not* have been so foisted. All these women were too sure of their identity for that. They knew who they were in a way one never feels Edith really did. It is, of course, true that to be unsure of one's identity is by no means unusual in either men or women. But if one is unsure in this way, then enforced independence with neither family life nor any particular career in prospect seems designed only to make things worse.

For one of the principles upon which Havelock and Edith had agreed was that each was to be economically independent of the other, since social equality and independence were inseparable from economic independence. Edith had a cottage at Carbis in Cornwall, while Havelock continued to live in London. Generally they spent the winters together in Cornwall and the summers seeing each other less frequently, alternating between the countryside near London, where they usually rented a cottage, and the city. In the early days of their marriage they constantly reiterated to each other this need for independence. Edith wrote to Havelock: 'I believe in folk separating at intervals, don't you? Yes, I know you do. How I should loathe a creature I was *always* near!'[29] And a year later he wrote to her: 'I'm afraid that I'm not altogether sorry that I shan't be able to go [to London] with you on Sunday . . . I don't at all like to feel that you are at all dependent on me in any way except of love. I don't feel dependent on you in those things and I'm sure I could never have loved you if I hadn't felt that you were strong and independent. You are, *really*, my sweetheart, are you not? – I can't bear to think that you are ever such a tiny bit like those wives who hang round their husbands' necks like millstones. I'm sure you aren't *really*.'[30] In short, Havelock absolutely refused to act as a social foil or escort for Edith: there was in their marriage none of that unquestioning social support which for many people is one of marriage's great boons. It might be there or it might not: it could not be taken for granted.

In many ways this was probably a good thing. Edith was a highly sociable person who sought company and sparkled in it, while Havelock was just the opposite: he hated company and was almost a recluse. 'If, like a St Bernard dog, he could express himself in his daily human life, through wagging a tail or lashing it, or barking and growling in turn, while keeping his written words for his more adequate expression, social life would not have such terrors for him as now,' Edith wrote some years later.[31]

But while Havelock was always perfectly happy with these arrangements, and insistent upon maintaining them, Edith did not find them so easy. Not that it was any problem for her to keep busy. For some years she kept a smallholding down at Carbis, then, when that got to be too much for her, she would do up cottages and rent them to summer visitors; and in the latter part of her life she published several novels and plays and books of essays, and undertook two lecture-tours of America. But she found it more difficult than Havelock either to make an adequate living or to bear the periods of separation upon which he continued to insist. For his part, he had, even in his relationship with Olive, shown an extraordinary, almost abnormal capacity to do without the presence of the beloved, so that actual physical contiguity was something to be remarked upon. For example, 'I always feel so glad that we got so near to each other – physically near – that evening. We could never have got the effect of that by writing,' he wrote her on one occasion[32] – as though anyone but himself would ever have imagined for a second that writing could produce the same effect of intimacy as an evening together.

In fact, even Havelock, after Edith's death, expressed some reservations about this insistence on independence, but they concerned his inability to keep control over her extravagance rather than the evident loneliness for his company which she often expressed. 'The principle seems a sound one, and I should hesitate to admit that my faith in it has wavered,' he wrote after her death. 'Yet I cannot say that in our case it proved a success. In practice it gave greater scope to her than to me, because of her greater practical energy, of her more impetuous impulse and swifter decision. It enabled her to live out her own life in great freedom, and therein I often benefited, but it also led her into many mistakes from which I also, and sometimes chiefly, suffered. Again and again it would happen that, on her own initiative, with all the ardent precipitancy of her nature, she would take up a new scheme, without waiting even a day to consult me, and I could scarcely refuse, even when she left me free to refuse, to take up my share of all the burden, which sometimes proved grievous . . . The result was that during the whole of our married life we were rarely free from some degree of worry over money . . . During the first half or more of our life together the strain was about fairly divided though it was she rather than I who determined the level of our expenses. But during later years not only were her frequent serious illnesses a source of expense, but after she had given up farming and lecturing, novels and plays seemed to be holding out promises of success and, with her usual eager confidence, she anticipated and outran these prospects, so that while her income increased her expenses still more increased. Thus it came about that all the unused balance of my own income, which was also beginning to increase, was always transferred to her.'[33]

What Edith in fact did – a very reasonable reaction under the circumstances – was to make a career of her marriage, with its peculiar and particular demands. Soon after their return to London she wrote and had printed the first of many essays and lectures which she was to devote to this subject. It was called 'Democracy in the Kitchen', and was followed a year later by a pamphlet, 'A Novitiate for Marriage', of which she over-optimistically had a thousand printed of which few were ever sold: the box of 'Novitiates' followed her around throughout her life. These were among the lectures the giving of which occupied her for the first few years of her married life, and again at the end. They were mostly concerned with the propagation of the ideas upon which she and Havelock had based their marriage, though some were about famous relevant personalities, such as Edward Carpenter, Olive Schreiner and Havelock himself. The novels and plays with which she was occupied in the intervening years were all autobiographical – one, *Seaweed*, or *Kit's Woman*, as it came to be called, most peculiarly and relevantly so – as we shall see.

To an extent, then, it might be said that the imposition of child-lessness upon Edith – for that, in effect, is what it was – transformed her along with the marriage itself into a sort of case study, in both the social and medical senses of that term. That this might even have been partly conscious is confirmed by Ellis's almost bizarrely cool language when he describes his state of mind at the outset – usually, after all, a time of great excitement and happiness, whatever may happen later. Ellis was quite aware of this. 'I can never be too thankful that I escaped a marriage of romantic illusions. Certainly, I was not a likely subject to fall victim to such a marriage,' he wrote after Edith's death. '. . . I was able to look on marriage as an experiment which might, or might not, turn out well. On her part it was, and remained to the end, a unique and profound experience which she never outgrew. Yet had anything happened to the marriage it is unlikely that either of us would then have suffered from a broken heart. The most passionate letters I wrote her were, as she realised, not written until some years after marriage . . . Much as each of us suffered through marriage I have never been convinced that our marriage was a mistake.'[34]

Perhaps such an approach was inevitable, given who Ellis was – not only his character, so deeply prone to exhaustive and exhausting self-examination, but his quasi-divine mission to enlighten the world about sexual variation and relieve it of its sexual guilt. How could such a man not regard his own life peculiarly objectively, as a kind of lived experiment? The hoary notions he retained and acted upon with regard to insanity, were compatible with the most modern social scientific ideas and interests. 'The medicine of perversions and the programs of eugenics were the two great innovations in the technology of sex of the second half of the nineteenth century,' writes Michel Foucault.[35] Ellis was a leader in the former field and an enthusiastic propagandist in the other. How much both were bound up with the advanced thought and political activism of that time was perhaps summed up in the person of Olive Schreiner, who fell in love with the embodiment of first the one (in Ellis), then the other (in Pearson) – an attraction whose force was in both cases very largely intellectual. But Edith did not have Olive's strength of intellect; she could not counter Ellis on his own ground.

Foucault identifies four subjects who 'emerged from this preoccupation with sex, which mounted throughout the nineteenth century – four privileged objects of knowledge, which were also targets and anchorage points for the ventures of knowledge: the hysterical woman, the masturbating child, the Malthusian couple and the perverse adult'.[36] Between Edith and himself, Ellis had (as it turned out)

three of these four primary objects of interest to examine at leisure
on his home ground.

3

Some years after her marriage Edith wrote a novel, which she at
first called *Seaweed*, later changing the title to *Kit's Woman*. The
plot concerns a Lancashire woman, Janet, who marries a Cornish
fisherman, Kit, and comes to live in Cornwall with him and his old
mother. A short time later Kit is injured in an accident and loses the
use of the lower part of his body. Janet is understandably depressed
by this, as is Kit. After a while the gossips begin to hint that Janet
is having an affair; and indeed it turns out that she is seeing a man
whom she has met on the beach and who is in love with her. But
after he makes love to her she finds she cannot bear deceiving her
husband, whom she still loves, and runs to confess all to Kit. The
two of them are then reconciled.

Ellis was very proud of this, as of all Edith's literary productions,
which he was always urging upon their friends. Its relation to their
marriage seems unmistakable, though, strangely enough, he confesses
in his memoirs that he only made this connection many years later.

In the reconciliation scene, Kit is extremely magnanimous. Speaking in almost impenetrable dialect he says: 'We love one the t'other,
woman – love one another so well we ain't afraid of no one – not even
of someone who tells thee I'm a wolf over thee. I am a wolf, sure
enough, but thee's made me feel tonight a longin' to give that other
chap a handshake . . . Ah! lass, this night beats our marriage night
to fits. We'm married o'er again – more like they marry i' heaven,
I reckon. . . . I'm like a child i'the sun, woman – o'erjoyed at the
thought that I'd grudge thee nothin' i' the whole world, nothing,
mind – not even his chiel!'[37]

After reading this book it would be fair to assume that Havelock
had failed Edith sexually; that she had sought consolation elsewhere;
and that he not only did not mind, but gained an almost masochistic
pleasure from knowing that she had another lover, whom he did not
in the least grudge her. That indeed was the story as it should have
been; but, as so often, life was messier than fiction.

What was true was that, about fifteen months after their marriage, while Havelock was in London and Edith at Carbis, she began an affair with an old friend. What one might not have guessed was that the lover was not a man, but a woman. Edith did indeed write to tell Havelock all about it, and he did indeed respond generously and apparently without jealousy. But in fact he was deeply hurt, though he tried hard to keep this from Edith.

How shocked was Havelock by this new relationship, and the form it took? If we are to believe his autobiography, neither he nor (more surprisingly) Edith was really aware of her lesbian preferences. Discussing their lack of sexual attraction towards each other he says that 'I, *though I failed yet clearly to realise why*, [my italics] was conscious of no inevitably passionate sexual attraction towards her, and she, *also without yet clearly realising why*, had never felt genuinely passionate sexual attraction for any man.'[38] A little later he expands on this: 'I knew, for she had told me everything, of the sentimental and sometimes passionate attraction which from early school life up to a few years before marriage she had experienced for girl friends. I knew that when a schoolgirl the resulting relationships had sometimes possessed a slight but definite sensuous character, though she had not found that experience in later adult friendships with women. I knew that such feelings were common in young girls. But at that time I . . . was not yet able to detect all those subtle traits of an opposite sexual temperament . . . and really the roots not only of the disharmonies which tortured her but of much of the beauty and strength of her character. The masculine traits were indeed not obvious in Edith . . . most people, I believe, failed to see them, and I cannot too often repeat that she was not really man at all in any degree, but always woman, boy, and child, and these three, it seemed, in almost equal measure.'[39]

What is one to make of this curious outpouring? Quite apart from the surprise that one so versed in all forms of sexuality should suppose that masculine traits invariably accompanied lesbianism, the fact is that it is almost certainly untrue, at least as regards Edith.

The evidence for this comes from Edith's case history, which is generally accepted to be that of Miss H. in the section of the *Studies in the Psychology of Sex* dealing with 'Sexual Inversion in Women'. If this is to be believed – and it is written with much less constraint, and much nearer the time, than Ellis's memoirs – Edith had had several physical relationships with women before her marriage, so that she, at least, must have known what her preferences were. Referring, presumably, to the time just before and after their marriage, Ellis writes: 'She has sometimes resisted the sexual expression of her feelings, once for years at a time, but always in vain. The effect on her of loving women is distinctly good, she asserts, both spiritually and physically, while repression leads to morbidity and hysteria.'[40] Certainly if Havelock was aware of Edith's sexual preferences at the time of their marriage, this would have been yet another reason why she should not have children. In his conclusions to the section of the *Studies in the Psychology of Sex* dealing with sexual inversion, he makes it quite clear that homosexuality is, in his opinion, as likely to be inherited as insanity: 'For the sake of the possible offspring . . . marriage is to be avoided . . . It must be pointed out that homosexuality is undoubtedly in many cases inherited. Often, it is true, the children turn out fairly well, but, in many cases, they bear witness that they belong to a neurotic and failing stock.' In support of this he quotes the case of an invert 'of great intellectual ability' and 'except in so far as his perversion was concerned' perfectly healthy, who, advised by his doctor to marry, did so and had four children of whom the first was 'an epileptic, almost an imbecile, and with strongly marked homosexual tendencies; the second and third children were absolute idiots; the youngest died of convulsions in infancy'.[41] It is an extraordinary outburst of almost medieval prejudice.

At any rate, whoever did or did not know what, this relationship of Edith's with 'Claire', as Ellis calls her in his memoirs, irrevocably changed the nature of their marriage. The innocent idealism with which it began had left it, at least as far as Havelock was concerned. 'There remained beneath the surface the consciousness of a flaw in the ideal of married love I had so far cherished . . . enough to kill that conception of mutual devotion in marriage which all my purely intellectual interest in Hinton's doctrines had never destroyed as a personal aim.'[42] In later years, when he revealed to Edith how much her affair with Claire had hurt him, she riposted that there was very little in it, and that in any case he should not have left her so much alone. Indeed, her early letters to him about Claire have more of a sense of loneliness relieved than of sexual thirst slaked. Havelock himself describes Claire as 'made to be a staunch friend rather than a lover either of man or woman.'[43] Edith wrote to him at this time (February 1893, not much more than a year after their marriage): 'I told Claire you would be trusted with all and she smiled "You *are* two odd people!" . . . she is so childlike and unprudish and gives me like a child a love which has rested and comforted me and strengthened me in a way that amazes me.'[44]

As always happened with him, it was some time before Havelock was able either fully to realize or express his feelings. The affair with Claire started in the spring of 1892; it was not until early in 1893 that he began to express his misery and anger in his letters to Edith; misery and anger, but also love. The expression of that love, however, was very odd. 'That letter needn't have pained you so,' he wrote after one such outburst. 'It only showed that I love you a great deal more than is wise . . . Love is funny and I am funny. It needs it's wifie's little breasties every two hours like a baby, and if they seem far off – it do shriek! (But you know, my Love, when the mother hears her baby, and knows that she has that within her to soothe it, she doesn't feel that she must yell too!)'[45]

Edith was quite happy to assume the role of the protective mother. 'My own sweet Baby, eh! man! thee ought not to go far from your mammy's apron-strings for thee wants thy bottle sadly!'[46] Indeed, it was to all appearances the thought of a wholly adult relationship that frightened her: 'I love to feel you my child, but I get "uppish" when the man of science is too rampant; the best thing we can all be is to be little children,' she wrote.[47] Sometimes the roles would be reversed: when she hurt herself he would run to her crying 'My Baby!'[48] This sense that to be a child was somehow preferable to being an adult, something to which adults should aspire, seems to have been something Havelock conveyed to his women: even the unassuageably adult Olive Schreiner would sometimes sign herself, in her letters to him, 'your little child', while he liked to assume the child's role even with her: 'You know I don't feel like a man in heart: much more like a child. If I did, I should probably have behaved to you differently. But I think it is when you are most like a child that I love you most.'[49] On Olive's side this particular fantasy had to do with the purity and innocence of response which those pre-Freudian days attributed to children, and towards which she always strove. But as far as Havelock was concerned there seems to have been more of an unwillingness to be a man, with that state's concomitant sexual and emotional responsibilities.

By now there was another woman in Havelock's life, too. Despite all the protestations that passed between them, the advent of Claire meant, as far as Havelock was concerned, that he, too, was free to seek elsewhere the satisfaction he could not find with Edith. 'Even my strong sense of justice could scarcely have tolerated so one-sided a sexual freedom in marriage. It might be true that I was exclusively heterosexual and she was not, and that therefore there was no demand on me to go outside marriage for love. But it was also true that the very qualities in her nature which made her largely homosexual were qualities which, fortifying as they might be to our comradeship, were inimical to the purely feminine qualities of sweetness and repose which a man seeks in a woman, and therefore opposed in our case to a strict conjugal fidelity,' was how he put the position in his memoirs.[50]

The woman in the case was called Mneme Barker-Smith. She was then twenty-four, the daughter of an old friend and colleague of Ellis's; he had known her from a child. He had never paid her any special attention – she was very quiet, and he had other things to discuss with her father. But now she entered his life, ironically, through Edith. They had rented a bungalow at Haslemere in Surrey, and Edith wanted someone to keep her company there during Havelock's absences: he suggested Mneme, and, thrown together with her as he had not been before, began to feel attracted to her – to become aware of her 'sweet, soothing, unselfish qualities'. One day, when they were out walking alone together, he gave her a kiss. 'It was but a single, simple kiss, and for months, even years, afterwards there was but little further progress in intimacy, for with me relationships developed with extreme slowness, and [Mneme] was much too inexperienced to make, or to invite, any advances.'[51]

It seems unlikely that Mneme was quite so guilelessly innocent as Havelock supposed. She had watched and admired him for years, and the story of their relationship as it muddily emerges from the tortuous pages of his memoirs seems rather to suggest that she was happy to take things at his pace and make herself indispensable to him, as did indeed happen. He saw in her the feminine virtues of sweetness, gentleness and compliance which he missed in Edith, but outside observers often saw a rather small-minded and spiteful person. She and her friendship with Havelock long outlived Edith, and outlived even Havelock. She was one of the executors of his will, and took every opportunity to make things difficult for the loving companion of his later years, Françoise Lafitte-Cyon. Edith hated Mneme and was terribly jealous of her, refusing to recognize that Havelock was doing no more to her with Mneme than she had done to him with Claire. Her indignation had two results: 'In the first place the injustice of her attitude aroused an opposing sense of justice in me and stimulated a firmness the emotional impulse itself might have been too weak to attain. In the second place the original impulse was fortified by the attention which, through Edith's attitude, I concentrated on it, whereas in a calm and free atmosphere it might soon have withered.'[52] From now on Havelock and Edith were not only to live independently, they were to carry on independent sex lives, the proviso being that nobody would ever replace the total love and trust, emotional and spiritual, which was the great binding tie between them.

So the next few years passed, more or less satisfactorily, but never without a plethora of letters on both sides assuring one another that really, despite appearances, they were when it came down to it all in all to one another. 'It was probably somewhere about this time,' wrote Ellis, 'that she wrote out and sent me Emily Dickinson's poem "Proof" on the tests of love, ending: "This dost thou doubt, sweet?/ Then have I/Nothing to show/But Calvary." . . . But as all Christendom has testified, the path of Calvary is not the path of failure.'[53]

It was at this point that, at Edith's suggestion, 'our marital relationship in the narrow sense was permanently brought to an end'. The nature of this relationship remains as unclear in this passage as in all the others discussing the matter. All that can be gleaned is a certain relief felt by Havelock at being released from this particular obligation: 'I made not the slightest objection . . . The loss was in our case a gain. We had secured all that that "golden key to the deepest secrets of intimacy" has to give and we could now develop our relationship better without it. In all other respects our physical intimacy remained the same . . . Only one thing was left out, a real and definite thing, yet so small in comparison to all that was left that we scarcely missed it.'[54] When Edith, some time after this, suggested that they revert to what had been the situation at the beginning of their marriage and drop all other lovers for each other once again, Havelock was so unwilling even to consider the matter that (as we have seen) he simply never mentioned the proposal, and she, not surprisingly, did not try to bring it forward again. 'The whole matter seemed entirely to pass from our minds,' he wrote; at least, it did from his.

4

It was at this time – to be precise, after the publication of his fourth book, *Man and Woman*, in 1894 – that Ellis began the work to which he had felt dedicated ever since his mystical experience in Australia, and for which he is now chiefly remembered: his *Studies in the Psychology of Sex*.

In many ways, he might have seemed a somewhat inappropriate person to embark on such a study. He himself recognized this, or recognized that this was how he might appear to others. In his memoirs he wrote: 'I am regarded as an authority on sex, a fact which has sometimes amused one or two (though not all) of my more intimate women friends. But, after all, it is the spectator who sees most of the game.'[55]

The fact was, of course, not so much that Ellis was a 'spectator' as that what is generally regarded as the normal sexual act did not, by itself, excite him very much. It is interesting to note that Sigmund Freud was in no doubt that this must be the case. In conversation with an analysand, Joseph Wortis, who was a devoted disciple of Ellis, Freud observed that 'Everybody has some slight neurotic nuance or other, and as a matter of fact, a certain degree of neurosis is of inestimable value as a drive, especially to a psychologist; and it is on the other hand possible to have strong character defects inside the limits of so-called health. . . . I feel sure, for example, that Ellis must have some sexual abnormality, else he would never have devoted himself to the field of sex research.' (He added: 'You might of course say the same of me, but I would answer that it is first of all nobody's business, and second of all it is not true.')[56]

Ellis's preference was the somewhat unusual one that he himself dubbed 'Undinism' or 'urolagnia': what excited him was the sight of women urinating. His earliest definite memory of early childhood was of 'once accompanying the nurse who was wheeling the perambulator [containing his infant sister] along [the] road. The nurse stood still and I heard a mysterious sound as of a stream of water descending to the earth. I recall no feeling of interest or curiosity on my part, but the fact that I recall the incident at all seems to indicate that at that moment I was for the first time touched by the strange mystery of woman.'[57] Ellis's own opinion was that he might have inherited this trait from his mother. Although he pronounced his early childhood free from all 'those complications to which the child's affection for his mother is now supposed to be liable' he did recall several flirtatious moments with her, all of them associated with her urinating in a semi-public place while her son watched in delightful complicity. In later years many of his happiest moments were associated with the act of female urination. He found it transcendently beautiful, and the piece of writing he always considered his 'finest piece of poetic prose' was a description of such a moment (the woman in question was Hilda Doolittle, the poet H.D.): 'The tall form languidly arose and stood erect, taut and massive it seemed now with the length of those straight adolescent legs still more ravishing in their unyielding pride, and the form before me seemed to become some adorable Olympian vase, and a large stream gushed afar in the glistering liquid arch, endlessly, it seemed to my wondering eyes, as I contemplated with enthralled gaze this prototypal statue of the Fountain of Life . . . the image of creative arrogance; while on the firm austere lines of the face one read, not pride, but a shy and diffident smile, the fear lest to the merely human spectator that which is transcendent should be mistaken for what is gross.'[58] He quarrelled with the novelist Dorothy Richardson for missing out vital details on account of self-censorship with a conventional public in mind: 'We are told in the most minute detail all that had happened at breakfast, and after breakfast we are told how Miriam went upstairs, and how she passed the little lavatory door, but we are not told why she passed that little door just when we might have expected her to enter in.'[59] In the *Studies*, a hundred pages are devoted to urolagnia, including arresting descriptions of how, with practice, a man may defeat normal physiology and learn to urinate while inside his partner, thus causing exquisite pleasure to both parties. (The lady in the case, not surprisingly, reported a feeling of 'fullness'. This particular account admits that these practices may be hard on the bed linen, but concludes that a few dirty sheets are a small price to pay for such delights.)

However, the first volume of the *Studies* did not include this interesting section but was devoted to sexual inversion (i.e. homosexuality). This was due partly to the fact that, although this subject had until a few years earlier interested him relatively little, he had since found that several of his closest friends, such as Edward Carpenter and of course Edith, were wholly or partly homosexual; partly because he had recently begun to correspond with John Addington Symonds, whose work he had admired for years and who was deeply interested in this subject. Symonds, though married with children, was himself homosexual, and partly for this reason chose to live abroad. He now proposed to collaborate with Ellis on this volume, and set to work collecting case histories for it among his friends, which were duly included in the book when it was published. But before the two had even met Symonds died suddenly in Rome during an epidemic of influenza. The loss of this collaboration was not regretted by Ellis, since he felt this would have been very difficult, perhaps almost impossible, between two highly individual and idiosyncratic writers. But by then work on the book was well advanced, and in 1896 the book, with both names on the title page, was published in German translation; the translator, Dr Hans Kurella, a friend and colleague of Ellis's, had found a German publisher before one could be found in England. When it came to the English version the Symonds family took fright, and bought up all the copies which acknowledged Symonds as a co-author.

But before an English edition of any sort could be brought out, it was necessary to find an English publisher – and that was not so easy. Ellis at first selected the small, reputable firm of Williams and Norgate. They in turn asked the distinguished alienist Dr Hack Tuke for his opinion of the manuscript. Dr Tuke (whom we have already had occasion to mention as a leading proponent of the hereditary theory of insanity) was, as it happened, an old and valued friend of Ellis's, whom he had invited to his country house and introduced to his wife. But in spite of this friendship he felt he had to advise Williams and Norgate against publication, being, as Ellis put it, 'a Quaker brought up in an old-fashioned school, which could not possibly view sympathetically any detailed approach to the problems of sex'. He told Ellis of the advice he had given, and explained that whereas he had nothing to say against the study as a book for specialists, there could be no guarantee that it would be confined only to specialist hands: at the very least, 'there are always the compositors!'[60]

It was at this point that another old friend of Ellis's, F. H. Perry-Coste, told him of a new publisher he had heard of who sounded most promising. This was a Mr J. Astor Singer, who was interested in scientific and philosophical subjects and was proposing to set up a small publishing house which would bring out some books on these subjects even though they might have little appeal to the wider public. Mr Singer sounded just the kind of publisher Ellis needed. But in fact it turned out that Mr Singer himself was never available. He was said to live on the Riviera, and when much wanted was usually travelling in Mexico. Ellis had to deal with his London agent and brother-in-law, a Dr Roland de Villiers, a mysterious fellow who seemed to be of German extraction and who lived not with his wife but with a lady he introduced as Mrs J. Astor Singer.

The really extraordinary thing – or one of the many extraordinary things – about this affair was that Ellis could ever have persuaded himself that de Villiers or the legendary J. Astor Singer were persons with whom it was desirable or even possible to deal. Either he was a complete innocent when it came to business affairs, or else he was so desperate to get his book into print in England that he was ready to seize any opportunity which presented itself and to shut his eyes to any suspicious circumstances surrounding it.

Of some such circumstances it was impossible to remain oblivious, however hard he tried. For a start there was the improbable nature of the mysterious and always invisible Mr Singer, who whatever the source of his millions possessed two of the most authentically moneyed names of his time. Ellis came to the conclusion that he probably did not exist but was 'a creation of de Villiers' brain'. But who, then, was the Mrs Singer who lived in de Villiers' large and splendid house? She was supposed to be his sister-in-law, and the money used in the transactions was mostly in her name; but it seemed most probable that she was his wife. Ellis even began to doubt the identity of 'Dr de Villiers' himself, and his worries were compounded when de Villiers chose to call his publishing house 'The University Press, Watford' when, as everyone knew, there was no university at Watford. Still, when it came down to business dealings de Villiers could not be faulted. He readily agreed to publish the book on generous terms – indeed, Ellis commented, 'it is quite possible under the circumstances that the author obtained more money from the book than the publisher'. Nor could any objection be made to the other books on the Watford University Press list, which included Edith's novel *Seaweed*.

So far, so unobjectionable. Ellis's (and de Villiers') bad luck was to get the book's distribution mixed up with some anarchists, in whom the police at that time took a keen interest.

The anarchists in question were attached to a society called the Legitimation League. When it was founded in 1895, the League's main aim was to legitimize acknowledged illegitimate children. It acquired a certain notoriety when in 1896 it took up the cause of Miss Edith Lanchester, the socialist daughter of a prosperous London architect. In the course of her political work (which included acting as secretary to Eleanor Marx) Miss Lanchester met a handsome young Irish railway clerk, James Sullivan, and the two of them set up house together. Her father's reaction was to kidnap her and have her sent to a private lunatic asylum on an 'urgency order' signed by his doctor, who gave the cause of her insanity as 'over-education'.

Edith Lanchester's case became a *cause célèbre* in socialist and feminist circles, though it presented some difficulty for those such as Belfort Bax, editor of the Social-Democratic Federation newspaper *Justice*, who could not bring themselves to sympathize with feminist aspirations and believed that, when push came to shove, the place for socialist daughters was in the home being obedient to their fathers. This was an old quarrel between socialists and anarchists, the socialists wishing to maintain respectability and distance themselves from any taint of free love, the anarchists, naturally enough, having no such inhibitions. Bax ritually deplored Miss Lanchester's father's action, and hoped that the present marriage laws would before long be rendered inapplicable by radical changes in the economic status of women. But until that happened 'we Socialists cannot effectively enter our protest against capitalism by individual anarchistic action or personal revolt . . . neither can we usefully determine that each of us shall go his or her own way in business, in pleasure and particularly in sexual intercourse . . . We ought not to take a serious step of this kind, we say, without considering the injury we may do to our own comrades; to our immediate family connections; or – which is perhaps the most important point of all – to the children we may bring into the world.'[61] But the anarchists of the Legitimation League, as may be imagined, were unworried by the thought of such children (Miss Lanchester went on to live happily with her lover for many years and produced several children, including the actress Elsa Lanchester) and vigorously took up Edith Lanchester's case with the Commissioners in Lunacy, who acted promptly and saw to it that she was released immediately from the asylum.

Among the leading figures in the League was one George Bedborough, and soon after the Lanchester case he became its secretary. Under his leadership the League broadened its aims to advocate the abolition of the marriage law and to support the doctrine of free love, a position which it urged in its periodical publication *The Adult*. Bedborough organized weekly meetings of the League at the Holborn Restaurant, and these were attended by a number of anarchists, who were interested in abolishing not only the marriage law but all laws. It was because of the anarchists that the League, and with it Bedborough, started to attract the attention of the police.

The League was infiltrated by Inspector John Sweeney, who gained Bedborough's confidence and soon became quite friendly with him. Needless to say, Sweeney deeply disapproved of the League, *The Adult*, and all they stood for, but when he placed his report before the public prosecutor 'a grave difficulty presented itself. The Public Prosecutor was anxious to protect the public from all the objectionable features of an open and unashamed free-love movement in its midst, but he was equally anxious to abstain from interference with legitimate freedom of speech.'[62] Unfortunately for the police, the language used in *The Adult* was carefully chosen to keep within the law, and there was never any suggestion of indecorous behaviour at League meetings.

What was needed was a legally viable pretext to close down the League and *The Adult*; and this was conveniently provided by Havelock Ellis's book on sexual inversion. This had been published by the Watford University Press in 1897, and early in 1898 de Villiers arranged with Bedborough that the League should undertake an agency for the sale of the book from its offices in John Street, Holborn. Sweeney was delighted. 'There was never any hesitation on the part of the authorities as to the illegality of the sale of Ellis's book, and I was instructed to find out whether Bedborough had any other objectionable works on sale. In the midst of my inquiries, we received at the Yard a complaint from Liverpool that a young man there had received a copy of the book without ordering it, and his parents were indignantly demanding the suppression of such literature.'[63] A warrant was immediately issued for Bedborough's arrest, and Sweeney set out accompanied by a Chief-Inspector and half a dozen men. 'They imagined that the man who could influence so many great ones, magnetise the masses, and attack single-handed one of the oldest institutions in the world, attracting to his standard the commonplace discontented person as well as the most fiery Anarchist, must essentially be a manufacturer of bombs, or at least an Anarchist plotter himself. Nothing of the kind. My meeting with Bedborough to arrest him was a unique experience. He was just leaving his home in John Street accompanied by two friends . . . He saw me coming and stepped forward with his usual *bonhomie* to shake hands and ask after my welfare. I asked him to leave his friends for a moment, and I explained my mission and introduced my chief. Bedborough's cheery spirits and *sang froid* never left him and we three took a hansom to Bow Street, gaily chatting as we went along.'[64]

Needless to say, the news of Bedborough's arrest was not received with quite such gaiety in all quarters. It took place on 31 May 1898. The same day Ellis, then at Carbis Bay, received a telegram telling him what had happened from one of the friends who had been with Bedborough at the time, and soon after heard the same news from de Villiers, who added that he had heard privately that Ellis was also to be arrested.

Ellis was alone at the time; Edith had been staying with a friend in London and was now visiting the home of Claire, her lover, in the north. She had been having a wonderful time, enjoying the amenities of a comfortable London life, and her only worry had been that she felt she would never want to come back to Carbis. Havelock wrote at once to tell her what had happened and she replied: 'My love, I'm just starting off on my way to you, – you poor old Love. Never mind, I'll stick to you and help you, and I'm at last *glad* to come home to you and cheer you and love you and comfort you. We'll live in England and spit at them, and two together can pull a boat that else would sink. If I get a wire to-night I shall be off to-morrow to you as fast as civilisation can bring me. Claire sends love and hopes all will be well. Your own Wifie. Here is cheque for £2.'[65]

It is hard to escape the impression, now and throughout this whole episode, that Edith, although of course she was worried on Havelock's behalf, was delighted that there was now a genuine reason for them to be together, and that Havelock would now be in some way dependent on her for support. 'Through all those trying and vexatious days,' he wrote, ' – and by repeated delays they were spun out for nearly six months – she was as often as possible by my side, always bright and cheery, always helpful.'[66] She made little of the fact that her own book, *Seaweed*, just published, had been caught up in the general débâcle of the Watford University Press, so that it had virtually no circulation until brought out in a new edition and with a new title some years later.

The next few months were a time of great confusion. The first count in the case *Regina vs Bedborough* was the charge that Bedborough, who really had no connection with Ellis's book, had 'sold and uttered a certain lewd wicked bawdy scandalous and obscene libel in the form of a book entitled *Studies in the Psychology of Sex: Sexual Inversion*'. Other counts related to the publications of the Legitimation League. The difficulty as far as the defence was concerned was that people who might have been prepared to come forward in Ellis's support were not necessarily happy to appear for the Legitimation League, and vice versa. For this and other reasons, although Ellis received handsome testimonials from a number of leading medico-psychological authorities, no one was prepared to testify for the book in person; and he was not even prepared to testify himself, as he felt he could not possibly give proofs of the reality of case histories which constitute the principal matter of the book and which had been given to him in strict confidence – as his solicitors wanted him to do. However, despite these difficulties, there was no question of abandoning the defence. Its main thrust would not be a medical one, but one which many people considered far more important – that of freedom of the press. A 'Free Press Defence Committee' was set up, whose supporters included a regular roll-call of advanced thinkers, from Edward Carpenter and H. M. Hyndman to Frank Harris, Belfort Bax and Bernard Shaw. A brilliant young counsel, Horace Avory, was retained for the defence. He was most enthusiastic about the case, which he believed offered the great occasion for which he had been looking in order to make his name (he was later to become one of the most famous judges of his day).

However, all this effort and excitement came to naught, for the case was never defended. Bedborough, who was a weakling, was persuaded, either by the police or by his solicitor, to plead guilty, and his solicitor, who had been given £200 with which to pay the barrister's fee, failed to hand the money over to Avory. This being so, the etiquette of the Bar meant that Avory could not appear. (After the case was over the solicitor was struck off for this conduct, but by then it was too late.) As Bedborough was the sole defendant, there was nothing anybody else, be it interested party or lawyer, could do. The case came to trial on 31 October 1898. Ellis's solicitor thought that the judge might possibly call for him to appear, so, accompanied by Edith, he remained in a room off the court; as it happened, undisturbed, for neither his name nor the book was specifically mentioned in the proceedings. The defendant, having pleaded guilty, was released on his own recognizances. The Legitimation League and *The Adult* were, *ipso facto*, defunct. As for *Sexual Inversion*, the judge remarked gnomically to the defendant: 'You might at the outset perhaps have been gulled into the belief that somebody might say that this was a scientific book. But it is impossible for anybody with a head on his shoulders to open the book without seeing that it is a pretence and a sham, and that it is merely entered into for the purpose of selling this filthy publication.'[67]

As to the book, Havelock was determined that his work should not be in any way interrupted – he at once started work on Volume 2 – but he would not try and publish any more of it in England. De Villiers, who had been noticeably absent during the whole of the police proceedings, now reappeared and agreed to reissue the book from Leipzig, under the imprint of 'The University Press'. Later it was revealed why he had been so chary of having anything to do with the police. De Villiers, it emerged, was a well-known confidence trickster. His real name was Georg Ferdinand Springmuhl von Weissenfeld, the son of a judge who had become estranged from his father and spent the past twenty years conducting swindles of one sort and another, often by obtaining money from prospective shareholders in fictitious companies of which he was the only officer (the Watford University Press seems to have been an unusually above-board venture). After the showdown regarding the *Studies*, the police felt it was unlikely that he would show his face in England again.

However, in 1902 a tip-off assured them that he had indeed returned and was living under the alias of Dr Sinclair Roland in a large house in Cambridge – for he always liked to live in the most luxurious style, with large houses and many servants, though even these were as much of a mystery as the rest of his life: just as his wife sometimes posed as his sister or sister-in-law, so the servants might sometimes pose 'as housemaids, nurses, or cooks, at other times, prodigiously smart in dress, they sat in the drawing-room and were introduced to visitors as wives and daughters of statesmen, ambassadors and celebrities'.[68] The police determined to beard the villain in his lair, which had (Sweeney assured his readers) been chosen for its safety from observation and its plethora of hiding-places. But this time all exits were blocked and a systematic search was instigated. 'At length a secret panel was discovered revealing a passage just large enough to hold one man. At the risk of his life Sergeant Badcock entered stealthily into the dark passage, and flung himself upon a man he found there. Dragged into the light de Villiers faced his pursuers, a haggard fugitive at bay. Fortunately in the struggle a loaded revolver had been knocked out of his hands, and all his courage fled when the handcuffs were put on. . . . A few minutes later he seemed to develop sudden symptoms of a strange excitement. He called for water. One of the servants of the house ran and filled a glass which was standing on the drawing-room table. De Villiers swallowed a few drops of water which seemed as if it were choking him. A few gasps followed, and he fell dead.'[69] Such was the first publisher of the unwinkingly serious *Studies in the Psychology of Sex*.

To read the *Studies* is a curious and indigestible experience. One of Ellis's aims in writing it was to convey the sense that all forms of sexuality, or 'anomalies' as he liked to call them, were, on their own terms, normal (whatever that might mean) and acceptable. Although when he started work on the *Studies* he felt that sex should generally be directed towards procreation (except, presumably, in special cases such as his own), as the years and the work progressed he became much less prescriptive. Thus, in writing about 'Erotic symbolism', he concludes on a positively triumphant note, a hymn to fetishism, no less: 'The phenomena of erotic symbolism can scarcely fail to be profoundly impressive to the patient and impartial student of the human soul. They often seem absurd, sometimes disgusting, occasionally criminal; they are always, when carried to an extreme degree, abnormal. But of all the manifestations of sexual psychology, normal and abnormal, they are the most specifically human. More than any others they involve the potently plastic force of the imagination. They bring before us the individual man, not only apart from his fellows, but in opposition, himself creating his own paradise. They constitute the supreme triumph of human idealism.'[70]

What is bizarre to the modern reader is the combination of modernity with Victorianism. The modernity is in the subject-matter. Michel Foucault talks about 'the existence in our era of a discourse in which sex, the revelation of truth, the overturning of global laws, the proclamation of a new day to come, and the promise of a certain felicity are linked together'.[71] This is a pretty exact description of that quasi-mystical call which had drawn the young Havelock to this particular study and inspired the older Havelock with missionary zeal.

Yet this exceedingly modern crusading tolerance is grafted onto a technique of presentation which is entirely Victorian. The work, all seven volumes of it, is nothing more than an immense heap of piled-up examples, demonstrating by sheer force of numbers the absurdity of a concept of 'normality' or 'abnormality'. Two things become clear: the huge range of sexual expression, and the comparatively limited part played in it by the reproductive act. But what is so strange to the twentieth-century mind is the absence of theory. The emphasis is wholly upon categorization: taxonomy is all. It is possible to deduce what may be the author's particular interests in such details as the space allotted to one thing rather than another – as for example the section on 'Undinism' discussed earlier. But in no other sense, except in so far as it is indicated by the very choice of subject, does the authorial voice intrude.

The reason why this concatenation seems so odd is of course that we have got into the habit of theorizing. On this subject in particular the anomaly (to borrow Ellis's favourite word) is that this habit was introduced at just about the time he himself was beginning to work on the *Studies*. It was of course introduced by Sigmund Freud, and yet Ellis, who purported to be so modern and must (indeed, certainly did) know about Freud's work seems to have been completely unaffected by it, in manner as well as in matter. It is impossible not to compare the two, and there is no doubt that in the comparison Ellis comes off far the worst. The reasons why he does so are the reasons why it is clear that Freud was a genius while Ellis was not. (Ellis himself described Freud as 'an extravagant genius'.[72]) These have nothing to do with either of them being correct or incorrect in their ideas, for Ellis never ventured any controversial pronouncement, while Freud's ideas in their detail are frequently contested. What Freud did was to change the way people thought about things, so that it is impossible now to be unaffected by his work even if one has not read it. What Ellis did was choose to remain rootedly pre-Freudian – a stance which now, especially given his subject-matter, dates him irretrievably.

It is interesting in this connection to see what Freud had to say about Ellis (Ellis was always perfectly polite about Freud, simply unaffected by him). We have already seen that he assumed Ellis was drawn to writing about sex because he had some sexual abnormality – and that this was indeed true. In the course of the same analysis (of Joseph Wortis) he also remarked that a man who makes so few judgments is suspect of being impotent.

Wortis became very angry at these suggestions of Freud's. He immediately connected the remark about impotence with Edith Ellis's childlessness (a connection which, as we have seen, Ellis himself pointedly failed to make in his memoirs, or indeed, from what one can gather, in his discussions on the subject with Edith). Wortis defended Ellis against this supposition, insisting to Freud that 'He had no children because his wife was diabetic – besides, he was too poor.'[73]

Ellis, when faced with Freud's conclusions, rejected them out of hand. He wrote: 'I am interested in F.'s remarks about me, and not at all annoyed at the suggestion that my interest in sex was due to a perversion. It is precisely my own feeling about many sex-obsessed people, and it is often correct. But I am quite ready to accept F.'s statement that it was not true of himself. Neither is it true of me!' Passing on to the question of childlessness, he explained that Edith was not diabetic until the end of her life, and gives her neurotic and fragile constitution as the main reason why they decided against children. He obliquely rejects any question of his own impotence as being part of the reason, harking back once again to the old incident when he produced some sperm to satisfy Olive Schreiner's scientific curiosity: 'My own spermatozoa looked quite healthy under the microscope!' On the question of whether he was able to convey these spermatozoa to their destination, however, he remains silent. On impotence in general he continues: 'With regard to impotence, F.'s notion that it is associated with a lack of decision in intellectual judgments is new to me. The notion seems based on a false analogy. In most of the cases that come to me, the impotence is not due to any hesitation or lack of decision, but is a hyperaesthetic over-rapidity of nervous reaction marking the whole of our modern civilisation.'[74] If we may extrapolate from this the notion that Ellis was here discussing himself as one of the cases of impotence with which he was best acquainted (and the rather defensive tone seems to make this not improbable), then it seems likeliest that he suffered from premature ejaculation and that the normality or otherwise of his sperm had little to do with the case.

However that may be, by 1898, after seven years, the Ellis marriage had reached an even keel. Certain basic facts had become incorporated into it: they would have no children; there would be no more sex of any sort between them; and each overtly willingly, but in fact more or less grudgingly, accepted that the other was free to find sex elsewhere, according to taste. It may be a measure of Havelock's greater tolerance, or his greater detachment, that while his involvements continued to pain Edith, he became increasingly unaffected by hers. But for the moment all that was suspended. When the Bedborough trial ended, after spending a few days in Cornwall, the Ellises set off together to spend the autumn and winter months in southern Spain and Tangier. It was a time of great happiness for Edith: she had 'joyous memories of Spain, which she always desired to revisit though circumstances never again permitted; whenever I went to Spain afterwards it was always alone'.[75]

ELEANOR AND EDWARD:
END OF THE LONG, SAD YEARS

I

In March 1898, a couple of months before Bedborough's arrest and the ensuing panic, Edith, who was then in Carbis, received a 'rather urgent' letter from Eleanor Marx, asking to see her.[1] It was some years since Havelock and Eleanor had been in close touch, since the main links between them had been Olive Schreiner, who had left Europe in 1889, and the editorial work which Havelock had been able to offer Eleanor, which had come to an end. Both of them, besides, were fully occupied along very different lines. But Edith was friendly with Eleanor, and would certainly have gone to see her had she been able to do so. Unfortunately, since she was in Cornwall, this was impossible to arrange. She later regretted this deeply: for a few days later, on the morning of 31 March, Eleanor committed suicide by taking poison.

Although it was generally known that her life with Aveling was not happy, this dreadful event shocked everyone who knew her. For in the last few years Eleanor's life had seemed, materially at least, to be taking a turn for the better. In 1895 Friedrich Engels had died, and although she missed him extremely, as her oldest and closest friend and mentor, and the last remaining link with her beloved father, nevertheless her share in his estate enabled her to buy a house in Sydenham and freed her from the grinding day-to-day worry of penury. In a letter to her sister Laura, inviting her and her husband, Paul Lafargue, to visit the new domain, her happiness is apparent: 'I want Paul badly to help me with the garden! There! The cat's out of the bag. If Paul has any little affection left for me he'll come and teach us to garden,' she wrote. 'As to our house (I am Jewishly proud of our house in Jew's Walk), voilà. Ground floor: Large room (Edward's study and general room combined); dining room (opens on back garden), kitchen, scullery, pantry, coal and wine cellars, cupboards, large entrance hall. One flight of stairs (easy), bedroom, spare bedroom (*yours*), servant's room, bathroom (large enough to be another spare room on special occasions). My *study*!!! . . . Finally, as to furnishing all this I ought to let you know that . . . Edward . . . is buying all the furniture that unluckily one can't do without. I want you to know this as it would not be fair to think *I* was paying for it all.'[2] From which one can glean that the ineradicable bourgeois desire to be able to feel pride in her surroundings was finally satisfied and that she was still deeply committed to Edward, and wanted to present him in the best possible light. To her 'Den' she took a special delight in inviting all her old friends; and from it she worked harder than ever in the socialist cause.

The summer of 1897 was a particularly busy one in both these respects. Johnny Longuet, Jenny's eldest son, to whom she had always been particularly close, was staying with her; on 2 June she wrote to her old friend Wilhelm Liebknecht that he was 'a very great anxiety' to her because although he was 'undoubtedly gifted' he was 'hopelessly (I fear) lazy; incapable of real work or any sustained effort . . . He is 21 and seems no more minded to work seriously than if he were 10 . . . It is heartbreaking for me to see Jenny's children going wrong and to stand by helpless.'[3] Then Edith Lanchester, who had given birth to a son and was 'very ill after her confinement' arrived for a few weeks' nursing. Liebknecht himself, the 'dear old Library' of her childhood, came for a visit on 11 July. Edward, too, needed constant looking after. His health had for some time been very poor (he was suffering from kidney disease). In the same letter to Liebknecht in which she confessed her worries about Johnny Longuet Eleanor wrote: 'I am very much worried too about Edward. The abscess in his side (now open for over 2 years) *may* necessitate an operation (though we hope not), which would be a serious one. He yesterday saw one of our best surgeons and sees him again tomorrow.'[4]

Meanwhile political work went on unabated. Eleanor had started language and debating classes for the Social Democratic Federation, feeling that British delegates to international conferences were noticeably lacking in both these skills. She was busy editing and sorting out the mass (and mess) of papers for which, since Engels' death, she was now responsible. In the second week of June the miners held an international congress in London for which, as usual, she did the translating. And in July began the great confrontation between the Amalgamated Society of Engineers and the engineering employers. The Engineers had determined to win an eight-hour day from employers in the London area; and the employers in their turn had formed an organization, the Employers' Federation of Engineering Associations, which was determined to stop them. This Federation set up a London committee under the German Alexander Siemens, which co-ordinated a national lock-out of union members. This began in July 1897, and help and support for ASE members flooded in from friends and supporters in Europe. In this dispute Eleanor, with her contacts, her languages and her experience of union action, was naturally much involved. When Siemens admitted that the object of the lock-out was to smash the union, the London correspondent of Liebknecht's *Vorwärts*, probably Eleanor, wrote: 'It is no mere strike, no mere lock-out – it is civil war.' In response to the German Siemens's declaration she urged, 'German workers, do your duty!'[5] And they did: the German donations amounted to more than £14,000, about a half of the entire overseas contribution to the union's lock-out funds.

Aveling was now at last free to marry again. His wife, the unfortunate Bell, had died some time previously, alone in a room in Holborn. She was intestate, and Aveling, still her lawful husband, was granted the administration of her personal property, which amounted to about £126.[6] As his brother had prophesied, he had not married Eleanor. This, however, had in no way affected her habit of assuming that he was in every real sense her husband. The law, of course, would not agree; and so, in the will she made after she had come into her share of Engels's estate, she made sure that financially at least (always, as far as he was concerned, the important consideration) he would be treated as such. All the interest in royalties from her father's works was left to Jenny's children, and the residue of her estate and effects to Aveling, who was also her sole executor. That was in 1895; it was not enough for Aveling. In 1896, a codicil was added to the effect that the royalties were also to be given to Aveling in his lifetime.[7]

For many years – indeed, ever since they had started living together – people had asked themselves and each other how Eleanor could possibly tolerate Aveling, with his constant and undisguised sexual infidelities, his dishonesty, his shameless habit of sponging. In socialist circles, Eleanor's old friend Engels was virtually the only person wholeheartedly to like or accept him; and, loved as Engels was in those circles, not to say central to them, there were even people who preferred not to visit him if this meant having to meet Aveling.

In *The Doctor's Dilemma*, in which the central character, the painter Louis Dubedat, is an undisguised and (by all accounts) accurate portrait of Aveling, Bernard Shaw also gives a picture of the way Eleanor dealt with the aspersions and accusations so generally levelled against him:

MRS DUBEDAT: – Listen. I know Louis as nobody else in the world knows him or ever can know him. I am his wife. I know he has little faults: impatience, sensitiveness, even little selfishnesses that are too trivial for him to notice. I know that he sometimes shocks people about money because he is so utterly above it, and can't understand the value ordinary people set on it. Tell me – did he – did he borrow any money from you?

SIR COLENSO RIDGEON: He asked me for some – once.

MRS DUBEDAT: [tears again in her eyes] Oh, I am so sorry – so sorry. But he will never do it again: I pledge you my word for that. He has given me his promise: here in this room just before you came; and he is incapable of breaking his word. That was his only real weakness; and now it is conquered and done with for ever.

RIDGEON: Was that really his only weakness?

MRS DUBEDAT: He is perhaps sometimes weak about women, because they adore him so, and are always laying traps for him. And of course when he says he doesn't believe in morality, ordinary pious people think he must be wicked. You can understand, can't you, how all this starts a great deal of gossip against him, and gets repeated until even good friends get set against him?[8]

Shaw himself by no means personally disliked Aveling, whose political and intellectual integrity as a militant atheist, a Shelleyan, a Darwinian and a Marxist, was, he thought, absolute. (He also had a soft spot for him because Eleanor's defection to him from Shaw early in their acquaintance had been instrumental in convincing Shaw that matters of attraction between men and women had nothing to do with logic or personal worth, something that appealed to Shaw both intellectually and personally.) Aveling's invariable kindness to his old dog also endeared him to Shaw, who told his biographer, Hesketh Pearson, that Aveling's case was by no means unique in his experience: 'he had been on equally pleasant terms with three others, two clergymen and a retired colonel, all of whom combined a pleasing absence of aggressive vices with a total lack of conscience in money matters and sexual relations.'[9] Shaw was always happy to appear on the same political platform as Aveling, and contented himself with warning off friends from whom he tried to borrow money. 'His exploits as a borrower have grown into a Homeric legend,' he wrote Ellen Terry after Aveling had tried his luck with her. '. . . For some years past he has been behaving well, because Marx's friend Engels left Eleanor £9,000. But the other day he tried the old familiar post-dated cheque on Sidney Webb – in vain. And then, I suppose, he tried you. Must I really not tell anyone? If you only knew how utterly your delicacy is wasted!'[10]

Others, however, were less prepared to be tolerant. J. L. Mahon, for example, a Scottish socialist for whom Eleanor had a very high regard, simply refused to work with him, even if this meant forgoing Engels's financial support for his political work. 'Dear Comrade Engels [he wrote in July 1887] . . . From my conversation with you . . . I understand that your financial help to the provincial propaganda will only be given on the conditions that I treat Aveling with the fullest confidence, consult him in all party matters & regard him as an essential person in the movement. You insist on a clear understanding in this matter & therefore I am compelled to say bluntly that I *do not* accept these conditions . . .' Engels insisted that he clarify the matter with Aveling himself, and this Mahon did. Aveling wrote: 'I do not ask why you do not regard me as essential in the English movement, as no one can be that – in a word, why you have joined the ranks of those who are anxious, as Engels puts it, to shove me out of the movement.' To which Mahon replied: 'It cannot be of much consequence to you what I think of you. We were never very close comrades or friends and often, perhaps generally, very much the opposite. As I am not *breaking off* any relations with you, nor making any attack upon you, but simply *refusing an invitation* to work with you I don't see why I should be called upon to formulate any charges. Nor do I see what good would come of it if I did.'[11] But among those who knew Aveling such charges hardly needed to be formulated. 'In spite of an exterior that almost recalled Quasimodo, he always exercised a remarkable fascination for women, and the effect of his lecturing tours in the provinces was frequently discounted by tales of victims that he left behind him,' ran an obituary notice of him. 'That these offences were only known to a few persons, who were unable to speak in fear of injuring the innocent, is the explanation of the position he occupied in the political world. In order to shield the unfortunate lady who had united her fortunes with his own, silence was necessary.'[12] The same veil was also drawn over many rumoured peculations: Aveling, it was said (but never too loudly), was not a person to entrust with the party funds.

Naturally people hesitated to confront Eleanor with these whispered accusations. Not only did common tact demand a certain reticence where she was concerned, so did affection: she was as much loved as he was distrusted and disliked. But of course she was aware of them: they were the terrible burden she had to carry during all the years she spent with Aveling – a burden which he in no way shared: from very early in their relationship his complete indifference to what people thought of him – his blithe unawareness, indeed, that their thoughts either mattered or existed – had been a source of wonder and pain to her.

This aspect of her relations with Edward was something about which she rarely unburdened herself. In her letters to her sister Laura and to old family friends such as Liebknecht she invariably put the best face on things. She would say that Edward was ill, but never that he was unfaithful or a sponger – rather the contrary. And this was wholly understandable. She had allied herself to him, she did not intend to part from him, and she neither wanted to worry them nor be disloyal to him. Olive had always known the truth, both about Edward and about her own misery, and so had her other close friend, Dollie Radford; but Olive was now in South Africa while Dollie had her hands full with her own husband, Ernest Radford, who, not long after their marriage, had suffered an irreversible mental collapse. But she did discuss her life with Edward at this time with one person.

This was a young man called Aaron Rosebury, an immigrant from Russia. He had first met Eleanor in 1891, when he approached her on some business for an association of Jewish socialists in the East

End of London. She had invited him to the flat she then shared with
Edward in Chancery Lane and entertained him to tea and seed-cake.
It seems clear that young Rosebury fell somewhat in love with her
(he was then twenty-four, she, thirty-six) and from then on went
back to see her fairly regularly, about once a month. Aveling was
usually away – on theatrical business, Eleanor said; and even a
young newcomer like Rosebury knew enough about the real state
of affairs not to enquire more closely. On one occasion when they
did meet, Aveling, to Eleanor's horror, touched the young man for
half a crown – a considerable sum of money in those days, and one
which Aaron could only find by dipping into some union funds which
he was carrying with him. Eleanor watched, appalled but unable to
intervene, while Edward promised to repay the money in a week and
assured young Rosebury that if he didn't, 'Tussy' would. After this,
some years passed before they met again. Then, in 1895, Aaron asked
Eleanor if she would help him with some details of her life, so that
he could complete a notebook he had been keeping about her. She
agreed, on condition that what she said should remain confidential
during her lifetime, and then talked to him, frankly and despairingly.
(This must have been very near the time of Engels' death, which of
course would have affected her mood.)

'You see, my good friend, my conception of the purpose of life
is different from other people's,' she said. 'The movement has
been my life, and now only two alternatives remain for me. If I
can't reconcile them soon . . .

   She was referring, evidently, to the movement and Aveling,
her need somehow to hold on to both. . . . The public nature
of her dilemma was aggravating it beyond endurance.
   . . . 'I suppose you are puzzled by the attacks on Edward. Alas,
they are based on fact. But I have been with him for twelve years
. . . All my friends are worried, but most of them are half-blind
to the problem. You are one of the few who understand. One
alternative is to leave Edward and live by myself. I can't do that;
it would drive him to ruin and wouldn't really help me. I'm a
strange mixture, my friend. My father used to say that I was more
like a boy than a girl. It was Edward who really brought out the
feminine in me. I was irresistibly drawn to him . . . Our tastes

were much the same . . . He was a popular agnostic lecturer. We agreed on socialism. We both loved the theatre. Neither of us cared for money. My father liked him. We could work together effectively . . . If I sacrificed something . . . it was no more than my mother had done. . . . But although these last few years have been unhappy, I have had the good feeling that, like my parents, I've been true to my convictions and not yielded to hypocrisy. I could not have known that Edward would fail me. Even so, to turn away from him now would be to succumb to despair.'[13]

To stay with Edward, then, was for Eleanor an important part of her affirmation – to herself as much as to the rest of the world – that her life was not a failure. It was in this frame of mind that she resolutely, optimistically, even joyfully, looked forward to the new life they were to lead together in the Den.

2

For some time Aveling, under his theatrical *nom de plume* of Alec Nelson, had been friendly with a young actress named Eva Frye. Miss Frye, who was twenty-two in 1897, had taken part in two fund-raising 'dramatic entertainments' organized by the SDF and directed by Aveling/Nelson. In the first of these she performed under the name 'Miss Richardson' and in the second under her own name. This, which took place in January 1897, opened with an overture played by the SDF String Band conducted by H. W. Lee, followed by a curtain-raiser by Nelson entitled *The Landlady*. 'Nelson' had by now given up any real hopes of achieving a commercial success on the West End stage, although this was still a line to be used if he wanted to borrow money or defer repayment; but he could not resist writing plays, even if they were not very good, or acting in them. On this occasion the author took the male leading role and Miss Frye was his leading lady.[14]

There is no way of knowing whether or not Eleanor was present at this entertainment. It seems improbable. She had few illusions about the quality of Nelson's dramas – though, like him, she lived in hopes – and, more to the point, the last thing she wanted was to see him in pursuit of his current inamorata. She had come to accept that living with Edward entailed putting up with his sexual proclivities, but there was no reason for her to know more of them than she was forced to. Besides, she had her own exceedingly busy life to get on with. So there seems little reason to imagine that she gave more than a passing thought to Miss Frye, if indeed she knew of her existence.

The second week of June that year was, as we have seen, particularly busy even by Eleanor's standards. The house was full of guests and the International Miners' Congress was in full swing at St Martin's Hall. On 8 June, while Eleanor was busy there, Alec Nelson, widower, and Eva Frye, actress, were married at Chelsea Register Office. After the ceremony Nelson returned to his other life as Edward Aveling, the sick husband of Eleanor Marx – a life to which he was tied, not by conscience, but by more practical considerations. He could hardly expect his new young wife to start her married life as a sick-nurse; and, even more to the point, what would they have to live on? Miss Frye was hardly in a position to support him as Eleanor and Engels's legacy did. So for a while everything went on as before. Eleanor, who was, as we have seen, exceedingly worried about Edward's health at this time, reported to her old friend Karl Kautsky, the Austrian socialist, that on 19 June he was off to the sea for twelve days on doctor's orders. Presumably Mrs Nelson joined him there. Then he returned to the Den to welcome Liebknecht in July, and went off to Northampton for the annual conference of the SDF (with which he and Eleanor were now reconciled) at the beginning of August. There he was elected to the SDF executive, eloquently urged Federation members to join and co-operate with trades unions, and embarked on a lecture tour of South Wales, where he spoke at SDF branches. On 22 August he spoke at a mass meeting in Trafalgar Square on behalf of the Spanish Atrocities Committee.[15] Some time soon after this he left the Den, taking with him everything of value that he could find. Possibly Mrs Nelson was putting her foot down; possibly he manufactured a quarrel. At any rate, Eleanor was, as may be imagined, distraught.

One of the minor attachments of the Marx household since before Eleanor's birth had been a son, Freddy, born to the faithful Marx housekeeper and family friend, Helene Demuth. 'Lenchen' had stayed with the Marxes and had Freddy fostered out. The Marx girls did not think much about him, but in so far as he did impinge on their consciousness it was under the assumption that Engels was Freddy's real father. One of the many terrible shocks with which Eleanor had to deal at this period of her life was the discovery that this was not true. She had sometimes wondered at the kindly Engels's brusque treatment of Freddy, whom he would not see even when, after Marx's death, Lenchen moved into his house at Regent's Park Road and became his housekeeper. When Engels was dying she found out why. Freddy was not his child but Marx's; it may be that Engels's harsh treatment of him stemmed from a not unreasonable resentment at having another man's child fathered upon himself. Eleanor refused to believe this story until, at the very last, when he was almost beyond speech, it was confirmed to her by Engels. But after she had been forced to believe it, her attitude to Freddy changed completely. She was filled with remorse and affection for her half-brother, who had been so shamefully treated by his family, had never known family life, had received no education. By the time Engels died Freddy had married and had a son, but his wife had left him, and he was bringing up the boy by himself. It was in Freddy alone, this half-brother so recently discovered, and of whom she had now grown so fond, that Eleanor found herself able to confide. She could not take her troubles to her political friends; Liebknecht, almost the last of her father's and Engels's generation, was in Germany and busy; with Laura, her sister, there was a certain front to keep up, admissions that her pride would not let her make (for certainly she never made them). Anyway, Laura lived in France and was always singularly unwilling to take the trouble to come to England, even in the direst emergency. But none of this applied to Freddy. With him there need be no worries about false pride or unavailability. So that it is through the letters Eleanor wrote him at this time that we can follow what happened.[16]

The first letter is dated from the Den, 30 August 1897. Aveling had told her that he was not letting her know his address, but that if she must write to him she could do so through an intermediary, 'M'.[17] It is clear that by then Freddy knew the circumstances and had already written to Aveling on Eleanor's behalf.

My dear Freddy,
Of course not a line this morning! I have at once sent on your letter. How can I thank you for all your goodness and kindness to me? But, indeed, I do thank you from the bottom of my heart. I wrote once more to Edward this morning. No doubt it

is weak, but one *can't* wipe out 14 years of one's life as if they had not been. I think anyone with the least sense of honour, not to mention any feeling of kindness and gratitude, would answer that letter. Will he? I almost fear he will not . . .

To-morrow evening is the Executive of the S.[DF]. I *can't* go – because if he is not there I can't explain. I hate to give you all this trouble; but could you go? They meet at 8 o'clock and sit till 10, so that if you went about 9 or 9.30 you could find out. You could ask if he had been. You would then know, at any rate. If *he is* there you can get at him – before others he can't get away – and wait for him till the sitting is over. Then you can *assume* he is coming here; if you find he simply lies – *go with him to London Bridge.* Then go with him and *say* (you can tell him *that* from the outset) that you had told me you were coming, and must come late because of your work, but that I had replied I would put you up for the night. Then he either must tell you he is *not* coming – and you can get your chance of speaking to him – or he will come. I don't know that it is very probable; but in any case I hope that you will go . . . and find out if he is there.

Ever your
Tussy.

She had also written to Arthur Wilson Crosse, the solicitor who had acted for her in sorting out the complications regarding Engels's will. This indicates that Aveling was making new financial demands upon her: possibly his new wife, to whom it must have been perfectly clear that he was very ill, was worried that he might die before Eleanor, in which case his (and her) main source of funds would be entirely cut off. Eduard Bernstein, the joint executor with Eleanor of Engels's will and an old family friend, hints in a long article he wrote about these events for *Die Neue Zeit*, later translated and printed in *Justice*, that he had been nagging her to sell off Marx's papers, but that 'with all her weakness in money matters' she had always refused to do this. Maybe the suggestion was that, if she did agree to finance him, he would return and no one need be any the wiser. Certainly one of the remarkable features of this whole episode is that none of Eleanor's acquaintances other than Freddy did know what was going on: she continued throughout to write her usual calm, collected letters about political matters to Liebknecht, Kautsky, Laura, as though nothing was happening. And maybe we should not wonder at this. When she was seventeen Eleanor's mother had written of her that 'Tussy is political from top to toe'; and so she remained. Although the fact of her being a girl prevented her from being taken as seriously as she should have been by her father, the fact that her politics were revolutionary and extra-parliamentary meant that she was always able to lead a full political life in a way that her friend Olive Schreiner, desperately directing her male acquaintances from the sidelines, was not. This in turn meant that Eleanor's life was far less restricted than that of most women. Love was extremely important to her but it was not, to quote Byron's old saw, her 'whole existence'. Even when love, or rather the lack of love, rendered her distraught, she was able to find relief in politics, her other abiding passion.

The next thing that happened was that Aveling appeared to have a change of heart. On 1 September she received a note saying 'Have returned. Shall be home early to-morrow', followed by a telegram: 'Home for good 1.30.'

I was working [she wrote to Freddy] – for even with all the heartbreak one must work – in my room – and Edward seemed surprised and quite 'offended' I did not rush into his arms. He has so far made no apology and offered no explanation. I – after waiting for him to begin – therefore said one *must* consider the business position – and that I should never forget the treatment I had been subjected to. He said nothing. Meantime I said you *might* be down, and if you can come to-morrow or any evening this week, I trust you will. It is right he should have to face you in my presence, and me in yours. So, if you can, come to-morrow – if not, let me know when you can come.

Dear Freddy, how can I ever thank you! I am *very*, very grateful. When I see you I will tell you what C[rosse] said.

Always, dear Freddy,

Your Tussy.

Next day there was another letter. There had been a terrible crisis:

My dear Freddy,

Come, if you possibly can, this evening. It is a shame to trouble you; but I am so alone, and I am face to face with a most horrible position: *utter* ruin – everything, *to the last penny*, or utter, open disgrace. It is awful; worse than even I fancied it was. And I want someone to consult with. I know I must finally decide and be responsible; but a little counsel and friendly help would be invaluable. So, dear, dear Freddy, come. I am heartbroken.

Your Tussy.

What was the nature of this terrible crisis? Various guesses have been hazarded. Eduard Bernstein can tell us little. 'Naturally Demuth hastened to Sydenham. But his visit was almost fruitless. Eleanor had by the time he arrived lost courage to tell him anything.' Bernstein adds: 'As regards the question of money, Aveling had the advantage that neither Eleanor nor Demuth understood all. His declaration that the last penny of Eleanor's fortune was not claimed disarmed them.'[18] So clearly what happened was that Aveling was blackmailing Eleanor and pointing out that there was still money left for her to give him. It seems possible that he was insisting upon the sale of some of Marx's papers, something which to Eleanor would have seemed little short of sacrilege.

What was his handle? One of her biographers thinks it was the secret of Freddy's birth. Another, Yvonne Kapp, thinks that it was possibly at this point that Aveling told her of his marriage, the deal being that if she gave him everything he asked for he would not openly leave her and set up home with Mrs Nelson. Kapp also posits the possibility that Aveling revealed he had been embezzling political or trade union funds, something which certainly would have been enough to bring Eleanor to her knees, but makes it clear that this is pure guesswork. The fact is that nobody knows or can know for certain.[19]

Whatever happened, it seems that Aveling got his way, because he remained with Eleanor and, for the moment, things quietened down. Freddy advised her to leave Aveling, but she could not do it. 'She was moved to renew even more firmly their union on his promise of reformation,' writes Bernstein.[20] In the middle of September the pair of them left for France to spend two weeks with the Lafargues in their splendid new home at Draveil, on the banks of the Seine, and as far as

Laura and Paul could see, things were quite as usual between them. Edward was ill and overworked and Eleanor was worried about him, but this was nothing out of the ordinary, and, between discussing all that had happened since their last meeting two years before and the wonders of the new house (also a result of the Engels legacy) the fortnight passed easily. In October Edward was still at Sydenham, for he added a postscript to a letter Eleanor wrote Kautsky. Then he and Eleanor set out on a November propaganda tour of Lancashire. Eleanor described it in another letter to Kautsky: 'we had "real" Lancashire weather. What *that* is only those who have experienced it can say. But certainly if Dante cd have dreamed of a Lancashire factory town in bad weather he wd have added circles to his hell, & to his "lowest depths a lower deep". Getting wet through daily was not calculated to cure an invalid.'[21]

Indeed, it did not do so: back in Sydenham, Eleanor reported to Natalie Liebknecht, whose husband was now serving four months in jail under the 'Little Anti-Socialist Law', that 'by the time we got back here, his neglected influenza developed into congestion of the lungs and a touch of pneumonia',[22] while to Liebknecht himself, on Christmas Eve, she wrote that she was 'busy looking after Edward and after Barnes' correspondence. [Barnes was the leader of the locked-out engineers, now enduring dreadful winter hardships.] In both cases it is a labour of love. And now, my dear old Library, goodnight.'[23]

To say that much was being demanded from her on both the personal and political fronts at this point hardly begins to state the case. Throughout December Aveling was seriously ill: his doctor warned Eleanor that she ought to get in touch with his relatives. 'Of course I did not,' she wrote Laura, 'because (except perhaps his sister, now living in Devonshire) there is not a relation he wd want to see at any time.'[24] He required constant nursing. Meanwhile, the engineers' struggle was reaching a crisis. On New Year's Day 1898 she wrote to Kautsky: 'I am translating all the many foreign letters Barnes gets, & am writing or answering letters right and left on the great fight . . . If only we could now spread our Socialist nets properly we should get a splendid haul – but I fear our fishers are not capable of using their opportunity.'[25] It was not only the employers she had to fight, but also other socialists, for, as usual, schism was part and parcel of left-wing politics. Now it was Eduard Bernstein, of all people, who was no longer to be trusted. He was editing *Vorwärts* while Liebknecht was in prison, '& his wet-blanket articles . . . are not exactly useful at the present moment,' she grumbled to Laura. 'Assuredly the critical attitude is necessary and useful. But there are times when a little enthusiasm – even if "uncritical" – is of greater value. Bernstein's position is a most unfortunate one for the movement, & one that makes *our* position very difficult. It is impossible to defend his attitude, & I am in daily fear that someone will tell Barnes & that Barnes will insist upon answering Bernstein – Barnes would be sure to get me to help him – & then I should be most awkwardly placed.' There was also a more bitter and personal quarrel with Bernstein: in the same letter, she told Laura that she had just discovered that Bernstein was using for his book her father's correspondence with Engels, access to which she had been vainly seeking since Engels's death.[26] In the middle of January the engineers' union capitulated, withdrew its claim for an eight-hour day and accepted the employers' terms of settlement. Eleanor sent her regular despatch to the socialist *Hamburger Echo*: 'The fight has been a heroic one and has been counted among the great battles of the world . . . We cannot be beaten. But we have our wounded to take care of. . . . May I ask help for these brave fighters who were wounded for our cause?'[27]

By the middle of January Edward was getting a little better, and on the thirteenth he left for Hastings 'on the doctor's orders, where I hope the warm air and bright sunshine may do him good.'[28] On the same day Eleanor replied to a discouraged letter from Freddy, who had been ill and was evidently feeling depressed: 'I sometimes feel like you, Freddy, that *nothing* ever goes well with us. I mean you and me. Of course, poor Jenny had her full share of sorrow and of trouble, and Laura lost her children. But Jenny was fortunate enough to die, and sad as that was for her children, there are times when I think it fortunate. I would not have wished Jenny to have lived through what I have done. I don't think you and I have been very wicked people – and yet, dear Freddy, it does seem as if we get all the punishment. When can you come? *Not this* Sunday, but next? Or during the week? I *do* want to see you. Edward is better, but very weak. Your Tussy.'

Things did not improve. Freddy was not well enough to come and see her, while, on his return, it turned out that although Edward's

lungs were better, the abscess in his side had got worse again and
he might have to undergo a serious operation. What was more, he
was proving an increasingly difficult patient (perhaps Mrs Nelson
was grumbling about his continued attachment to Eleanor). It says
much for Eleanor's continued hopefulness regarding him that this
ingratitude should have surprised or disappointed her, but it did,
for on 3 February she wrote once again to Freddy:

> My dearest Freddy,
> I am glad you are even a little better. I *do* wish you were well
> enough to come, say from Saturday to Monday, or at least Sunday
> night. It is brutally selfish, I know; but, dear Freddy, you are
> the only friend I can be quite frank with, and so I do love to
> see you.
> I have to face such great trouble, and *quite* without help (for
> Edward does not help *even now*), and I hardly know what to do.
> I am daily getting demands for money, and how to meet them,
> AND the operation and all else, I don't know. I feel I am a
> brute to trouble you, but, dear Freddy, you *know* the situation;
> and I say to you what I would not say to anyone now. I would
> have told my dear old Nymmy [the family pet name for Helene
> Demuth, Freddy's mother] but as I have not her, I have only
> you. So forgive my being selfish, and *do* come if you can.
> Your Tussy.
> Edward has gone to London today. He is to see doctors, and
> so on. *He would not let me go with him!* That is sheer *cruelty*,
> *and* there are things he does not want to tell me. Dear Freddy,
> you have your boy – *I* have nothing; and I see nothing worth
> living for.

Clearly, Edward was going to see Mrs Nelson (and from this letter
it seems as if Eleanor did not at this stage know of the marriage; what
seems most probable was that Edward had promised to be faithful in
return for whatever settlement he had extracted in September, and
that Eleanor now realized he had never intended, or was perhaps
constitutionally unable, to keep his word.) Freddy, in any case,
did not wish to see him, and so refused Eleanor's invitation. On
5 February she wrote:

My dear Freddy,

I *am* sorry you are not coming to-morrow. In common justice, let me say that Edward had *no idea* of asking you again for money. You don't know how ill he is. He wanted to see you because he believes he will not see you again after the operation.

Dear Freddy, I know how kindly your feeling to me is, and how truly you care for me. But I don't think you quite understand – I am only *beginning* to. But I do see more and more that wrongdoing is just a moral disease, and the morally healthy (like yourself) are not fit to judge of the condition of the morally diseased; just as the physically healthy person can hardly realise the condition of the physically diseased.

In some a certain *moral* sense is wanting, just as some are deaf, or have bad sight, or are otherwise unhealthy. And I begin to understand that one has no more right to blame the one disease than the other. We must try and cure, and, if no cure is possible, do our best. I have learnt this through long suffering – suffering in ways I would not even tell you; but I have learnt, and so I am trying to bear all this trouble as best I can.

Dear, dear Freddy, don't think I have forgotten what Edward owes you (I mean in money: in loving-kindness it is beyond calculation), and you will, of course, get what is owing to you. For that you may take *my* word. I expect Edward to go into hospital early next week. I hope soon, for this waiting is trying him terribly. I will let you know anything definite, and I do hope with all my heart *you* will soon be better.

Your Tussy.

Clearly Freddy was sceptical of this diagnosis of incurable moral decay absolving responsibility, for two days later Eleanor took up her theme again: 'I daresay I am so worried I did not make myself clear. But you have not understood me at all, and I am too troubled to explain. Edward goes to the hospital to-morrow for the operation on Wednesday. There is a French saying that to *understand* is to *forgive*. Much suffering has taught me to understand – and so I have no need even to forgive. I can only love. Dear Freddy, I shall be quite near the hospital at 135 Gower Street, and I will let you know how things go on. Your old Tussy.'

Aveling went into hospital on 8 February and was operated upon next day. Because he was a Fellow of University College he got the very best, privileged treatment, but Eleanor was still beside herself with worry, both about Edward and about the problem of meeting all the medical expenses. She was convinced he would not survive the operation; but he did, and on 17 February Eleanor was allowed to take him back to Sydenham, which she did, in a carriage. On 20 February she wrote almost apologetically to Freddy:

> My dear, dear Freddy,
> I brought Edward home on Thursday, as the doctors thought he would have a better chance here than at the hospital (oh! how *awful* a hospital is), and they want him taken to Margate. It is all so surely *going to the one thing* that I am giving up all the little I have left. You will understand – *I* can get on anyway, and I must now see to *him*. Dear Freddy, do not blame me. But I think you will not. You are so good and so true.
> Your Tussy.

The doctors recommended that Edward should convalesce by the sea, so Eleanor went to Margate to book rooms on 19 February. On the 22nd they left to spend a month there together. To say this was something they could hardly afford was no more than the truth; but Eleanor was fatalistic. She was convinced that Edward was going to die, and as for herself, she would survive somehow. She wrote to Natalie Liebknecht giving some idea of the strain she was under, describing how she changed his dressings, the invalid routine of their days, the terrible pain he had to endure and her own distress at witnessing it. 'One of the things that helps us both is that the time for our dear old Library's release is drawing near,' she wrote, with her usual generosity of spirit. 'Tell Library that in all his pain and suffering Edward never misses a day without saying "only – days now for Library!" – I think Library will be glad to know that. You wd not know my poor Edward if you saw him now. He is a very skeleton and can hardly walk a few yards . . . Sometimes I hardly know how I shall hold on! It is not only the awful anxiety, but the actual material difficulties. Our joint income is (for London) very small and my present expenses are enormous. – Doctors, chemists' bills, "chairs" for going out and so forth, added to the home that must be kept up – all this means a great deal. – I speak so frankly, because I know you will understand.'[29]

To Freddy, she expressed herself even more openly. Her life with Aveling had finally lost all its point for her.

It is a bad time for me [she wrote.] I fear there is little hope, and there is much pain and suffering. Why we go on is the mystery to me. I am ready to go, and would gladly. But while he *wants* help I am bound to stay.

The beautiful thing, and the one thing that helps me, is the kindness of everyone. I can't tell you how good to me all sorts of people are, I am sure I don't know why.

And I am quite proud of it, the Miners' Federation and Miners' Union, as I would not be paid for my work of the translating at the International Miners' Congress (it *was* work!) last June, have sent me a beautiful little writing case and stylographic pen. I am ashamed to accept such a gift, but I can't help doing so. And it *does* please me!

Dear Freddy, how I wish I could see you! But I suppose that can't be just now. Your Tussy.

This was the last of the letters Eleanor sent to Freddy. To Kautsky on 15 March she wrote that she was afraid 'there is *very* little hope of ultimate recovery'. Her last letter was to Liebknecht, her 'dear, dear old Library', to whom, as it happened, she had addressed the very first letter she ever wrote in her life. It was sent from Margate on 16 March:

In a very few hours now you will be free, and it is good to know that this letter will find you in your home. We shall be with you all on Friday, and with all our heart we wish we could be with you in the flesh as well as the spirit.

Our love to you, dear old Library, and
Welcome home!
Your
Tussy
Edward.

On 23 March 'Library' replied:

> My dear, dear Tussy!
> I am well, but how are *you*? . . .
> I should have written before; only you had promised me some notes about the Engineers' Struggle.
> But now I cannot wait any longer. How are you? How is Edward? Write only a few lines – I don't expect a long letter.
> We all send our love! And we all wait anxiously for *good* news.

Natalie added: 'Meine liebe, liebe Tussy.'[30]
But there was to be no more good news.

3

Eleanor and Edward returned to the Den on 27 March. Edward seemed a little better, and Eleanor immediately set about the ordering of her interrupted working life. She made arrangements with the publishers Swan, Sonnenschein for the publication of her father's address to the General Council of the First International, *Value, Price and Profit*, which she was editing. To this end she placed an advertisement in the *Reynolds's News* and the *Labour Leader* for a file of the *Eastern Post* which contained reports of the Council's sittings. She accepted, on behalf of them both, an invitation to attend a dinner in May in honour of Hyndman, the SDF leader.

Then, on the morning of 31 March, she received a letter. What it contained is not known. Robert Banner, a socialist friend who read it, reported that it threw 'a very discreditable light on a certain person'.[31] Since the letter was soon afterwards destroyed by Aveling, it may safely be assumed that he was the person in question. It also seems not implausible that it was this letter that was the final straw, finally pushing Eleanor over the brink of what was bearable. Perhaps, as Tsuzuki, one of her biographers, has guessed, this was a letter from Mrs Nelson, who had finally run out of patience, disclosing the real state of affairs with regard to herself and 'Alec Nelson'. Assuming that Aveling had not revealed to her the secret of his marriage (and this was known only among a very small circle of his theatrical friends)

– this, after so many months of strain, agony and selfless devotion, might well have had a devastating effect. We know that the fact of not being legally married to Aveling had not been an easy thing for Eleanor to accept; and although that feeling might well, after fourteen years, have receded into the background, there seems little doubt that the question must have been re-opened – if only in Eleanor's mind – after Bell's death (unless that, too, had been concealed from her). And whatever the situation, there could be no more final slap in the face than the fact that he had, in the end, married someone else. Even if, as she hinted to Freddy, she had at last steeled herself to finish with Aveling, the revelation of such monstrous ingratitude and duplicity on the part of the man she had loved for so long would have been enough to push mere reason quite out of her mind.

Certainly her actions in the days immediately preceding give no indication that she had been thinking about suicide. But now there were no longer any doubts left. At about ten o'clock the maid, Gertrude Gentry, was sent down the road to the chemist with a note reading 'Please give bearer chloroform and small quantity prussic acid for dog, E.A.' Aveling's card was enclosed. Gerty returned with a packet containing two ounces of chloroform and a drachm of prussic acid, the normal quantities for poisoning a dog. She brought the poison book, in which all such sales had to be recorded, into the front room, and Eleanor signed it E.M.A., after which Gerty took it back to the chemist. When she got back, at about ten forty-five, she found Eleanor in bed, undressed and scarcely breathing. Gerty called a neighbour and went for the doctor, but by the time he arrived Eleanor was dead.

She left two notes. The first was to Aveling:

DEAR. It will soon be all over now. My last word to you is the same that I have said during all these long, sad years – love.

The second was to her nephew, Johnny Longuet:

My dear, dear Johnny.
My last word is addressed to you. Try to be worthy of your grandfather.
Your Aunt Tussy.[32]

Waterloo, where coffins were conveyed by a special train to the crematorium. There were wreaths and tributes from many socialist organizations, and also from the Hyndmans and the Lafargues: Laura was 'too overcome by grief' to feel able to make the journey from Draveil, so marking this crisis, as so many others, by her absence. There were several speeches, from Aveling, Robert Banner, Eduard Bernstein, Pete Curran, Hyndman and Will Thorne, the leader of the Gasworkers' Union, of which Eleanor had for many years been a mainstay. Aveling spoke, as usual, theatrically and effectively; Will Thorne could hardly speak for tears. Afterwards, Aveling went to a cricket match.

He was granted probate of Eleanor's will on 16 April. The gross estate was £1,909 3s. 10d., £1,467 7s. 8d. net. Crosse, the solicitor, told Bernstein that hardly a quarter of the money left to her by Engels remained at the time of her death. 'I do not know how much of it was spent as hush-money to cloak his infamies with women or children, but it must have been very much,' wrote Bernstein to a friend.[36]

Eleanor's death finally removed all brakes on his colleagues' expressing their hatred of Aveling. Nobody would have anything to do with him. He accepted his lot with apparent equanimity. Towards the end of April he resigned from the SDF executive, and in June gave up the auditorship of the Gasworkers' Union which he had held for some years. Soon after Eleanor's death he moved to Mrs Nelson's apartment at No. 2, Stafford Mansions, in Albert Bridge Road, overlooking Battersea Park, which he furnished lavishly on the proceeds of the will. It was rumoured that he planned a tour to New Zealand for his health, but in the event he made it only as far as Ireland, returning to Stafford Mansions to die in his study there, peacefully among his books, on 2 August, just four months after Eleanor. 'What a pity he didn't die a little before!'[37] wrote Hyndman to Liebknecht. All his property went, naturally, to Mrs Nelson.

All Eleanor's friends and relatives concurred in blaming Aveling for her death. Eduard Bernstein was quite sure that he had driven her to suicide. In April, not long after the funeral, Bernstein wrote to Laura: 'He has been seen . . . with a woman in a fashionable restaurant feasting and joking. And there is no doubt that he lives with a woman. I don't know if I told you at the time that a rumour went [round] here that Aveling had at [sic] Tussy's lifetime secretly contracted a *legal* marriage, and that the news of this drove Tussy into death. The matter seemed to me incredible, but there are things which, otherwise inexplicable, could by it be explained . . .' Bernstein went on to recount how the son of an acquaintance starting for Newcastle the previous November had met Aveling with a woman, not Eleanor, about to travel to Newcastle on the same train. 'When the young man returned he spoke to his father with words of utter contempt about Av. Called to account for this he told his father that Aveling had a woman with him on the journey, that he told it to him (the young man) adding that *Tussy was not his legal wife*! Now this was in November last, a few months, nay weeks since the journey to Paris, which as far as we can judge was a kind of reconciliation journey after the cruel affair of the end of August . . . Why the rogue had returned to Tussy at all we can only suspect, but for me it is sure that it was her money.'[38]

Even Liebknecht, who, like Engels, had always taken Aveling at Eleanor's valuation, was forced to admit that 'these are terrible things, that people are saying about Aveling. I cannot believe it all,' he wrote Laura, 'and I wait anxiously for news from you and Paul. In any case, it was cowardice to say that Tussy might have a morbid tendency towards *suicide*. It *is not true*. . . . But a trial against Aveling, as Bernstein wishes, does not seem to me very reasonable.'[39]

It was indeed true that Bernstein and some others contemplated bringing Aveling to trial over the affair. They consulted A. K. Donald, a socialist lawyer, as to the practicability of this. 'It was rather funny,' Donald wrote to J. L. Mahon, Aveling's old adversary – though it is hard to see how anyone could have found the situation very humorous. 'Her friends came to me for advice as to whether or not Aveling could be prosecuted for complicity in the suicide. I went into the matter and took additional evidence from what was given at the inquest but I strongly advised them not to proceed owing to the want of evidence. I showed them a way how the will (value about £1,700) of the woman in favour of the man could be virtually upset, but they would have nothing to do with that. If they could not proceed criminally they would not act at all. Brilliant geniuses they may be, but not much sense . . .' The letter continues with a description of how Donald met Aveling in the Gaiety Bar, 'glaring at me like a fiend of hell . . . Had it not been for me very likely he would have had to stand the racket of a trial for being accessory to E.'s suicide at the

Old Bailey. He would certainly have been acquitted, however. He cannot live long now; he looks very ill, kidney disease.'⁴⁰ Donald was right: Aveling had at that time just two months left. Thwarted of legal revenge, Bernstein had to content himself with publishing the whole sad story, including Eleanor's letters to Freddy Demuth, in the English and German press, thus ensuring that no one could be under any illusions about Aveling.

Eleanor's biographer, Yvonne Kapp, tends to discount the notion that Aveling alone, however wicked, could have driven Eleanor to kill herself. She believes that he was simply the last straw – that many other factors contributed, most of all the sense that she was no longer needed by the working-class movement to which she had devoted her life, and the awareness, especially during those long weeks at Margate when there was so much time to sit and brood, and indeed so little else she could do, that 'the British working-class movement – her native element – was flowing ever more swiftly, broadly and deeply into channels far removed from Marxism, to leave her in a rivulet whose current would not be strong enough to bear her forward'.⁴¹

It is certainly unrealistic to imagine that a person as strong, intelligent and fundamentally hopeful as Eleanor could be driven to despair easily. Nor is it possible to think she would have killed herself had she had any such tangible reason to hold on to life as (to mention the most obvious example) a child. Indeed, her childlessness was much in her mind when she moved to the Den, having just turned forty, and now for the first time owning a spacious house which would never be filled with children. When Kautsky was coming to visit her there in 1895 with his wife and three little boys she wrote to him, 'Like Mohr [her favourite pet-name for her father] I wd rather have the good opinion of a child than of all the grown-ups.' Later, to Laura, when her second Christmas at the Den was approaching, she wrote: 'This is a stupid & a sad time where there are no children. I sometimes wonder if it is worse to have had & lost little ones than never to have had them?' And to Kautsky again, 'If you knew how I love children you wd know that every little detail about them is a joy to me.'⁴² But Aveling was unable to give her even a child.

There is, too, no doubt that her political life was of the most fundamental importance to Eleanor. 'She admitted to being sometimes tired of life, especially when the movement no longer needed her,' wrote Aaron Rosebury. But it seems more probable that this political engagement kept her on an even keel than that it led to depression. All the evidence is that on the occasions when Eleanor succumbed to depression, it was on account of personal disasters. There was a depressive, anorexic episode when, after her mother's death, she was looking after her sick father, overwhelmed by grief, guilt that her mother (on account of the quarrel over Lissagaray) had died not knowing how much Eleanor loved her, and worry about what she was to do with her life. There was the time when, in the early years of her life with Aveling, she had written despairingly to Olive Schreiner, and had indeed been rescued from a suicide attempt by Havelock Ellis and some other friends: this had presumably been precipitated by its being impossible any longer to ignore the full extent of Edward's depravity. And there was the final terrible time when, as we have seen, her absorption in political activity would have borne her through if anything could. But, in the end, even that was not proof against the repeated, almost unimaginable betrayals and miseries of her personal life.

5

THE USES OF PRINCIPLE
2: H.G.'s NEW UTOPIA

I

In many ways the uniquely tragic and brave figure of Eleanor Marx dwarfs her contemporaries. She is altogether more serious, more heroic, than they are. The depth and energy of her political commitment make introspective idealists like Havelock Ellis seem solipsistic to the point of triviality. The extent to which, having committed herself to Edward Aveling, she stood by that commitment and indeed, having given all for love, could not do otherwise, makes the deliberately emotionless politicking of such figures as Bernard Shaw and the Webbs seem pallid and ghostly. When Eleanor died, Shaw, her one-time affectionate admirer, could bring himself to note in his diary only 'the news of Eleanor Marx's suicide in consequence of Aveling having spent all her money'.[1] For Shaw, Eleanor personified, in her life with Aveling, everything from which, in his own relations with women, he instinctively recoiled. Unbridled passion appalled and terrified him; and while he had nothing against clandestine sexual relations in which appearances were preserved, he thought any woman who set herself up in an open union with a man to whom she was not married, thus taking on all the disadvantages of wifehood without any of the legal protection and status of marriage, was a fool. In a curious way, as Hesketh Pearson points out, Aveling was a character more sympathetic to the Shavian temper: his absolute shamelessness, the way in which he never even bothered to conceal his various wrongdoings, his gaiety and *désinvolture* in the face of the world's disapproval, were very much in the Shavian style.

The split between the Fabians and the New Lifers had, it will be remembered, occurred because some – the New Lifers, including Havelock Ellis – felt that it was useless to try to make a better world without first concentrating on making better human beings, while others, including Bernard Shaw, the Blands and Sidney Webb, felt that this would mean postponing the hope of improvement more or less indefinitely and preferred to concentrate on betterment through politics. To a figure such as Eleanor, both approaches were partial and almost irrelevant: the political and the personal life were one, to be lived as a whole. Now, in the years immediately following her death, a figure joined Fabian circles for whom life – and therefore, as an essential part of life, politics – without passion was equally unthinkable. That figure was H.G. Wells.

Wells had become, by the time he met the Fabians in 1901, a rather glamorous personage. But he had certainly not started out that way. Born in 1866, he was the same age as Karl Pearson, but had had none of Pearson's advantages of family wealth and education, nor even the more modest openings enjoyed by Havelock Ellis, who, even if they had little money, enjoyed educational encouragement from his family, or Bernard Shaw, who, though utterly penniless, grew up surrounded by music and literacy. Everything Wells was, he had become not only by his own efforts but in the teeth of his mother's opposition. His father was a gardener and professional cricketer and his mother ran an unsuccessful drapery business; later, his father suffered a crippling fall and his mother resumed her previous career (the one she had been following until she was so unfortunately diverted into marriage) as housekeeper at Uppark, a great house in Sussex. As soon as young Herbert was fourteen his mother had him apprenticed to a draper, abandoned the family business and returned to Uppark; but the boy hated every single thing about his new life, would not stand it and ran away. Much against his mother's will he returned to school, where he worked his way as a pupil teacher, and eventually, after many setbacks, won a place to train at South Kensington as a science teacher, specializing in biology under T.H. Huxley. He was a brilliant student, but he became ill, gave up science, and took up journalism. It was at this point that he first ran into Shaw, also then scraping a journalistic living. However, as everyone knows, it was not as a journalist that Wells made his name, but as an imaginative writer. When he was thirty he started to publish that series of books about imaginary worlds – *The Time Machine, The First Men on the Moon, The Invisible Man, The War of the Worlds* – which were to make him famous and which still remain among his best-known works.

It was as an up-and-coming litterateur that he first got to know the Fabians.

But Wells was not only, or even primarily, a literary man. His stories were first of all good yarns, but they were also serious speculations as to what possibilities might await man and his planet. Indeed, given Wells's background, it was impossible that they should not be speculative. For Wells, too, was of the generation whose religious certainties had been displaced by Darwinism – in his case, in the most literal way: he had rejected his mother's Evangelical religion, while his science teacher, T.H. Huxley, was the man who had originally defended *The Origin of Species* in the famous debate with Bishop Wilberforce, Slippery Sam himself. The great power of Wells's science-fiction stories is the way in which they weld together an almost biblically apocalyptic vision with plausible – and sometimes, as in his prefiguring of the atom bomb in *The World Set Free*, prophetically and minutely accurate – scientific deduction and extrapolation.

Wells's speculations were not confined to the scientific. He had experienced the miseries of poverty and ignorance, and he did not forget them. In a piece called *The Misery of Boots*, published in 1905 (and later reprinted as a Fabian pamphlet), he wrote about 'the figure of a badly fed but rather pretty little girl of ten or eleven, dirty, and her hands coarse with rough usage, her poor child's body in ungainly rags, and, on her feet, big broken-down boots that hurt her. And particularly I think of her wretched sticks of legs and the limp of her feet and all those phantom owners and profit-takers I spoke of, they are there about her martyrdom, leech-like, clinging to her as she goes . . . I want to change everything in the world that made that; and I do not greatly care what has to go into the process. Do you?'[2]

In short, Wells was a socialist – a visionary socialist; and in many of his imaginary societies the emphasis was not on scientific speculation but on the possible form of that new social order which he saw as a *sine qua non* of man's evolution if the world was not to end in disaster.

It was (for though the details differed from book to book, these were variations upon a constant theme) by no means an egalitarian social order. Wells had an essentially Platonic world-view in this respect. His model societies were invariably ruled by a special governing order of the best and the brightest. In *Anticipations* and *Mankind in the Making* they are called New Republicans; in *A Modern Utopia* they appear as Samurai; in *The New Machiavelli*, as Aristocrats. In the *Modern Utopia* the Samurai are explained by an informant to the visitor from Earth:

'The order is not hereditary – we know just enough of biology and the uncertainties of inheritance to know how silly that would be – and it does not require an early consecration or novitiate or ceremonies and initiations of that sort. The *Samurai* are, in fact, volunteers. Any intelligent adult in a reasonably healthy and efficient state may, at any age after five and twenty, become one of the *Samurai* and take a hand in the universal control.' . . .

'I have heard the phrase "voluntary nobility".'

'That was the idea of our Founders. They made a noble and privileged order – open to the whole world. No one could complain of an unjust exclusion, for the only thing that could exclude from the order was unwillingness or inability to follow the Rule.

'The Rule aims to exclude the dull and base altogether . . . Save in specified exceptional circumstances, the *Samurai* must bathe in cold water and the men must shave every day; they have the precisest directions in such matters; the body must be in health, the skin and nerves and muscles in perfect tone, or the *Samurai* must go to the doctors of the order . . . They must sleep alone at least four nights in five; and they must eat with and talk to anyone in their fellowship who cares for their conversation for an hour at least, at the nearest club-house of the *Samurai*, once on three chosen days in every week. . . . Every month they must buy and read through at least one book that has been published in the last five years . . . So far as the *Samurai* have a purpose in common in maintaining the State and the order and discipline of the world, so far, by their discipline and denial, by their public work and effort, they worship God together. But the ultimate fount of motives lies in the individual life . . . For seven consecutive days in the year, at least, each man or woman under the Rule must go right out of the life of men into some wild or solitary place . . . Partly it is to ensure good training and sturdiness of body and mind, but

partly also, it is to draw the minds of the *Samurai* for a space
from the insistent details of life . . . from personal quarrels and
personal affections and the things of the heated room.'[3]

Such elitist sentiments would not have sounded in the least paradoxical
to Wells's generation of socialists, convinced enthusiasts for eugenics
that they all were. The secret, of course, was that they all saw
themselves as members of the *Samurai*, or something very like it. For
instance, in 1886, fifteen years before *Anticipations*, Olive Schreiner
had written to Karl Pearson along very similar lines: 'Most human
beings, all but one in ten or twenty thousand, need to be roused and
stimulated: they are engines in which the fire must be heaped up and
more steam created if they are to get anywhere at all. It is difficult for
the few to see that their problem is quite different . . . and while all
others must have their fires made up and their steam generated, for
us there [is] only to let the fires low and the steam off. Our danger
is that we will reach the goal and sweep wildly past it into space! We
can get *any*where; but the question is whether we can stop there when
we get there!'[4]

It was almost inevitable that Wells would be taken up by the
Fabians, who were (especially Beatrice and Sidney Webb) the very
personification of Samurai and New Republicans, reading all the new
books, leading healthy country lives and belonging to gentlemen's
clubs as they did, not to say sharing a special predilection for government. Beatrice Webb commented in 1901 that *Anticipations* was
'the most remarkable book of the year'; and early in 1902 Edward
Pease, the Fabian Secretary, wrote to ask Wells, 'if you've yet met
the Webbs: they are the pioneers of your New Republic. We have
lived for years on Webb's new ideas of politics. We want someone
else who can think ahead.'[5]

In March 1902, the meeting was effected. Beatrice's views of Wells,
recorded in her diary after the event, are revealing of both her subject
and herself: 'An interesting, though somewhat unattractive personality
except for his agreeable disposition and intellectual vivacity. His
mother was the housekeeper to a great establishment of forty servants,
his father the professional cricketer attached to the place. The early
associations with the menial side of the great man's establishment has
left Wells with a hatred of that class and of its attitude towards the

"lower orders". His apprenticeship to a draper, his subsequent career as an assistant master at a private venture school, as a "government student" at South Kensington living on £1 a week, as an "army crammer", as a journalist and, in these last years, as a most successful writer of fiction, has given him a great knowledge of the lower-middle class and their habits and thoughts, and an immense respect for science and its methods. But he is totally ignorant of the manual worker, on the one hand, and of the big administrator and the aristocrat on the other . . . A world run by the physical-science man straight from his laboratory is his ideal; he does not see that specialized faculty and knowledge are needed for administration exactly as they are needed for the manipulation of machinery or [natural] forces. But he is extraordinarily quick in his apprehensions, and took in all the points we gave him in our forty-eight hours' talk with him, first at his own house and then here. He is a good instrument for popularizing ideas, and he gives as many ideas as he receives . . . He has no great faith in government by the "man in the street", and, I think, has hardly realized the function of the representative as a "foolometer" for the expert.'

Beatrice went on: 'His wife is a pretty little person with a strong will, mediocre intelligence and somewhat small nature. She has carefully moulded herself in dress, manners and even accent to take her place in any society her husband's talents may lead them into. But it is all rather artificial, from the sweetness of her smile to her interest in public affairs. However, she provides him with a charming, well-ordered home, though I should imagine her constant companionship was somewhat stifling.'[6] That Wells was perfectly aware of what she was thinking about his wife became clear when he published *The New Machiavelli* with its malicious portrait of Beatrice as Altiora Bailey. 'Altiora had been very emphatic and uncharitable upon the futility of the Socialist movement. It seemed that even the leaders fought shy of dinner-parties . . . "Most of them have totally unpresentable wives," said Altiora, "totally!!" and quoted instances, "and they *will* bring them. Or they won't come! Some of the poor creatures have scarcely learnt their table-manners. They just make holes in the talk." '[7]

As far as wives went, Wells, by the time he began to make his name, was already on his second. As a young man he had married his cousin Isabel, with whom he was much in love. But she could not respond to his eager sexuality, and although he was, and remained, very fond of her and deeply attracted to her, he found that as his life expanded and his horizons broadened she could not really give him the kind of companionship he wanted. What he *did* now want was symbolized for him by a very bright girl student of his at South Kensington called Amy Catherine Robbins, and at the beginning of 1894 he left Isabel and ran away with Amy Catherine.

Wells, in his *Experiment in Autobiography*, written forty years after that elopement, emphasized that sexual passion had little to do with his shift of allegiance, although at the time, given the expectations on both sides, they assumed it had. What was more to the point was that Miss Robbins shared the new Wells's hopes and expectations in a way that Isabel could not. At any rate, the new couple were very happy together and got married as soon as Wells's divorce was through, in 1895. They were to remain together, through thick and thin, until Jane Wells's death in 1926 (H.G. disliked both Amy Catherine's given names, and they soon agreed that she was to be called Jane).

Exactly what that thick and thin consisted of is explained in Wells's autobiography. Naturally it was all thought out. Wells was a man of his time, and for him, as much as for Havelock Ellis or Olive Schreiner, principle was all. If religion was to be replaced by rationalism, rationalism must have its own ethics, and the best part of Wells's intellectual energies throughout his life were devoted to formulating just what those ethics should be.

The problem in Wells's second marriage was that it did not satisfy him sexually, although (he emphasizes) in every other way it did. 'So long as we were in the opening phase of our struggle for a position and worldly freedom, this question was hardly a practical issue between us. There was neither time nor energy to indulge in any form of wanderlust. But with the coming of success, increasing leisure and facility of movement, the rapid enlargement of our circle of acquaintance, and contact with unconventional and exciting people, there was no further necessity for the same rigid self-restraint. The craving, in a body that was gathering health and strength, for a complete loveliness of bodily response, was creeping up into my imagination and growing more and more powerful. This craving dominated the work of D.H. Lawrence altogether. For my own part, I could never yield it that importance. I would justify it if I

Olive Schreiner and Havelock Ellis,
pictured at about the time they first met

Olive in 1882,
uncharacteristically
corseted

'You looked like a tall angel,'
wrote Olive to Havelock

Eleanor Marx and Edward Aveling, 1886

Eleanor is wearing her favourite blue velvet dress. She has already discovered what Edward was really like, after less than two years together; it was to be another twelve years before this knowledge finally destroyed her.

Edward Aveling

Karl Pearson, about 1882
*(University College,
London)*

Elisabeth Cobb
*(University College,
London)*

Karl and Maria Pearson, their son Egon (left) and daughter
Ilse, about 1896. An ideal family. *(University College, London)*

Olive and Cron, Kimberley, August 1895. This picture was taken about three months after Olive lost her baby.
(National English Literary Museum, Grahamstown, S.A.)

Beatrice Potter and Sidney Webb, 1891
(Passfield Papers)

'Let me have your *head only* – it is the head only I am marrying!'
wrote Beatrice to Sidney

H.G. Wells and Jane enjoying a day on the river, 1895. H.G. is
dreaming or possibly looking at a pretty girl, Jane is concentrating
on H.G. *(University of Illinois, Champaign-Urbana)*

Amber Blanco-White
with H.G.'s daughter
Anna-Jane, about 1911
*(University of Illinois,
Champaign-Urbana)*

Rebecca West and H.G.'s
son Anthony, 1916

Margaret Sanger on her
return from Europe,1915
*(Sophia Smith Collection,
Smith College)*

Edith Ellis just before she
left for her American
lecture tour, 1915

Margaret Sanger leaving the Court of Special Sessions after her
arraignment, October 1917
(Sophia Smith Collection, Smith College)

could, but not at the price of that joint attack upon the world to
which I was committed with Jane.'8

Wells presents the arrangement he and Jane arrived at as a joint
affair, although it seems clear that the impetus must have come from
him – in dealings with Wells, on any level, the impetus generally
did come from him. One imagines that, over some long period,
the subject was brought up; Wells argued and persuaded with that
enormous charm and vivacity always characteristic of him; and Jane
assented, conceivably with some relief: the bottom line being that
their marriage would always come first.

It is evident [writes Wells] that this marriage of ours had some
very distinctive features. Its originality did not end at that perfect
business confidence and that queer play of silly humorous fantasy,
mental caressing and imposed interpretations . . . At the back
of all that, two extremely dissimilar brains were working very
intelligently at the peculiar life problem we had created for each
other. We came at last to a very explicit understanding about the
profound difference in our physical and imaginative responses.

Jane thought I had a right to my own individual disposition
and that luck had treated me badly in mating me first to an
unresponsive and then to a fragile companion. About that she
was extraordinarily dispassionate and logical and much more
clearheaded than I was. She faced the matter with the same
courage, honesty and self-subordination with which she faced
all the practical issues of life. She suppressed any jealous impulse
and gave me whatever freedom I desired. She knew as well as
I did that for all its elements of artificiality, our alliance was
indissoluble . . . and she realized perhaps sooner than I, how
little that alliance demanded a monopoly of passionate intimacy
. . . The French with their absurd logicality distinguish between
the *passade*, a stroke of mutual attraction that may happen to
any couple, and a real love affair. In theory, I was now to have
passades.9

This arrangement developed after 1900. The couple had been together
six years, and Wells was beginning to make some money. He commissioned a house on the south coast at Sandgate from the up-and-coming

young architect Alfred Voysey; gave Jane two babies, Gip and Frank, born respectively in 1901 and 1903; and, supported by this background of tolerant and comfortable domesticity, where any or all of his increasing circle of friends would be welcomed in fine style and without questions, resumed his attack upon the world with a new freedom.

The compromise was not perfect. 'All life is imperfect,' Wells comments; 'imperfection becomes a condemnation only when it reaches an intolerable level. Our imperfections we made quite tolerable . . . the more marked the individuality the more difficult it is to discover a complete reciprocity.'[10] About this particular compromise, years after the event and some years after Jane had died, he was able to be quite honest: 'the spreading knowledge of birth-control . . . seemed to justify my contention that love was now to be taken more lightly than it had been in the past. It was to be refreshment and invigoration, as I set out quite plainly in my *Modern Utopia* . . . and I could preach these doctrines with no thought of how I would react if presently my wife were to carry them into effect, since she was so plainly not disposed to carry them into effect.'[11]

Such were the Wellses as they presented themselves eagerly to an eager world. Jane ran the house and brought up the boys, and Wells sallied out, unquestioned, in search of *passades* and other picturesque items.

2

For people like Havelock Ellis and Edward Carpenter, the question of sexual conduct entered the public domain because it was an essential part of that self which must be discovered and fulfilled before a better world of any sort would be conceivable. It therefore followed that their own lives were an essential part of their propaganda. Carpenter, by publishing *The Intermediate Sex* with its unemotional discussion of homosexuality, and his own quietly open homosexual household in Derbyshire, effectively set himself up as a living example of his intellectual and social preaching. In the same way Ellis, by the example of his 'semi-detached marriage' (as she called it) with Edith, could demonstrate the broad possibilities open to a truly modern marriage; and although it is impossible to imagine that reticent, almost reclusive man actually going so far as to cite his own personal example in his writings other than in the most oblique way (his memoirs were published posthumously) Edith, as we shall see, did not hesitate to do so. But the aim was definitely not to shock. Wherever topics of a dangerously sexual nature arose, the utmost decorum prevailed. The necessity of acknowledging the variety of sexual needs for the sake of a person's mental and physical health might be discussed, and so might the sexual implications of the widely-acknowledged need for women's economic equality. Sex might be acknowledged to be beautiful and poetic and it was without doubt essential and unavoidable. But the one thing nobody said was that it might be fun. *That* would not have been at all respectable, and when one was putting forward dangerously subversive policies, respectability was all – as Shaw, in his paradoxical way, never tired of preaching.

H.G. Wells changed all that; and one reason why he did so was that he was very possibly the first among that solemn band of theorists for whom sex *was*, absolutely and undeniably, fun. Indeed, it must be said that they were, sexually speaking, a very peculiar lot – which is no doubt why, as Freud pointed out, they interested themselves so particularly in these things. They were obsessive because sex was not easy for them, and they found in their radical groups not merely a sympathetic and tolerant audience for their points of view but in many cases – Edith Ellis, Olive Schreiner, Bernard Shaw spring immediately to mind – a warmth of friendship and acceptance among like minds absolutely lacking in their early lives; that is to say, in that portion of their lives from which so many of their sexual difficulties undoubtedly stemmed. (Shaw, of course, was full of fun, but not about sex, of which – and especially of its frequent concomitant, love – he was, like many philanderers, terrified. Indeed, for him the use of fun was more often to defuse potentially threatening sexual situations.)

In another way, too, Wells was different from people such as Ellis and Olive Schreiner. They started with their painfully worked-out ideals and principles and then spent their lives trying to live according to them. Wells did things the other way about. First of all he worked out the lines along which he would run his own life; then he set about constructing principles to fit them.

Having, then, achieved a happy and satisfactorily-arranged marriage, a delightful family life, an enviable position in the world of letters and a wide and increasingly influential acquaintance, Wells sat down to describe his ideal world. He did this in the series of books already mentioned between 1901 and 1915. Some of these, such as *Anticipations* and *A Modern Utopia*, were more or less theoretical; some, such as *In the Days of the Comet*, were cast in the form of a novel; others, such as *Ann Veronica* and *The New Machiavelli*, were novels based upon his recent life in which his behaviour and principles were described and expounded. In all of these the most notable and controversial idea, and certainly the one which received the most critical attention, was that of free and guiltless sexual choice between men and women, initiated from either side and with the tolerance of all.

This was not, as Wells explained at great length, to be an irresponsible society. In so far as children were concerned their upkeep would be the responsibility of the state: Wells favoured a scheme for the 'endowment of motherhood', much touted at that time, which would ensure that all children were provided for. This being a given, there was, so far as he could see, no reason why the old habit of exclusive monogamy need prevail. 'The ordinary civilized woman and the ordinary civilized man are alike obsessed with the idea of meeting and possessing one peculiar intimate person, one special exclusive lover who is their very own, and a third person of either sex cannot be associated with that couple without an intolerable sense of privacy and confidence and possession destroyed. It is difficult to imagine a second wife in a home who would not be and feel herself to be a rather excluded and inferior person. But that does not abolish the possibility that there are exceptional people somewhere capable of, to coin a phrase, triangular mutuality, and I do not see why we should either forbid or treat with bitterness or hostility a grouping we may consider so inadvisable or so unworkable as never to be adopted, if three people of their own will desire it . . . I do not want to force people who would otherwise be useful citizens into rebellion, concealments and the dark and furtive ways of vice, because they may not love and marry as their temperaments command, and so I want to make the meshes of the law as wide as possible . . . Then marriage . . . does not necessarily mean cohabitation. All women who desire children do not want to be entrusted with their upbringing. Some women are sexual and philoprogenitive without being sedulously maternal, and some are maternal without much or any sexual passion. There are

men and women in the world now, great allies, fond and passionate
lovers who do not live nor want to live constantly together.'[12]

By the time he wrote this, Wells was no longer thinking in terms
of delightful generalities, but had very particular instances in mind.

In his *Modern Utopia* (which, he wrote in his autobiography in 1933,
'remains my last word' with regard to sexual theory) Wells, following
Plato, visualized his Samurai 'of both sexes, a hardy bare-limbed
race, free lovers among themselves – and mutually obliging. Like
the people of the original Oneida Community in New York State
they constituted one comprehensive "group marriage." . . . the
book was popular among the young of our universities; it launched
many of them into cheerful adventures that speedily brought them
up against the facts of fixation, jealousy and resentment. It played a
considerable part in the general movement of release from the rigid
technical chastity of women during the Victorian period.'[13] Probably
this was no more than the literal truth: for to young women frustrated
by the narrowness of their lives (which then meant most intelligent
young women) Wells at that time appeared as a bright star of hope
formulating their thoughts more clearly than they could themselves.
'I wanted to read you wild, splendid passages from Wells – how he
stirs the rebel in one!' wrote one such, Ruth Slate, to her friend Eva
Slawson in 1911.[14] The book which so aroused her enthusiasm was
The New Machiavelli; for girls like Ruth and Eva, Wells opened out
prospects hitherto unimaginable.

It was not only among the young that Wells was influential at
this time, but among their parents as well. *A Modern Utopia* came
out in 1905; in 1906 *In the Days of the Comet* drew a picture of a
society magically released from sexual jealousy (and all other base
emotions) by the gas emanating from the tail of a comet passing
close by the Earth. Like so many of Wells's productions at this
time, the book was savagely criticized for immorality. Soon after its
publication Wells addressed a packed meeting of the Fabian Society
on 'Socialism and the Middle Classes', in which he set out his ideas
for the endowment of motherhood with all that followed therefrom,
such as the dissolution of the proprietary nature of marriage. In it
he attacked the 'unimaginative' Webbs for promoting socialism like
'district visitors'. As might be imagined, the meeting – the largest the
Fabians had ever attracted – divided along age lines. The younger

members of the audience were wildly enthusiastic, the older ones suspicious – not surprisingly, since it was largely they who were under attack. Hubert Bland, husband of that Mrs Bland to whom Eleanor had written so entreatingly on first setting up house with Aveling, wrote to Edward Pease: 'I am afraid that Mr Wells' lecture did no sort of good to the propaganda. Judging by what I heard afterwards a lot of people were quite upset.' Beatrice Webb, too, was disapproving: she thought he was 'gambling with the idea of free love – throwing it out to see what sort of reception it gets – without responsibility for its effect on the character of the hearers. It is this recklessness which makes Sidney dislike him.' However, fair-minded as ever, she went home to read *In the Days of the Comet*, and reflected anew on the Woman Question. Early in her career she had signed (and almost immediately regretted signing) a letter denouncing the idea of woman suffrage; now, while she still rejected the idea of free love, she realized that her own advantages had blinded her to the difficulties faced by many – indeed most – other women, and was at last galvanized to recant. Two weeks after the lecture she wrote a letter to Millicent Fawcett, the suffragette leader, explaining that she had withdrawn her opposition to votes for women. To Wells she wrote, 'Mrs Wells will rejoice to see that I have at last thrown in my lot with Women's Suffrage. See what you have accomplished by your Propaganda!'[15]

Wells and the Webbs were never, at this period, on more than arms'-length terms. It was unthinkable that they should be: their styles were too different. But not all the Fabians were as stiff and serious as the Webbs. Among those who were less serious was Edith Bland; and between the Blands and the Wellses a friendship very soon sprang up.

3

Hubert and Edith Bland were an exceedingly odd couple. Of an age with Bernard Shaw (Hubert was eleven years, Edith eight years older than Wells), they, like Shaw, had been in the Fabian Society almost from its beginning: indeed, Shaw was first introduced to it by Bland in 1884. Hubert Bland was an unsuccessful businessman and a rather more successful journalist, while Edith turned her hand to stories for ladies' magazines, pictures for birthday cards, poetry, romantic fiction and, most successfully, children's stories, for which, as E. Nesbit, she is still remembered and widely read.

The Bland ménage had, from the start, been highly irregular. Edith had been seven months pregnant when in 1878, at the age of twenty-one, she married Hubert against her mother's will (her father had died when she was a small child). What she did not then know was that Hubert was already engaged to, and indeed had a child by, another girl named Maggie, whom he continued to see. When Edith did eventually find out about this, she and Maggie became great friends – a reaction characteristic of Edith, who was a Bohemian to her soul.

It seems obvious that there could have been no possible reason for the Blands to disapprove of the Avelings, as Eleanor was so afraid they might and so much hoped they would not. And yet Eduard Bernstein, Eleanor's old friend, when he first visited London and was introduced to them at this time, sensed definite reservations on their part. 'About the end of the first year my wife and I received a social invitation from Mr and Mrs Hubert Bland, who belonged to the inner circle of the Fabians. They and their guests were interesting people, and the conversation was very natural and spontaneous. But when in some connection or other I spoke of the Avelings, there was suddenly a suspiciously unanimous chorus of praise for them. "Oh, the Avelings are very clever people." "Oh, everybody must admit that they have been of great service to the movement," and so forth, in the same key, so that it was at once clear to me that there was something in the air.'[16]

In fact Edith Bland was a friend of Eleanor's; as we have seen, reservations about 'the Avelings' generally boiled down to reservations about Edward Aveling. But in this case there might have been something different at work; because, although Hubert Bland led such an irregular personal life himself, he made a point of publicly disapproving of irregularity in others, and would certainly have been very equivocal about a publicly-flaunted unmarried union such as that of Eleanor and Edward.

In short, he was a terrible hypocrite. It was a quality that Wells, in his later view of the Blands, held mercilessly against him. 'The incongruity of Bland's costume with his Bohemian setting, the costume of a city swell, top-hat, tail-coat, greys and blacks, white slips, spatterdashes and that black-ribboned monocle, might have told me, had I had the ability then to read such signs, of the general imagination at work in his *persona*, the myth of a great Man of the World, a Business Man (he had no gleam of business ability) invading for his own sage strong purposes this assembly of long-haired intellectuals,' he wrote in his autobiography. 'This myth had, I think, been developed and sustained in him, by the struggle of his egoism against the manifest fact that his wife had a brighter and fresher mind than himself, and had subtler and livelier friends.'[17] She was also, by the time Wells knew her, far more successful professionally – it was her children's books that paid most of the family bills; another blow to Bland's self-image which had to be compensated for.

How and why, then, did Edith put up with him? The answer can only be that she was in love with him. She put up with him because she had to if she wanted to live with him; but not without asserting herself in her own way.

We have seen that before she began living with Aveling, and indeed until that ménage threatened to split apart, Bernard Shaw had been fond of Eleanor Marx and had seen a lot of her. This had set the pattern for a good many relationships during the years until his own marriage in 1898, in which he played the 'Sunday husband', the companion and consolation – but not, in the strict physical sense, the lover – of women who were safely but unsatisfactorily married. One of these ladies was Edith Bland.

Edith first got to know Shaw well in 1885, but she did not become seriously involved with him until the summer of 1886. Then, she fell in love with him, and at first Shaw, in his usual way, did nothing to discourage her. They met (of course) at the British Museum; they walked around London. In her novel *Daphne in Fitzroy Street*, which is in some ways an account of that affair, Edith wrote: 'When Daphne looks back at that summer, it seems to her that the sun always shone.'[18] She also pokes fun at Shaw himself:

'We went to "Man and Superman,"' she said. 'I think it's silly.'

'Didn't you like it? Most young ladies rave over Mr. Bernard Shaw.'

'Oh, it was clever,' said Daphne, 'much cleverer than anything I ever saw. But – '

'But?'

'People don't run after people like that in real life. It's simply caricature.' . . .

'I wonder,' said he. 'Well. I wonder. You think it's always the men who do the running?'

'Isn't it?' said she.

'Yes,' he said, 'in books.'[19]

Shaw tried to imply to Doris Langley Moore, Edith's biographer, that on the contrary it was Edith who had done all the running, although this seems implausible and his diary belies it. But in the end he, as usual, took flight when emotions threatened to get out of hand. 'You had no right to write the preface if you were not going to write the book,' Edith later upbraided him.[20] But for her, too, a pattern had been set, and she went on to have a number of affairs with younger and more insignificant men (not difficult, since most men were more insignificant than Shaw) which were consummated. Not that sex was of particular importance to Edith, who was more romantic than passionate, and who was in fact essentially rather shy and prudish about bodily matters: Wells remarks on 'an essential physical coldness in her'.[21] But she needed these affairs to maintain an equal footing with her husband, who was generally acknowledged among their circle to be 'rather hot-blooded', and who was about to make even greater demands of her tolerance.

In 1886 Edith gave birth to a still-born child, and a journalistic friend, Alice Hoatson, helped nurse her through the ordeal. Later the same year it was Edith's turn to help Alice, who was pregnant. She had often asked Alice to live with her and help as companion and housekeeper; now she saw a way out of Alice's plight which would be good for both of them. Alice would move in with the Blands, and Edith would bring up the child as her own. In October Alice gave birth to a little girl, Rosamund. She refused to say who the child's father was. Then, six months later, the secret of Rosamund's paternity emerged. The father was Hubert Bland.

Rosamund herself gave Doris Langley Moore two views of what happened next. Alice Hoatson's was that 'By this time [Edith] had

grown to love the baby so much that she could not part with it.'
Hubert Bland's, explained Rosamund, was rather different: 'When
it transpired who was the father, there was, quite naturally, the hell
of a scene, and I and my mother were to be ejected then and there
into the street. Whereupon my father said that if we went, he went
too. He said that he had never loved his other children as he loved
me and that he was passionately in love with my mother. Finally the
matter was thrashed out and the decision was taken that they should
all remain together. This business recurred several times during the
first years of my life. I mean, there were other occasions when A.H.
was told to go and take me with her, but my father prevailed and the
situation continued until it became permanent.' Speaking of her father
and Edith, Rosamund describes 'The tremendous hold he certainly
had on her from the moment he met her until he died. It wasn't
simply that she came nobly up to scratch over a big crisis. She could
not have borne losing him and there was a danger of that.'[22]

The secret of Rosamund's parentage was not generally known, but
Edith seems to have confided in Olive Schreiner, who was at that
time on one of her brief visits to London, and who wrote letters to
Havelock Ellis and to Edward Carpenter hinting at Edith's heroism
and dark, untellable secrets in her life – 'If I *could* tell you about her
you would love her so!'[23]

When Alice Hoatson moved in with them the Blands were not
well-off: they lived in a large but extremely shabby house in Lewisham,
a setting which will be familiar to all readers of Edith's books about
the Bastable family. Then, in 1898, when Edith was forty, the family
fortunes suddenly changed. In that year she published *The Treasure
Seekers*, the first of the Bastable books, and it was a great and
immediate success. On the strength of this the Bland household
moved to Well Hall, a big moated Tudor mansion on the edge of
south London; and it was at this time that the Wellses first got to
know the Blands.

In fact the first meetings between the families did not take place at
Well Hall but at Sandgate and Dymchurch, just along the coast, where
the Blands had a seaside house. At first relations were cordial but formal, both sides admiring each other's work, enjoying visits, addressing
each other as 'Mrs Bland' and 'Mrs Wells'. But by December 1904
Wells was writing to Edith: 'Steamed Lady, I never told you how we

like *The Phoenix and the Carpet* . . . It is the best larking I ever saw. Your destiny is plain. You go on every Xmas never missing an Xmas, with a book like this, and you will become a British Institution in six years from now. Nothing can stop it. Every self-respecting family will buy you automatically and you will become rich beyond the dreams of avarice.'[24] In return Edith plied him with adulatory young guests, and by the summer of the following year they were intimate and relaxed enough for Wells to arrive unannounced to spend a week at Well Hall. His letter of thanks – 'roofer' in their terminology – speaks for itself: 'Dear Lady, A roofer! the thing cannot be written! Jane I think must take on the task of describing the departure of a yellow, embittered and thoroughly damned man on one Thursday and his return on the next, pink . . . exultant, with a beautifully hand-sewn wreath in one pocket and a programme in the other and his manner – full of the most agreeable memories. If – as I have always said – the gratitude of a lifetime . . . Fine impalpable threads of agreeable association trail from Lodge to stair way, hold me to your upstairs and downstairs bedrooms, take me under the trees of your lawn, and to your garden paths, to the green seat in the garden and all about you. It was a bright dear time.'[25]

This evident warmth contrasts with the extremely ambivalent description of Well Hall and its inhabitants Wells gives in his autobiography.

They were the strangest of couples . . . E. Nesbit was a tall, whimsical, restless, able woman who had been very beautiful and was still very good-looking; and Bland was a thick-set, broad-faced aggressive man, a sort of Tom-cat man, with a tenoring voice and a black-ribboned monocle and a general disposition to dress and live up to that. The two of them dramatized life and I had as yet met few people who did that. They loved scenes and 'situations.' They really enjoyed strong emotion. There was no such persistent pursuit of truth and constructive ends in them as in their finer associates. It was not in their imaginative scheme. . . . She earned the greater part of the joint income. She ran a great easy-going household at Well Hall, Eltham, an old moated house with a walled garden. Those who loved her and those who wished to please her called her royally 'Madame' or 'Duchess', and she had a touch of aloof authority which justified that. A miscellany of people came and went there . . . And there also I and Jane visited and learnt to play Badminton and gossip and discuss endlessly.

At first it seemed to be a simple agreeable multitudinousness from which literary buds and flowers sprang abundantly, pre- sided over by this tall, engaging, restless, moody woman. Then gradually the visitor began to perceive at first unsuspected trends and threads of relationship and scented, as if from the moat, a more disturbing flavour . . . You found after a time that Well Hall was not so much an atmosphere as a web . . . At the first encounter it had seemed so extraordinarily open and jolly. Then suddenly you encountered fierce resentments; you found Mrs Bland inexplicably malignant; doors became walls so to speak and floors pitfalls. In that atmosphere you surprised yourself. It was like Alice through the Looking Glass; not only were there Mock Turtles and White Queens and Mad Hatters about, but you discovered with amazement that you were changing your own shape and stature.[26]

Wells also speaks of people coming to Well Hall and going, 'and some of them went for good. There had been "misunderstandings".' Exactly such was the case with Wells. The misunderstanding in this case was that he had tried to seduce Rosamund – had possibly even succeeded – and had been punched in the nose for his pains by Rosamund's outraged father on the platform at Paddington Station, where the romantic pair had been hauled off a train en clandestine route for the Continent.

Rosamund was a member of what was known as the 'Fabian nursery', a group of the children of older Fabians and their friends who were now growing up, eager for the cause, but eager also for innovation and fresh thinking. Wells, who was at this time setting himself up against the 'Old Gang' in Fabian politics, was a particular focus of admiration for them.

Nearly thirty years after the event, Wells wrote:

In that hothouse atmosphere of the Bland household at Dym- church and Well Hall . . . I found myself almost assigned as the peculiar interest of Rosamund, the dark-eyed, sturdy daughter of Bland and the governess, Miss Hoatson. Rosamund talked of love, and how her father's attentions to her were becoming unfatherly. I conceived a great disapproval of incest, and an urgent desire to put Rosamund beyond its reach in the most effective manner possible, by absorbing her myself. Miss Hoatson, whose experiences of life had made her very broad-minded, and who had a queer sort of liking for me, did not seem to think this would be altogether disastrous for her daughter; but presently Mrs Bland, perceiving Hubert's gathering excitement in the tense atmosphere about us, precipitated accusations and confrontations. Bland stirred up her strain of anti-sexual feeling. She wrote insulting letters to Jane, denouncing her tolerance of my misbehaviour – which came rather oddly from her. Rosamund was hastily snatched out of my reach and in the resulting confusion, married to an ambitious follower of my party in the Fabian Society, Clifford Sharp – and so snatched also out of the range of Hubert's heavy craving for illicit relations. It was a steamy jungle episode, a phase of coveting and imitative desire, for I never found any great charm in Rosamund . . . But in that damned atmosphere that hung about the Blands, everyone seemed impelled towards such complications; it was contagious.[27]

Doris Langley Moore records that when she went to visit Wells to discuss E. Nesbit with him he was uncharacteristically embarrassed and evasive; this would have been just about the time when he was writing his autobiography, with its uncomplimentary view of the Bland ménage, in which case the embarrassment is understandable.

Of course, things did not seem quite like that at the time. In fact, in March 1907, which would have been just about the start of his affair with Rosamund, he wrote to a mutual friend: 'I have a pure flame for Rosamund who is the Most – Quite!'[28] As for being thrust together with Rosamund, he was certainly encouraged to nurture her literary aspirations. But for the rest his account is probably fair enough. Of what Alice thought of H.G. and his intentions we can have no idea; but it seems not improbable that Edith would have had little to say about the affair until she saw that Hubert was getting upset about it. She was not an especially fond mother, despite the deep understanding of children that her stories show (and which probably sprang from clear memories of how she had felt during her own childhood rather than from observation of her children). She was especially uninterested in her daughters. Her real daughter, Iris, told Doris Langley Moore that 'My mother was never really interested in girls, or in women for that matter.'[29] As for Rosamund, relations between them became particularly difficult after the death of her beloved youngest son, Fabian, during a mishandled operation to remove his tonsils in 1899. Then, though she did not know the reason why until she was eighteen, Rosamund heard Edith scream at Hubert 'Why couldn't it have been Rosamund?' To Doris Langley Moore Rosamund wrote: 'It wasn't just that she did not feel for me what she felt for her own children. How could she? She actually, I think, always *subconsciously*, at any rate, had a lot against me. She did not forgive my existence.'[30]

Otherwise, everything we know or can deduce about Hubert Bland seems to indicate that Wells was probably entirely justified in his judgments and accusations. The depths of his hypocrisy can be deduced from the fact that in his *Letters to a Daughter*, published in 1906 and dedicated, of course, to Rosamund, he coolly discussed the phenomenon of the *ménage à trois* as though the Blands had not been conducting one for the past twenty years. As for the suspicion of incestuous fumblings, there is a distinct over-insistence by Bland that 'His daughter is the only woman in all the world for whom a man five-and-twenty years her senior can feel no stir of passion, no trace of . . . sex-love; the only woman from whom he cannot possibly evoke passion in return. That fact of itself gives his daughter a chamber all to herself in the man's heart, a chamber guarded by an angel with a flaming sword.'[31] As for Rosamund's feelings about all this, her own keen description of her father's attractions may indicate that she was not entirely immune to them: 'He was absolutely irresistible to the women he paid court to, not only before the event of capture, but after. He had a tremendous hold on anyone he had ever possessed. . . . He endowed every affair with the romance of his own imagination.'[32]

The next year, 1909, Rosamund married Clifford Sharp, then a young man with a brilliant future, who was to become the first editor of the *New Statesman*. But the brilliant future soon receded into the past, and to the middle-aged Rosamund, whose husband had by now become a chronic alcoholic, the episode with H.G. stood out as one of the high points of her life. In about 1929 she wrote him a sad letter: 'Clifford has no work and no income now, and I don't really any longer believe he will get anything . . . Strangely enough, I remember I gave you a promise – the seashore at Dymchurch *twenty-two* years ago that I would tell you if ever I was stranded. You told me then that Clifford would be no good to me. How horribly, terribly right you were! Of course, a promise like that doesn't mean anything on either side, except that I remembered it and you probably didn't. As you have stated, in print, you are not the person you were once upon a time – there have been hunderds of H.G.s, and there is still an H.G., and the one I spoke to on the sands at Dymchurch was only one of them and he is dead. . . .' Later in the year, having seen a photo in the *Tatler* of a new portrait of H.G. by Orpen she wrote: 'This is the real H.G., the H.G. who writes unforgettable, & darling things, the H.G. one loves, and always loved and couldn't misunderstand. This was once my H.G. and I think in some deep place in me is still my H.G.'33

The spectacle of Wells and Bland at each others' throats on account of an attempted seduction was not uncomical. Even Rosamund, after being snatched off the train, taken home by her father and instructed on the notorious laxity of Wells's morals, retorted that he was hardly in a position to talk since, according to Wells, he was a 'fearful roué' himself.34

But the fact was that, from Wells's point of view, there was an enormous and vital difference between the two of them: and that difference was principle. Wells, in his seductions, was acting on principle, while Bland in *his* was entirely unprincipled and gloried in the fact.

In company, in public, Bland talked and wrote of social and political problems and debated with a barrister-like effectiveness, but when I was alone with him, the fundamental interest insisted upon coming to the surface. He felt my unspoken criticisms and I could not check his assertive apologetics. He would give hints of his exceptional prowess. He would boast. He would discuss the social laxities of Woolwich and Blackheath, breaking into anecdotes, 'simply for the purpose of illustration.' Or he would produce a pocket-worn letter and read choice bits of it – 'purely because of its psychological interest.' He did his utmost to give his perpetual pursuit of furtive gratification, the dignity of a purpose. He was, he claimed to me at least, not so much Don Juan as Professor Juan. 'I am a student, an experimentalist,' he announced, 'in illicit love.'

'Illicit love'! It had to be 'illicit' and that was the very gist of it for him . . . What he seemed most to value was the glory of a passionate triumph over openness, reason and loyalty – and getting the better of the other fellow . . . [Wells goes on to contrast Bland's behaviour with his own, on the surface so similar, in reality so different:] It is curious how opposed this mentality of what I may call the seventeenth and eighteenth century "Buck," is to the newer, rationalist, go-as-you-please of the Shelley type, to which my own mind was being attracted in those days. I wanted to abolish barriers between the sexes and Bland loved to get under or through them. The more barriers the better. . . . He exalted chastity because so it meant a greater sacrifice, and I suppose he would have thought it a crowning achievement to commit incest or elope with a nun.'[35]

Wells survived the Rosamund affair with his reputation more or less intact. There was of course gossip – tremendous gossip – among the Fabians: gossip was one of their preferred activities. But none of the principals ever talked about it, perhaps because all of them felt slightly sheepish, and the ripples began to die down.

No sooner had they done so, however, than Wells found himself in hot water again: and this time things were not so easily dismissed.

4

'I would not drop the subject of the passionate daughter,' wrote Wells, referring to the fuss made about the publication of *Ann Veronica* in 1909 and that of *The New Machiavelli* two years later. But it would be just as accurate to say that neither would he drop the passionate daughters.

Among the Fabian couples the Wellses found most agreeable –
just as agreeable, indeed, as in the first years they found Edith
and Hubert Bland – were the Reeveses. William Pember Reeves
was a New Zealander of socialist leanings who had been eased out
of politics at home by his enemies and sent over to be Agent-General
in London, where the Webbs took him up and persuaded him to
become Director of the newly-founded London School of Economics.
Pember Reeves was a rather pompous man, not particularly to the
Wells taste; Wells remembered him as a bully who never allowed his
wife access to either birth control or funds of her own. But Maud
Reeves was another matter. She was much younger than him, 'then
about forty; still full of humour, a very bright talker, and working
out a sort of liberation for herself from the matrimonial flattening
she had undergone.'[36] Maud found her salvation in politics. She was
on the Fabian Executive and also became a leading suffragette, in
which guise she travelled the country campaigning, quite outside her
husband's control.

The two families soon became intimate friends. Maud wrote to
Jane to say how she had enjoyed H.G.'s latest books, how Will
hated the French seaside, how she hoped the Wellses would join
them for a week at a Norfolk rectory, how she was dying of boredom
plodding round Torquay with her dear but elderly father – in short,
the daily prattle of a good friend. It was clear that Maud found the
Wellses' free and easy ways much more to her taste than her husband's
solemnities. She became a great partisan of H.G., one of his few
supporters on the Fabian Executive in the political manoeuvrings he
was then engaged upon, and a wholehearted admirer of his works.
She was also enthusiastic about the general Wells ambience as far
as her family was concerned – there were three Reeves children,
of whom the eldest was a daughter, Amber, a little younger than
Rosamund Bland. 'Tell Mr Wells that if Mr Henry James ought to
have been a nursery maid H.G. Wells ought to have been a finishing
governess,' Maud wrote Jane after a week spent together by the two
families. 'How those girls revelled in him and how excellent was his
influence.'[37]

Amber was then preparing to go up to Newnham College,
Cambridge. 'She was then a girl of brilliant and precocious promise,'
wrote Wells. 'She had a sharp, bright, Levantine face under a shock

of very fine abundant black hair, a slender nimble body very much alive, and a quick greedy mind.'[38] She spent a lot of time with the Wellses, and Maud Reeves was delighted. 'Amber is panting to be with you,' she wrote in August 1907, '. . . Tell Himself that he grows younger and younger. I have grave doubts whether Amber is not too motherly for him now.' The next April Amber was with them again, this time convalescing: 'Thank you so much for your goodness to Amber. I think she is much better though not well yet. She adores you both and talked of nothing else when she came back. She has gone to Cambridge full of spirits and confidence. I hope she will realise all her desires, dear soul. You are good fairies to all those young people.'[39]

Amber was indeed realizing her desires. She was conducting a passionate affair with H.G., and reading her mother's correspondence after the event it seems almost impossible that Maud did not, at some level, realize the fact. 'Her mother encouraged the development of a very intimate friendship between us,' Wells wrote. 'It did not seem possible to her that any harm could possibly arise from our constant association. Her mind was engaged in repudiating some of the most important facts in the human make-up. Just as she would hear nothing of fatigue or indigestion or illness [the Reeveses were Christian Scientists] so she was doing her best to dismiss all love, romance, and, above all, desire, as a kind of unaccountable silliness that could not affect the kind of people one really knew and lived with.'[40]

In his autobiography Wells describes how what began as a high-minded friendship soon developed, pretty much inevitably given Wells's predilections and Amber's determination, into a love-affair. According to him it was Amber who made the running, to be met more than half-way by an eager H.G.; after which, in her excitement, she confided in several of her friends and teachers at Cambridge, and also in her mother (who, after the affair came out, had to pretend to her appalled husband that she had known nothing of it).

It is clear from Wells's description that the affair with Amber was a great emotional high-point, not only in her life but also in his. He describes how just before her Cambridge finals she spent some days with him in a lodging in Southend, after which she returned to take a double First; how 'after our luggage had gone down to the waiting cab, we hesitated on the landing, lifted our eyebrows, and went back gleefully for a last cheerful encounter in the room we were leaving'; how 'it seemed very fresh and keen to make love among bushes in a windy twilight' and 'a great lark to get a heavy key from the sexton to inspect the belfry of – was it Paddlesworth? – Church, and embrace in the room below the bells.' 'My memory of all these experiences glows still with unregretted exhilaration and happiness,' he concludes.[41] 'A lark'; a phrase which sums up all that differentiates H.G. from the rest and encapsulates his immense attractiveness. Not only can one not imagine Havelock Ellis, Olive Schreiner or Karl Pearson having a lark – the very notion is alien to their deep seriousness – but, in such a context, they would thoroughly have disapproved of larking as being unworthy of the gravity of the undertaking.

Of course, it was impossible to maintain the delicate equilibrium of the affair as time went on. No relationship is static, and the essence of one like this is that while it inevitably affects everyone in the immediate circle of the protagonists, it cannot – or could not then – be acknowledged to be doing so. That was one dilemma; the other was that both H.G., on account of his much-touted theories of the ideal sexual life, and Amber, because she was so proud of and delighted by the whole thing, wanted to be open about the affair while recognizing that, for a variety of reasons – for Amber's reputation, for Jane and the children, for Amber's family – they must keep quiet about it.

Wells's analysis of why things started to come unstuck is revealing in its assumptions. The main difficulty, as he saw it in retrospect, was that he had his own definite ideas of what this affair was to be and how it should affect his and Amber's lives, and that for various reasons they proved unrealistic. As far as he was concerned, there were three main reasons for this. The first was that Amber, for all her brilliance, did not share his powers of concentration. 'The theory of our relationship was that these excursions into sensuousness were the secret link that was to bind us in some very ambitious constructive work,' he explained. 'All this time my own output was unimpaired, and I wrote as vigorously as ever I did, and swept aside a number of irrelevant distractions, because I knew that in a few days I could be clutching Amber's fuzz of soft black hair. And she too was supposed to be working strenuously . . . I had never been satisfied with the Socialist, and particularly with the Communist, theory of social motives, and I wanted her, for her London thesis [Amber was now a research student at the London School of Economics] to attempt a more objective classification of motives and hindrances to social service. I wanted her to enquire, "Why and How are Men Citizens?" I think still that that might have been a very important piece of work. But it was never carried out.'[42]

The reason for this, according to Wells, was that although Amber had been a brilliant pupil, she could not cope when it came to striking out on her own. 'I have seen this happen to many successful students; travelling on beaten tracks is no training for the wilderness.' As a result, 'She became discouraged; she slackened and lost steering way; she did not get on with the job. This left her exciting love-adventure unbalanced and tremendous in her mind; she found herself with time on her hands and unsettled; and, while I was keeping our secret close and tight, she gave way to a desire to talk about it and elaborate it.'[43] Thus the responsibility for the failure of the Wellsian intellectual ideal, that ideal of a relationship between lovers which should be both a sensuous and a working fulfilment and which represented his dream of sexual perfection, is thrown on to Amber: when it came to the test she could not measure up as an independent intellect. That Amber herself quite accepted this is shown by the fact that it is what she told her family when, many years later, the secret of her eldest daughter's parentage was revealed.[44]

One may reasonably question whether this is a fair rendering of the realities of the case. Wells was a distinguished man with many preoccupations, not to say a wife and family; he was also twenty years older than Amber. However dazzled he was by her – and he was pretty comprehensively besotted – she was still only a section of his life; the other sections were too firmly established to melt away at the touch of an infatuation, however fierce that touch. She, on the other hand, still had her life to make. It is hard to imagine that even the most potentially brilliant intellect would have found 'Why and How are Men Citizens?' much of a focus for concentration when in competition with the conduct of a passionate affair with the most exciting man of his generation. The truth is that whatever Amber's intellectual potential might have been, she was never given a chance to realize it. By the time the obsession with H.G. had abated she had a husband and, more to the point, a baby. And as everyone knows who has experienced it, the toughest intellect must quail before the demands of a baby. Wells himself makes the point that Amber and her husband, Rivers Blanco-White, were not particularly well-off; they had three children; and that is the story of Amber's intellectual potential.

Jane, of course, knew what was happening – she had to, both because that was what she and H.G. had agreed, and also because she must have seen the beginnings of the affair during the frequent visits paid by Amber, as Maud Reeves's thank-you letters testify, to Spade House, the Wells home at Sandgate. 'Jane was invincibly the wife, and Amber the young mistress; we all understood each other, we asserted, beautifully,' Wells recalled, describing a situation modern only in the self-consciously declared contentment of all parties. But by now things were beginning to take on a momentum of their own. In the small, gossipy circle of the Fabians there were whispers. Wells makes it pretty clear that, in his opinion, the Blands, for reasons of their own, were the chief whisperers. In *The New Machiavelli* they are portrayed as the wholly malicious Booles, who make sure that the hero's character is blackened; a revenge for what H.G. saw as Hubert Bland's own revenge on him for the incessant and unashamed seduction of daughters. (It should be noted that Bland himself also enjoyed this hobby. There was a scandal about him and one of Rosamund's schoolfriends; and even at the very end of his life it seems probable that he seduced Alice Hoatson's niece, despite the fact that he was then blind and had a heart condition. But of course, as Wells would have pointed out, these were old-fashioned seductions untainted by any whiff of theory.) 'Boole, I found, was warning fathers of girls against me as a "reckless libertine," and his wife, flushed, roguish and dishevelled, was sitting . . . after dinner, and pledging little parties of five or six women at a time with infinite gusto not to let the matter go further.'45 Sooner or later things would be out in the open. What was to be done?

With hindsight, as Wells himself noted, 'As the older and more responsible lover I ought, since I could not leave Jane to marry her, to have helped Amber release herself from me. I ought to have realized that the splendid friendship had failed . . . It was not in me to do that, for the very simple reason that the erotic passion she had aroused in me was intense and would tolerate no separation . . . I could not think of other women, nor endure the thought of relinquishing her to any other man.'[46] So Amber took things into her own hands.

One of the paradoxes about Wells was that although he loved women, and especially modern, intellectual women, he was extremely old-fashioned in many of his attitudes towards them once he had, so to speak, got them. This was noted with her usual razor-sharp perception by Rebecca West (who, of course, had first-hand experience of the phenomenon) in an article on the literary 'uncles' of her generation. Of 'Uncle Wells' she wrote:

Uncle Wells arrived always a little out of breath, with his arms full of parcels, sometimes rather carelessly tied, but always bursting with all manner of attractive gifts that ranged from the little pot of sweet jelly that is *Mr Polly*, to the complete meccano set for the mind that is in *The First Men on the Moon*. And he brought all the scientific fantasies, and the magic crystals like *Tono-Bungay* and *The New Machiavelli*, in which one could see the forces of the age sweep and surge like smoke about brightly coloured figures that were blinded by them, that saw through them, that were a part of them, that were separate from them and were their enemies, that were separate from them and were their allies, and illustrated as well as it has ever been done the relationship between man and his times.

This impression of wild and surpassing generosity was not in the least one of youth's illusions. One had, in actual fact, the luck to be young just as the most bubbling creative mind that the sun and moon have shone upon since the days of Leonardo da Vinci was showing its form. The only thing against Uncle Wells was that he did love to shut himself up in the drawing-room and put out all the lights except the lamp with the pink silk shade, and sit down at the piano and have a lovely time warbling in too fruity a tenor, to the accompaniment of chords struck draggingly with the soft pedal held down, songs of equal merit to 'The Rosary.'

You know perfectly well what I mean: the passages where his prose suddenly loses its firmness and begins to shake like blanc-mange. 'It was then I met Queenie. She was a soft white slip of being, with very still dark eyes, and a quality of . . . Furtive scufflings . . . Waste . . . Modern civilisation . . . Waste . . . Parasitic, greedy speculators . . . "Oh, my dear," she said, "my dear . . . darn your socks . . . squaw. . . ."' But take him all in all, Uncle Wells was as magnificent an uncle as one could hope to have.[47]

This piece annoyed Wells extremely. 'I don't object to criticism but I do object to slighting . . . If the passage was "almost word for word" lifted from *The Passionate Friends*, why wasn't it lifted outright in quotes?'[48] But similar examples can be found in many of his novels. For instance, in *The New Machiavelli*, published in 1911 only two years after the affair with Amber ended, he portrays several aspects of himself and Amber in the novel's heroine, Isabel, and its hero, Remington, the narrator. Remington is safely married to a beautiful, rich and suitable wife when he meets and falls headlong in love with the much younger Isabel: 'I suppose . . . I should figure as a wicked seducer, while an unprotected girl succumbed to my fascinations. As a matter of fact, it didn't occur to us that there was any personal inequality between us. I knew her for my equal mentally; in so many things she was beyond comparison cleverer than I; her courage outwent mine. The quick leap of her mind evoked a flash of joy in mine like the response of an induction wire; her way of thinking was like watching sunlight reflected from little waves upon the side of a boat, it was so bright, so mobile, so variously and easily true to its law. In the back of our minds we both had a very definite belief that making love is full of joyous, splendid, tender, and exciting possibilities, and we had to discuss why we shouldn't be to the last degree lovers.'[49] Yet later in the story this intellectual paragon declares her wish to live with him: 'At the back of my mind I've always had the idea I was going to have you somehow presently for myself – I mean to have you to go for long tramps with, to keep house for, to get meals for, to watch for of an evening.'[50] Note that it is unquestionably the brilliant Isabel who is to do the watching in the evening.

Wells's novels were taken from his life; and this contradiction certainly reflects a contradiction that was at the centre of his attitude to women in real life. He was only interested in intelligent – extremely intelligent – women; but he never really imagined they were his equal.

Meeting Berta Ruck, a friend of Rosamund's who was to make her name as a novelist, at Dymchurch, he complimented her by calling her by her Christian name, which she considered, she told him, 'an honour'. 'He replied that I was one of the few women he knew who seemed to realize it is the woman's part to be the petrol of this world. "Most of them," said H.G. in gloomy mood, "want to be the engine."'[51]

Even clearer were his instructions to Rebecca West herself on the household she was to set up for him in Wales while she was waiting for their expected child: 'You are Mrs West, I am Mr West. . . . Mr West is in the cinematograph business, and he has to write things. He wants a quiet room to work in and he has to have a separate bedroom. (Though he proposes to spend much time in your delicious bed.) You also write. Make this clear and get everything comfortably arranged. That house has to be our home. We have to settle down and work there and love there and live there, and you have to see that it is all right. You have got to take care of me and have me fed and have me peaceful and comfortable. You are going to be my wife. We will have great mysteries in each other's arms, we shall walk together and eat together and talk together. You are the woman and you are to be the maker and ruler in all this life.'[52] As with Jane, he wished to know nothing of the boring mechanics of how this was to be achieved. The difference between Jane and Rebecca was that Jane devoted her life to these mechanics, while Rebecca 'also wrote'.

Another deep contradiction lay in his attitude to children. Within marriage, when he happened to be there, he was a model father, particularly good at inventing games for his two young sons and joining in with huge seriousness and enjoyment. But it was not only within marriage that Wells had to face the joys of fatherhood. He also had two children, a daughter and a son, outside his marriage.

One of these children was borne to him by Amber Reeves. This, Wells assures us in his memoirs, was all Amber's idea. 'A wave of philo-progenitiveness was passing through the intelligentsia,' he writes, an odd phrase which surely betrays something of his own odd attitude. At any rate, she began to talk about having a child by him; and the conversations they must have had are once again echoed by Isabel and Remington in *The New Machiavelli*.

'We can't have that,' I said.

'No,' she said, 'we can't have that.'

'We've got our own things to do.'

'*Your* things,' she said.

'Aren't they yours too?'

'Because of you,' she said.

'Aren't they your very own things?'

'Women don't have that sort of very own thing. Indeed, it's true! And think! You've been down there preaching the goodness of children, telling them the only good thing in a state is happy, hopeful children, working to free mothers and children [Remington in *The New Machiavelli* is, like Wells, an enthusiast for the Endowment of Motherhood] . . . Children get into a woman's brain – when she mustn't have them, especially when she must never hope for them. Think of the child we might have now! – the little creature with soft, tender skin, and little hands and little feet! At times it haunts me. It comes and says, Why wasn't I given life? I can hear it in the night . . . It's like a little fist beating at my heart . . . Little cold hands that tear at my heart. Oh, my heart and my lord!' She was holding my arm with both her hands and weeping against it, . . . 'I shall never sit with your child on my knee and you beside me – never, and I am a woman and your lover!'[53]

Wells did not welcome this talk. It 'did not at all suit my obsession to "get on with my work," and my disposition to treat love as an incidental refreshment in life.'[54] But this was not the only new topic Amber began to introduce. There was also the question of other young men. 'She set herself with an ingenious subtlety to remind [Wells] that there were other men in the world. The convenient fags, sometimes a little embarrassed, found their unobtrusive services being brought into the light before [his] eyes. . . . One was a contemporary . . . a man with a touch of Spanish blood and a suggestion of Spanish fire, who quite manifestly was very much in love with [Amber], and of whom she spoke with a slight perceptible difference of manner that made [Wells] feel uneasy.'[55]

This was a young ex-Cambridge mathematician, now a barrister, called Rivers Blanco-White. He appears as Sir Philip Easton in Wells's

The Research Magnificent, who in the end carries off the hero's wife Amanda, in whom, as in so many of Wells's heroines at this period, there is much of Amber. 'She told him of her intimacies with me and distressed him very much. . . . He determined to rescue Amber from herself at any cost – for himself.[56]

Wells saw that with the constant undertone of gossip, and with Amber determined to bring things to a head, he would before long have to deal with a crisis. This was precipitated by Blanco-White going to Pember Reeves and telling all, at the same time making it plain that despite her having been 'ruined' at the hands of H.G. Wells, he still wanted to marry Amber.

Pember Reeves saw red. He 'became all that an eighteenth-century father should be,' as Wells remarked. Until now he had, almost uniquely among the Fabians, been quite oblivious of the affair. Now he 'expressed his intention of shooting H.G. at the first opportunity. They were both members of the Savile Club, and the outraged father used to sit at one of the small tables in the big bow-window at 107 Piccadilly with a pistol beside him, waiting for H.G. to approach the Club from either direction. The Committee were naturally disturbed by the prospect and H.G. Wells was asked to resign. After the outraged father died some years later H.G. was warmly welcomed back to the Savile.'[57] Wells further enraged him, if that were possible, by writing a letter implying that Maud Reeves had known about the affair from the start and condoned it, which she hastily denied.

At this point, both central parties in the affair completely abandoned any attempt at logical thought – of which, indeed, as Wells himself makes clear, they were anyway by now hardly capable. Events had overtaken them. 'I was, by twists and turns, two entirely different people; the man for whom Jane's security and pride and our children and my work were the most precious things in life, and the man for whom Amber had become the most maddeningly necessary thing in life,' wrote Wells. '. . . Amber was perhaps divided as widely between her desire for a passionate isolation with me and a quite natural wish for social rehabilitation, a life of coming and going with all her friends about her . . . She knew she could not trust me except to make an outcast heroic life for her that would have been intolerably hard to live . . . There was no logical development in our conduct, but only jagged masses of inconsistent impulse . . . With the storm gathering over us, Amber got through to me by telephone, and we went to our room near Victoria for the last time. "Give me a child," said Amber, "whatever happens," and that seemed heroic to me . . . We set about the business there and then. She told Blanco White but he persisted in his resolve to separate us and marry her. She packed a couple of valises and slipped off to meet me at Victoria Station. I carried her off to Le Touquet in France and took a little furnished chalet there. We looked isolation in the face.'[58]

Having done this, Amber and H.G. had to face the future; and neither of them much liked what they saw. According to Wells, they reasoned thus: H.G. did not want to divorce Jane. Neither of them fancied wandering around Europe as social outcasts. What they wanted was London and life; but while H.G. was for braving it out there, Amber could not face the prospect, especially as she could no longer rely on her mother for support. There was nothing for it but to go back and marry Rivers. So she packed and left.

Amber's account of what happened, as she told it to Anthony West, Wells's son by Rebecca West, is (as one might perhaps expect) rather different. 'Living with him among strangers in a foreign country, she made discoveries about him and about herself. He wanted her to run the house and look after him. She had never given the art of running houses a thought, and had no wish to learn it. He couldn't endure her almost sacrilegious indifference to his creature comforts. He was soon darting back across the Channel for days at a time to take refuge from her casualness with Jane Wells, who knew how to look after him so beautifully . . . Amber . . . came to a full understanding of those absences one night while she was spending some unpleasant hours lying at the foot of the villa's steep staircase. [Wells] was in England with Jane, and she was alone. She had taken a fall down the steep staircase . . . When she had tried to get up, a stabbing pain in her back had told her to stay where she was. So she lay there, wondering how badly she was hurt, and if the baby was going to be all right, until the daily woman came in the morning. As the hours passed she had begun to realise that she knew Jane Wells almost as well as she knew [H.G.], and that she understood much more about that relationship than she had been admitting to herself. They were an ideally matched pair . . . Amber had no desire to upset Jane Wells's applecart; she didn't in the least want to take part in their game, much less break it up. And in her loneliness she also realised, as she hadn't before, how profoundly conventional and unadventurous her professedly liberal and advanced parents really were, how horridly she had shaken them, and how fond of them she was.'59

The upshot of this (and Amber's account rings truer than Wells's in almost all respects) was that when Wells got back to Le Touquet both of them were cross, Amber because of her bad night at the foot of the stairs, Wells because he found all this to-ing and fro-ing thoroughly tiresome. 'She told him that the whole thing was, indeed, becoming quite impossible. He asked her what, in that case, she wanted to do. She told him that she had no idea. She didn't see how she could go on with him, and she didn't see how she could give him up. He snapped at her, telling her that she was being childish and unrealistic . . . He told her that if she couldn't go through with what she had let herself in for, she had better take the obvious way out and get herself married to young Rivers Blanco-White, who was always dangling about after her. She was amazed by this suggestion. Was [Wells] asking her to marry a man for whom she felt nothing in particular just to get them out of a passing social difficulty? He would be recommending prostitution to her next! He exploded. She was a fool. She was a *damned* fool. She didn't understand anything.'60 Wells then returned to England leaving Amber to follow or not, as she pleased. So she sent a telegram to Blanco-White and spent a miserable crossing wondering what on earth she was going to say to him, should he actually be there to meet her. But he was there (one can imagine her relief), and he was as good as his word, and married her at the end of July 1909.

Wells, unable to bear either a return to the 'lustless decency' of Sandgate or solitude in Le Touquet, made good use of the remainder of his lease on the Le Touquet house. He summoned his family to a seaside holiday in France. They came accompanied by the Swiss governess, Mathilde Meyer, whom Jane had recently engaged, and who appears to have known nothing whatever of the situation: all she saw was that the boys 'enjoyed themselves very much indeed' on this, their first trip to France.61

Amber married Blanco-White in July; and by August, everybody in the Fabian Society knew all about it. 'The end of our friendship with

H.G. Wells,' recorded Beatrice Webb in her diary in early August. 'A sordid intrigue with poor little Amber Reeves – the coming of a baby, and the run to cover of marriage with another man, a clever and charming young Fabian (Blanco-White), who married her, knowing the facts, out of devoted chivalry. The story got about owing to Amber's own confidence to a Cambridge don's wife, and owing to H.G. Wells's own indiscretions. Moreover, after the hurried marriage, without the Reeves's knowledge, of Amber and Blanco, Amber and H.G. Wells insist on remaining friends – a sort of *Days of the Comet* affair.'⁶²

There was no doubt that *In the Days of the Comet* had had a considerable effect on a number of Fabians. At the time it was published, Beatrice had devoted much thought to the problems it raised, as her diary records. The novel 'ends with a glowing anticipation of promiscuity in sexual relations,' she wrote. 'The argument is one that is familiar to most intellectuals – it has often cropped up in my own mind and has seemed to have some validity. Friendship between particular men and women has an enormous educational value to both (especially to the woman). Such a friendship is practically impossible (or, at any rate, impossible between persons who are attracted to each other – and, therefore, most remunerative as friends) without physical intimacy; you do not, as a matter of fact, get to know any man thoroughly except as a lover.'⁶³ This had certainly been Beatrice's experience with Sidney, and a thoroughly rewarding one. Nevertheless, she could not convince herself that the Wells view could be right. Six weeks later, after long arguments with Wells, who had spent a couple of nights at the Webbs', she was even less convinced. Wells had first argued that 'it was a work of art and, therefore, could not be criticised from the standpoint of morality. "When Michael Angelo displayed groups of nude figures in stone or colour, it does not follow that he desired to see all his acquaintances sprawling about without clothes" . . . However, he afterwards admitted that he thought "free-er love" would be the future relation of the sexes when we got over the sordid stage of the masculine proprietorship of the woman. "At present [Wells had argued] any attempt to realise this free-er love means a network of low intrigue, assumes, and, therefore, creates an atmosphere of gross physical desire – but this is only an incident of a morality based on the notion of private property in women. No decent person has a chance of experimenting in free-er love to-day – the relations between men and women are so hemmed in by law and convention. To experiment you must be base; hence to experiment starts with being damned." There is, of course, truth in this argument,' Beatrice admitted, '. . . But I cling to the thought that man will only evolve upwards by the subordination of his physical desires and appetites to the intellectual and spiritual side of his nature. Unless this evolution be the purpose of the race I despair – and wish only for the extinction of human consciousness. Without this hope – without this faith – I could not struggle on . . . Oh! for a Church that would weld into one living force all who hold this faith, with the discipline and consolation fitted to sustain their endeavour.'[64] For Beatrice, the fervent religion of her youth had joined with the selfless satisfactions of public service in a celebration of the higher qualities of intellect and spirituality over the baser animal passions. The creed thus produced transmuted the comparative sexlessness of her own marriage, that triumph of mind over matter, into something loftier than the steaming marital beds of less evolved persons. Thus she, too, was able to use principle to justify the facts of her life. As for sex outside marriage – that was, for her, irretrievably associated with sin; this was a feeling deeper than intellect from which she could never detach herself, and from which Wells, however intellectually seductive his arguments, would never turn her. Beatrice, that stickler for the intellect, was in the end ruled by her emotions, and in this case her emotions were enmeshed with the Victorian religious proprieties and prohibitions in which she had been reared and which, unlike Wells and so many of her other socialist friends, she had never rejected.

Now the tangible results of Wells's experimentation once again set Beatrice thinking about sex. 'The whole case, and the misery that seems likely to follow, is a striking example of the tangle into which we have got on the sex question,' she wrote in her diary. 'We accepted Wells, in spite of his earlier divorce case, on grounds of tolerance. He and his wife were happy – the other wife had married again, and there seemed no reason, on ordinary enlightened principles, for us to hold back or object. The Reeveses knowing all these facts, and Mrs Reeves claiming to be "advanced" in her opinions (she did not object to *In the Days of the Comet*), were very intimate with him and allowed him to become Amber's guide, philosopher and friend. Amber being a little heathen, and H.G. being a sensualist, they both let themselves go, and start a surreptitious liaison. At first, both of them think that they will stand it out. But Amber gets into a panic, and marries the first faithful swain who will let himself be married to a lady with a "past" of an imminent character. . . . All this arises because we none of us know what exactly is the sexual code we believe in, approving of many things on paper which we violently object to when they are practised by those we care about. Of course, the inevitable condition today of any "sexual experiments" is deceit and secrecy – it is this that makes any divergence from the conventional morality so sordid and lowering. That is why upright minds are careful not to experiment except in the "accustomed way" (i.e. with prostitutes). It is hardly fair to become intimate with a young girl, fresh from college, on the assumption that you believe in monogamy, and then suddenly to propose a polygamous relationship without giving her guardians and friends any kind of notice. That is not playing the game of sexual irregularity even according to the rules of a game full of hazards, at any rate, for the woman.

'Oddly enough, Sidney had long had a settled aversion to H.G. Wells.'[65]

It can be seen from this that Beatrice took a fairly conventional view of the responsibilities in the case – that is to say, she blamed the grown-ups, Amber's mother and, of course, Wells, who still bore the stigma not only of his *outré* opinions but of his dubious marital past. This being so, her social response was clearly dictated by events. It was Wells, not Amber, who was to be denied the benefit of future friendship with the Webbs. 'If Amber will let us, we shall stand by her as Blanco's wife and drop H.G. Wells once for all, as he no doubt will drop us.' But there was a definite question as to whether Amber *would* allow this tame scenario. 'Apparently there is no breach,' wrote Beatrice wonderingly, 'and the household goes on being of a very mixed sort.'[66]

It certainly did. Amber, having married Blanco, had an 'immense recoil'. She could not bear him to touch her until the child was born; she could not bear to give up Wells. Wells sold the Sandgate house, with its 'all too healthy, all too unstimulating' life, and moved his family to Church Row, Hampstead, taking a cottage in Surrey for Amber, where she officially lived with Blanco but where Wells, to everyone's horror, visited her. There were also other, more hidden meetings between them, and, 'up to the very birth of our daughter, I would call for Amber at her nursing-home in Cambridge Terrace, and take her gravely and publicly for walks in Hyde Park'.[67]

These arrangements sent Beatrice into a froth of horror. 'The blackguardism of Wells is every day more apparent,' she confided to her diary on 27 September. 'He seduced Amber within the very walls of Newnham, having been permitted, as an old friend, to go to her room . . . Anyway, the position now is that Amber is living in a cottage that has been taken by Wells, and is receiving frequent visits from him while her husband lives in his chambers in London. And poor Reeves is contributing £300 a year to keep up this extraordinary *ménage*! Our advice to father and husband is to break off all negotiations with Wells, to employ a solicitor in dealing with him and to insist that Amber returns to her family's home if she refuses to live with her husband.'[68] The situation as Beatrice saw it was quite clear. She put it succinctly to Amber herself: 'You will have to choose – and that shortly – between a happy marriage and continuing your friendship with H.G. Wells. *That is the one essential fact in the present situation*.'[69] But a short time later she was frothing again: 'GBS has intervened and is trying to persuade the father and husband to condone everything and accept the situation in order to avoid a public smash! He has even suggested to Reeves that he should entertain all three to dinner every week to show his approval!'[70]

This typically Shavian suggestion, though on the face of it merely an irresistible dramatic device, was, it may be assumed, more than partly serious. Shaw took a quite different view of the affair from Beatrice. Though he, too, was guilty of the same inconsistency in reconciling theory and practice that characterized all the 'advanced thinkers' ('Aren't you funny,' the actress Ellen Terry wrote him in 1906, 'preaching against marriage and marrying. Against other things and doing 'em.'[71]) in some things he was quite consistent. One of these was his invariable assumption that in love affairs it was the predatory woman who took the initiative. This was certainly his assumption in the Amber-H.G. case, and in fact, if we are to believe Wells's account of how the affair started, it was more or less correct. 'One day,' wrote Wells describing the start of their physical intimacy, 'she broke the thin ice of my suppressions by telling me she was in love, and when I asked "with whom?" throwing herself into my by no means unwilling arms.[72] Such an action, although unthinkable in the kind of decent girl still envisioned by Beatrice, was no more than Shaw would have expected. Shaw in fact immortalized Amber as Hypatia Tarleton, the heroine of his play *Misalliance*, which he was then writing. As he portrays her, Hypatia is impatient, intolerant, very clever and filled with a desperate desire to experience life: 'My mother tells me that when I'm her age, I shall be only too glad that nothing's happened; but I'm not her age; so what good is that to me? There's my father in the garden, meditating on his destiny. All very well for him; he's had a destiny to meditate on; but I haven't had any destiny yet. Everything's happened to him; nothing's happened to me. That's why this unending talk is so maddeningly uninteresting to me,' she tells Lord Summerhays, the father of her fiancé, who is in love with her.[73] Beatrice did not like the play: 'It is amazingly brilliant – but the whole "motive" is erotic, everyone wishing to have sexual intercourse with everyone else,' she grumbled.[74]

Shaw also differed from Beatrice in that his view of the affair was wholly untainted by emotion.

My dear Beatrice [he wrote on 30 September from Ireland, whence he was trying to orchestrate a sane response to the affair.] Yes: the real difficulty seems to be that Amber brags of her exploit. However, I hope I have made it clear to W. that this must not be done.

I have had a long letter from Mrs Reeves giving me the whole history of the affair, the most astonishing part of which is the length of time it has been going on, and the fact that W. held out against his determined assailant for a whole year . . . Amber has a very strong hand if she plays it well and resists the temptation to boast. Nobody knows from the outside who pays for the cottage; nor would it greatly matter if they did. Why should not W. who, if not 70, is old enough to be Amber's father, pay for the young couple's cottage? . . . Suppose I pay a years rent of a cottage for Rosamund Bland and Sharp & furnish it & go down to see them often, will there be the faintest impropriety in it? Not a scrap. . . . Wells of course threatens: it is the right card for him to play against an enemy. He ought to know better than to play it against you; but I am not altogether sorry that he is doing it. I have told him flatly that if you asked my advice in the matter I should urge you most strongly not to commit yourself to a word of anything but sternest disapproval of the whole affair; that you must not be made an accomplice in questionable social experiments; that the Nat.[1] Committee & all you stand for must not be played with to amuse Amber . . .

Perhaps Sidney ought to join the Unionist party. But he wont; and there's an end to it. Perhaps Wells & Amber ought to recognize that they have behaved badly & part; but as they finally and certainly WONT, I am not going to waste time either giving advice that wont be taken or suggesting action on the basis of what will not occur. The only sane course is to calculate on what *will* occur, & make the best of it. What will occur, then, is that W. will stand by Amber until the 'ripping child' (who, alas! may not be a ripping child) is born. That much is certain. After that, we shall see . . . I think it very likely that the compact originally made with Blanco, and now repudiated by Amber, will keep itself no matter how much they may repudiate it. At all events we must give it a chance: there is nothing else to be done. [He added:] I havnt bothered about the right & wrong of the affair, which is clearly one of those in which the right & wrong are very largely conventional, but simply about the best way of avoiding the smash. Such unnatural detachment from the ethical interest of the problem is aggravating; but it has its value. Also there is something exasperating in the fact that the person who will suffer least by an explosion is H.G.W., and that therefore he will not say thankyou to us for warding it off, if we *do* ward it off.[75]

5

As things turned out, Shaw, who had dealt with more than one awkward amatory situation in his time – certainly more than Beatrice – and understood more than most about people's motivations, correctly prophesied the outcome of the affair. Amber stayed with Blanco – stayed with him, in fact, for the next sixty years – and had two more children; Wells stayed with Jane.

A real difference between Amber and Wells was in their attitude to the child. Amber cared for Wells and their coming child; Wells, for Amber and the grand gesture. As far as he was concerned, the child, after the 'heroic' moment of its conception which so appealed to him, was a nuisance and a complicating irrelevance. He makes this quite clear in his account of the affair: 'Both she and I clung most desperately to the idea that we were sustaining some high and novel standard against an obtuse and ignoble world,' he wrote. 'As a matter of fact, we had lost our flag long ago, when we allowed our liaison to be interrupted. We ought to have gone on meeting as lovers and saying "You be damned" to the world. If we had been separated for a time, we ought to have held out for our freedom and mutual preference. Then we should have done something. The child was an extraordinary irrelevance. It seemed a fine idea that afternoon, but it was destined to be the seed of a thin trickle of perplexing afterthoughts . . . The fiasco of our transitory elopement to Le Touquet was a development of that false situation. Thereafter we had no case.'[76] Such an attitude would of course be very hard for a woman to share, especially a woman pregnant with a child by a man whom she loves as much as Amber loved Wells. Perhaps this difference, with all that it entails, accounts for Wells's undoubted difficulty in accepting women as his true intellectual equals. For him detachment was (as we shall see) a necessary virtue, and it is hard for women to feel detached about their children.

The difficulty entailed by this contrast between the heroic gesture and its boring practical aftermath was one which Wells had soon to face again, with Rebecca West, with whom he started an affair in 1913 and whose son by him was born in 1914. While the baby was expected Wells was delighted about it: it was, like Amber's 'ripping child', part of the wonderful gesture, the fruit of the experiment. 'I think of that happy thing cuddled up in your soft flesh and your dear warm blood,' he wrote to her then. 'I'm so glad we've made it.' But he was much less enchanted by the tedious consequences it entailed – the constant arrangements about lodgings and servants which it made inevitable and which came so unromantically between him and Rebecca. He explored this aspect of their relationship in his novel *The Secret Places of the Heart*, in which Rebecca appears as a successful cartoonist, Martin Leeds, while her lover is Sir Richmond

Hardy. ' "She just let herself go at me," ' explains Sir Richmond to a doctor friend:

> 'And you?'
> 'Let myself go too. . . . All sorts of considerations that I should have shown to a sillier woman I never dreamt of showing her. I had never met anyone so mentally brilliant before or so helpless and headlong. And so here we are on each other's hands!'
> 'But the child?'
> 'It happened to us. For four years now things have just happened to us . . . When things go well – they usually go well at the start – we are glorious companions. She is happy, she is creative, she will light up a new place with flashes of humour, with a keenness of appreciation . . .'
> 'But things do not always go well?'
> 'Things,' said Sir Richmond with the deliberation of a man who measures his words, 'are apt to go wrong . . . At the flat there is constant trouble with the servants; they bully her. A woman is more entangled with servants than a man. Women in that position seem to resent the work and freedom of other women. Her servants won't leave her in peace as they would a man; they make trouble for her . . .'
> Thus Sir Richmond; who goes on to grumble, 'All she wants to do is just to settle down when I am there and go on with her work. But then, you see, there is *my* work.'
> 'Exactly,' replies the doctor, and concludes, 'After all it seems to me that your great trouble is not in yourselves but in social institutions. Which haven't yet fitted themselves to people like you two.'[77]

That, of course, was how Wells liked to see it; and one of the many functions of the novels he published at this period featuring variants of himself, Jane, Rosamund, Amber and Rebecca, was to display his behaviour in its theoretical context. (An aspect of the Amber affair that many people found particularly shocking was that *Ann Veronica*, which contained an unmistakable portrait of Amber enthusiastically conducting a love affair with a married man, was published even before the baby, Anna-Jane, was born.) The novels were about the social experiment. They were about his notion of the ideal companionship of equal men and women behaving freely; and yet, as we have seen, even in the novels the reality of what Wells wanted from women kept breaking through. What he wanted was the delight of companionship with his intellectual equals – which, in Wells's case, meant the most brilliant women of his day – who would suddenly, when the scene became domestic, feel able and willing to provide the uncompetitive, smooth laying-on of creature comforts he was used to at home with his wife. But, things being what they were – and here the question of social institutions was indeed relevant – they were not his wife, and as a result could not compete in the domestic department even had they been so inclined. Jane kept house in style at Sandgate, Amber was confined to a rented chalet at Le Touquet; Jane entertained expansively (and expensively) at Easton Glebe, the country house which the Wellses established as the boys grew older, while Rebecca was hidden away in squalid lodgings at Hunstanton; and in the end, as both Amber and Rebecca discovered, Wells was wedded to Jane and his comforts; those comforts which she made it her job to provide and which – as she must have been perfectly aware – made her position unassailable. Being a mistress, even Wells's mistress, was a hole-and-corner affair once the great gesture had been made and a child was expected.

Amber escaped by making the counter-gesture, which seemed to both of them abject, of marrying Blanco-White. By doing so, however, she contrived the best of all worlds, given that her intellectual career was a thing of the past: the constant reminder, in the person of her daughter, of her grand affirmation of freedom, together with a settled and happy family life. Blanco-White's one condition was that he should have a clear run. 'My parents' solution seems to have worked – we were so happy,' says Amber's second daughter, Justin.[78] Wells was never mentioned, and nobody in the family ever knew who Anna-Jane's real father was until she was told when she was sixteen, just as she was about to go off to the London School of Economics. By that time Jane had died, as had Pember Reeves, and Wells and the Blanco-Whites could and did resume amiable social relations. In 1939 Amber wrote to Wells: 'What you gave me – a love that seemed perfect to me, the influence of your mind, and our daughter – have stood by me ever since. I have never for a moment felt that they were not worth the price.'[79]

Rebecca West had a much more difficult time, and so did her son, Anthony. Not only did she suffer from the social restrictions imposed upon her by her unmarried status – living, for the first years of Anthony's life, in a succession of unsatisfactory houses tucked away in the country and chosen largely for their convenient access from Easton Glebe – but she had to put up with appalling frustrations: the rudeness of the servants at whose mercy she was because of her equivocal status, the difficulty of being able to get on with her work while living alone in the country with a small child, the consciousness that London literary life, at whose centre she should have been, was fizzing along without her; and, always, the inescapable fact of Jane, whose help and friendship she definitely did not want and whom she deeply resented. Rebecca could not understand, as Amber only too clearly did, why Wells did not divorce his mediocre wife and marry her. But Jane knew there was never the slightest chance – or danger, depending on whose viewpoint you took – of that.

What Jane thought about it all, and about life with her so frequently errant spouse, we do not know, because it was a part of her extreme discretion, which so annoyed many people and which was essential to her role, that she never confided her feelings, either in speech or in writing. But what seems clear is that, pretty early on, she made up her mind that running her husband's multifarious life was a career to which she would be happy to dedicate herself.

It seems impossible that she was not at the same time perfectly aware that, in doing this, she was placing herself in an invincible position as far as competition from mistresses went. She knew, because they had talked about it, that mistresses there would be. H.G. could not do without them and had gone so far as to construct an elaborate ethical scheme around this compulsion of his. But neither could he do without her.

Talking about the affair with Amber, Wells said: 'None of the people involved, except for Jane and Blanco-White, showed any singleness of purpose.' Blanco purposed to marry Amber; Jane purposed to keep H.G. Having caught her amazing husband, she was not about to let him slip away. If that involved subordinating her life to his – and he made it abundantly clear that those were the only terms upon which he would stay with any woman – that was a price worth paying. After her death H.G. wrote: 'We had to work out our common problem very largely by the light nature had given us. And I am appalled to reflect how much of the patience, courage and sacrifice of our compromises came from her. Never once do I remember her romancing a situation into false issues. We had . . . the sincerest affection and respect for each other. There again the feat was hers. It was an easy thing for me to keep my faith in her sense of fair-play and her perfect generosity. To the end I would have taken her word against all other witnesses in the world. But she managed to sustain her belief that I was worth living for, and that was a harder task, while I made my way through a tangle of moods and impulses that were quite outside her instinctive sympathy. She stuck to me so sturdily that in the end I stuck to myself. I do not know what I should have been without her. She stabilized my life. She gave it a home and dignity. She preserved its continuity. Not without incessant watchfulness and toil. I have a hundred memories of an indefatigable typist carrying on her work in spite of a back-ache; of a grave judicial proof-reader in a garden shelter, determined that no slovenliness should escape her; of a resolute little person, clear-headed but untrained in business method, battling steadfastly with the perplexities of our accumulating accounts and keeping her grip on them.'[80]

In writing of his theorizing about free love, Wells remarks that he failed to make allowance for 'personal fixation'. Perhaps both the failure and the phrase tell us something about him. It is, after all, such an extraordinary thing to forget, especially in one who had already twice suffered such a fixation. Perhaps the solution lies in the fact that fixations, although they constituted such a vital part of his emotional life, were not really fundamental with him. One friend wrote after his death: 'Behind all his responsive intimacies there was a very hard core that was unimpressionable and untouchable. As more than one found, not without distress, he never really gave himself in any personal association. In describing the relations between his autobiographical character "William Clissold" and the Clementine of that book, he makes the former say, "I have never given myself to anyone. I cannot conceive that anyone should ever be necessary to me." For good or ill . . . he was in the last resort immune from the influence of others.'[81]

Wells himself makes this clear. In his autobiography he talks at one point about family relationships and about his own feelings with regard to his children. He says: 'They mean much to me in friendliness, interest and happiness, but they do not go deeply into the living structure of my Self . . . We all rely on each other and trust each other. But all that is a matter of free association and preference and interest. What I am writing of here is the psychological inter-penetration and mutual service of *personas* . . . I think we should feel something embarrassingly incestuous about the idea of any such response.' Wells regards this detachment – so very different from that visceral bond felt by most people for their children – as a definite advance in human relationships, an advance towards that 'fearless individualism' which he takes to be necessary to the advance of world socialism. 'Maybe in the past the family concentration was psychologically more intimate and entangled; and the atmosphere of ideas in which my children have grown up may be exceptionally *modern*, with a real antagonism to emotional concentrations . . . We do not like concentration of feeling and we do not like being tied . . . Clustering is antipathetic to us. I have always been disposed to despise people who cluster close in families, gangs, clans and nations. That is my main objection to Jews. And Scotsmen. And the provincial French. I reveal perhaps the immunizing influence of a serum drawn from the very disease, when I say that roughly speaking the English have not this human disposition to remain clustered so highly developed.'[82] Once again, it will be noted, principle is invoked in order to claim for the general good a quality which to some might seem a weakness.

Perhaps it was this quality of detachment, allied to his enormous brilliance and charm, that gave him such power to bend others to his will. Bernard Shaw put it another way: 'Wells is a spoiled child. His life has been one long promotion. He was born cleverer than anyone within hail of him. You can see from his pleasant figure that he was never awkward or uncouth or clumsy-footed or heavy-handed . . . The world that other men of genius had to struggle with, and which sometimes starved them dead, came to him and licked his boots. He did what he liked; and when he did not like what he had done, he threw it aside and tried something else, unhindered, unchecked, unpunished, apparently even undisliked . . . Take all the sins he ascribes to his colleagues . . . Add every other petulance of which a spoiled child or a successful operatic tenor is capable; multiply the total by ten; square the result; cube it; raise it to the millionth power and square it again; and you will fall short of the truth about Wells. Yet, the worse he behaved, the more he was indulged; and the more he was indulged, the worse he behaved.'[83] Wells thought and hoped he was persuading women that the world was well lost for principle. But in fact all he succeeded in doing was to persuade them that the world would be well lost for Wells.

6

THE SAGE
AND THE WOMAN REBEL

I

H.G. Wells considered that his scheme for the endowment of motherhood was far to the left of current thinking, and attributed his lack of political success (as opposed to literary, financial and general success) to the fact that slower natures were not yet ready to accept notions so advanced. He set out the problem and its solution in his usual impassioned yet impersonal way, perhaps most clearly in *The New Machiavelli:* 'Women must become less and less subordinated to individual men, since this works out in a more or less complete limitation, waste, and sterilization of their essentially social function . . . After two generations of confused and experimental revolt, it grows clear to modern woman that a conscious, deliberate motherhood and mothering is their special function in the State, and that a personal subordination to an individual man with an unlimited power of control over this intimate and supreme duty is a degradation . . . I want to see them bearing and rearing good children in the State as a generously rewarded public duty and service, choosing their husbands freely and discerningly . . . It is no use pretending that this is not novel and revolutionary: it is. The Endowment of Motherhood implies a new method of social organisation, a rearrangement of the social unit, untried in human experience – as untried as electric traction was or flying in 1800.'[1]

The trouble – or one of the troubles – was that not even among women was there much enthusiasm for this particular form of social engineering. As Wells saw it, he was rejected by the socialists because they did not want to be tarred with the brush of Free Love, and by the feminists because they were essentially man-haters and wanted to concentrate on getting Votes for Women as the instrument by which they would eventually put the male sex in its place.

Left-wing feminists also distrusted the suffragettes' concentration of energy on getting the vote because the proposed age and property restrictions meant that this had nothing to offer young or poorer women. They saw it as an affair of the propertied and educated middle class, an irrelevant distraction as far as working-class feminists were concerned.

But these same women also rejected Wells's idea, seeing that, too, not as a daring left-wing innovation but as a deceitful ploy of the capitalist state. In March 1914, the first issue of a new paper called *The Woman Rebel* appeared in New York. Its masthead was NO GODS NO MASTERS and it declared that 'This paper will not be the champion of any "ism".' Among the 'isms' it rejected was the idea of what it called 'maternity pensions'. These it dismissed as a bourgeois liberal or cunning capitalist trap designed to entice women into bearing lots of children. Capitalists needed to be sure that there would always be more people than jobs, so that unemployment would remain high and, as a result, wages could be kept low. What was needed to defeat this strategy was sound advice about contraception. 'No plagues, famines or wars could ever frighten the capitalist class so much as the universal practice of the prevention of conception. On the other hand no better method could be utilized for increasing the wages of the workers.'

Accordingly, *The Woman Rebel* proposed to embark on a thorough programme of education on sexual and contraceptive matters. It was emphatically not man-hating: it stated that an early feature would be a series of articles 'written by the editor for girls from fourteen to eighteen years of age. In this present chaos of sex atmosphere it is difficult for the girl of this uncertain age to know just what to do or really what constitutes clean living without prudishness. All this slushy talk about white slavery, the man painted and described as a hideous vulture pouncing down upon the young, pure and innocent girl . . . could any more repulsive and foul conception of sex be given to adolescent girls as a preparation for life than this picture that is being perpetuated by the stupidly ignorant in the name of "sex education"?' It was *The Woman Rebel*'s opinion that, if one talked to prostitutes about how they came to be on the streets, most of them would say that their first sex experience 'was with a sweetheart or through the desire for a sweetheart or something impelling within themselves, the nature of which they knew not, neither could they control. Society does not forgive this act when it is based upon the natural impulses and feelings of a young girl. It prefers the other story of the grape juice procurer which makes it easy to shift the blame from its own shoulders.'[2]

The Woman Rebel, then, did not ignore or distrust the existence of what Wells called 'personal fixation'. Its concern was that a girl should know what to do when confronted by such a fixation, so that she might enjoy and benefit from it; and, in case she might be tempted to dispense with contraception on account of an over-rosy vision of the joys of maternity, 'other subjects, including the slavery through motherhood . . . will be dealt with.'

The editor, publisher and main writer of *The Woman Rebel* was a young woman of twenty-nine called Margaret Sanger. She had arrived at her beliefs through bitter personal experience. She was born the sixth of eleven children in the glass-making town of Corning, New York, in 1879 (though she always pretended to be six years younger than she really was, giving her date of birth as 1885). Corning was situated on the banks of the Chemung River; the glassworkers, mainly Irish Catholic, lived in the valley, while the middle classes in the surrounding hills. Margaret's family, although itself numerous and Catholic, lived in the hills, since her father, a mason, thought the good air up there would help his frail wife. But little Margaret very early on learned to associate the squalor of the valley dwellings with large families and poverty, and the pleasant pine-clad hills with smaller families and larger means.

When Margaret was seventeen her mother died, exhausted from overwork and the strain of too frequent childbearing, and her father, who had been a liberal and gentle man, now became, at least as far as Margaret was concerned, a petty tyrant. Missing his wife, he vented his misery on his daughters, and Margaret, as the eldest girl still living at home, took the brunt of it. She was held responsible for the house and her younger brothers and sisters and her social life was restricted: she saw her mother's life looming before her and refused to submit. She persuaded her father to let her attend a co-educational boarding school, from which she at first planned to go to Cornell University and study medicine; but, this not being practical, she entered a hospital to take up nursing. 'In the hospital I found that seventy-five

percent of the diseases of men and women are the result of ignorance of their sex functions. I found that every department of
life was open to investigation and discussion except the shaded
valley of sex. . . . So great was the ignorance of the women
and girls I met concerning their own bodies that I decided to
specialise in women's diseases and took up gynaecological and
obstetrical nursing. . . . A few years of this work brought me
to a shocking discovery – that knowledge of the ways of con-
trolling birth was accessible to the women of wealth while the
working women were deliberately kept in ignorance of this knowledge.'[3]

Meanwhile, Margaret had married and had children. Her husband was William Sanger, generally called Bill, an architect of
advanced views. When their first child was born Margaret had a
crisis of rejection. She turned away not so much from the child,
whom she kept with her, as from the whole of life. She refused to
eat and turned her face to the wall. A friendly doctor jolted her
out of this state and she returned with her baby, Stuart, to Bill.
As soon as she was strong enough they moved to a colony of liberal
professionals at Hastings-on-Hudson in Westchester County, where
Bill designed and (with great effort) built a dream house overlooking
the Hudson River, while Margaret settled down to domestic life and
had two more children: a son, Grant, and at last the daughter she
had always wanted, Peggy. On the day they moved into the new
house it burned to the ground, with all their possessions inside it:
luckily, Margaret and the children were able to escape – Bill was
away that evening. It was rebuilt, but the joy had gone out of it,
and Margaret was glad when Bill decided he was broke and must
move back to New York.

Hastings had been a sluggish rural backwater. New York, by
contrast, was a whirlpool of excitement. A fever of radicalism was
sweeping through the city. At the Armory, in 1913, an exhibition
of modern European painting revealed for the first time in America
one aspect of that intellectual and creative blossoming which characterized this period in continental Europe; while throughout the city
there was a ferment of that political and social rethinking which, in
anglophone America as in England, was the form into which native
radicalism seemed most naturally to fall.

The ideas of socialism and anarchism had first arrived in America during the 1870s and 1880s with German refugees. They had soon almost completely taken over the organization of socialist institutions in their new homeland. But now the Socialist Party in the United States was trying to separate itself from this German influence. A new, specifically American socialist party gathered around the inspirational figure of Eugene Debs. It expressed itself in the muckraking journalism of Lincoln Steffens and Ida Tarbell, and in such folk-heroes as the International Workers of the World leader Big Bill Haywood.

Margaret and Bill Sanger were part of this socialist group, and there were frequent gatherings in their apartment of all shades of radical, from pink liberals through to anarchists such as Alexander Berkman, Emma Goldman's lover, just released from prison after serving a fourteen-year sentence for trying to assassinate the steel magnate Henry Clay Frick; from rough Bill Haywood to John Reed, the young journalist just out of Harvard, whose eye-witness account, *Ten Days that Shook the World*, was to be many people's introduction to the Russian Revolution. Margaret's personal sympathies were with the anarchists, but she thought their ideals would have to be attained through socialism.

It was through this group that Margaret first became acquainted with the difficulties of sex education. She was invited to give some lectures for the *Call*, a socialist paper, and, knowing little of politics, decided to speak on health, which as a nurse she did know about. After the lecture there was a question-and-answer session at which the main questioners were young mothers wanting to know details of 'their intimate family life'. These lectures proved so popular that Margaret was invited to contribute a series of articles to the *Call* which she decided to entitle, *What Every Mother Should Know*. This series was a great success; it was decided to follow it up with another, to be called *What Every Girl Should Know*.

'These articles ran along for three or four weeks until one Sunday morning I turned to the *Call* to see my precious little effort, and, instead, encountered a newspaper box two columns wide in which was printed in black letters:

WHAT EVERY GIRL SHOULD KNOW

N
O
T
H
I
N
G

BY ORDER OF
THE POST-OFFICE DEPARTMENT

The words gonorrhea and syphilis had occurred in that article
and Anthony Comstock, head of the New York Society for the
Suppression of Vice, did not like them. By the so-called Comstock
Law of 1873 . . . the Post Office had been given authority to decide
what might be called lewd, lascivious, indecent or obscene, and
this extraordinary man had been granted the . . . power, alone of
all citizens of the United States, to open any letter or package or
pamphlet or book passing through the mails and, if he wished,
lay his complaint before the Post Office. So powerful had his
society become that anything to which he objected in its name
was almost automatically barred . . . During some forty years
Comstock had been damming the rising tide of new thought.[4]

It was Margaret's first brush with Comstock, a man who was to be
a momentous figure in her life.

During these years, Margaret contributed to the family budget by
working, when she could, as a nurse. The demands of her family
precluded working in a hospital; but at this time there was a great
demand for home nurses, as people were distrustful of hospitals. For
Margaret's speciality of gynaecological nursing, which in practice
meant mostly childbirth, the home was almost always used. A woman
gave birth in her own bed, and, since she could usually give the nurse
two or three weeks' notice of a lying-in, Margaret was usually able to
arrange her domestic life to fit in with her work.

Almost in spite of herself, Margaret found that more and more of her work was taking place among the very poorest families. It was not that she found any particular satisfaction in this, but 'I could see how much was wrong with them which did not appear in the physiological or medical diagnosis.'5 What was wrong generally boiled down to too many children and no way of preventing them. The constant question among her clients and their friends and visitors was, 'I am pregnant (or my daughter, or my sister is). Tell me something to keep from having another baby. We cannot afford another yet.' They rejected condoms or coitus interruptus, because that depended upon the husband's co-operation, which was rarely to be counted upon. And they could not believe that Margaret knew of no other method. But she did not: and she could not find out, for the dissemination of such material was against the law, and no doctor would enlighten her for fear of being prosecuted. The only advice a doctor could offer to one of Margaret's distraught clients, recovering from the effects of a septic abortion (and soon to die of another) was, 'Tell Jake to sleep on the roof.'6

That was in the summer of 1912; and that was the case that decided Margaret's future career. Come what may, she was going to find out about birth-control and get the information to the poor women who most needed it. As to how she was to do this, she had no idea. Meanwhile she was tired and run-down, so she took the children and went to spend the rest of the summer at Provincetown, a small fishing village at the tip of Cape Cod.

There, among other sympathetic spirits (for Provincetown was already starting to become popular among radicals) she found Big Bill Haywood, who had been brought there by his friend Jessie Ashley to recuperate from the rigours of the Paterson silk-workers' strike which he had been organizing. Big Bill's life was centred round the organization of the IWW or 'Wobblies', and, sympathetic as he was to Margaret's preoccupations, he could not see that the small-family question was important enough to be made a plank of the labour platform. Nevertheless he was very encouraging, and suggested that she should waste no time but should up sticks and go to France, where people had been restricting their families for generations on account of the provisions of the Code Napoleon which forbade primogeniture and instead laid down that inherited property had to be divided equally between all the children of a family. This had led to people limiting their families to one or two children in order to avoid family farms being subdivided until they were plots of land so small as to be useless. 'This struck me as a splendid idea,' she wrote later, 'because it would also give Bill Sanger a chance to paint instead of continuing to build suburban houses. The trip to Europe seemed so urgent that no matter what sacrifices had to be made, we decided to make them when we came to them. In the fall we sold the house at Hastings, gave away some of our furniture and put the rest in storage. Although we did not realize it at the time, our gestures indicated a clean sweep of the past.'[7]

The Sangers arrived in Europe in October 1913. They went first of all to Glasgow, which had been vaunted to Margaret as an example of socialism in action. She was expecting great things, but was depressed first by the incessant rain, and then by the shortcomings which lay behind what at first seemed an excellent system of social planning. For example, a model tenement specially constructed for 'deserving and respectable widows and widowers belonging to the working class', having one or more children with no one to care for them while the parents were at work, had been turned over to the exclusive use of widowers: widows were expected to shift for themselves. Moreover, all the new municipal dwellings were planned, on the basis of area and lighting regulations, for from two to five inhabitants; which meant that large families were debarred from them. These pettinesses, which led to so much misery in the cause of bureaucracy, distressed Margaret, and she was glad to move on with her family to Paris.

By February 1914, Margaret felt she had learned what she had come for in Paris and returned to America with her children, leaving Bill behind.

It is clear from letters Margaret received at this period that Bill regretted the separation much more than she did, and it is also clear why. 'William for a time was a bit upset – he does not enjoy being away from his sweetheart and children . . . He misses the racket the kiddies make every morning and is very anxious to get back,' wrote a mutual American friend, Walter Roberts, from Paris. He added, 'A thing which is necessary is the writing of what people may think of William being *alone in Paris*.'[8] But such considerations, what people thought and what they might think, had never mattered a jot to Margaret and mattered if anything even less now. Bill was still in love with her, but she was no longer in love with him – if indeed she ever had been. She had married on impulse, very young. Now she had grown up, and she felt that she had done her bit by Bill. There were three children, Stuart, Grant, and Peggy; she had given him a family; now she wanted to take up her own life.

It was a life one of whose most notable features was a plethora of lovers. One of the things that distinguished the new American brand of socialism from the imported German variety was the abandonment of those solid bourgeois family values which were such a mark of German home-life, and whose effect we have already seen at work upon the lives of the Marx girls. 'To most of these home-loving Germans, only the form of government needed change,' Margaret commented, implying that the Americans did not take so narrow a view.[9] Certainly she did not, and perhaps she now felt freer to indulge herself in that respect on account of the useful information which she had gone to Paris especially to acquire. At any rate she was now, on her return to New York, deluged with love letters from a variety of different men. She was small and lively, with red hair and a soft, mobile face. She was evidently quite irresistible, and saw no particular reason to resist. On the contrary, she rather gloried in her new situation; that February she sent on one of these letters to Bill in Paris with a note reading, 'Return this to me dear. This is an example of a fine clean feeling which two can have toward each other. Do you object to this Bill?'[10] He may well have objected, or at least minded; but they were separated by the Atlantic ocean and clearly, whether he minded or not, Margaret was going to go her own way.

It was that way which led to *The Woman Rebel*. Armed with her new information, she now lacked a means to dispense it. To open a clinic in New York was impossible: State law forbade it and it would be closed immediately. (This is what happened when she did open such a clinic in Brooklyn in 1917, although by then, as a result of her efforts, the climate of opinion was changing.) A monthly paper, on the other hand, might disseminate all sorts of information very widely before (as was almost certain to happen) Comstock forced it to close.

It was clear from the start that *The Woman Rebel* – and its editor – were out not just to influence opinion but to outrage it. Max Eastman, the editor of the *Masses*, the leading socialist paper, commented that it was 'very conscious extremism and blare of rebellion for its own sake'[11] – by inference, the production of a self-indulgent publicist rather than a serious political worker. Certainly the paper's tendency was anarchist rather than communist. The issue for August 1914, for example, carried an obituary paragraph for 'three revolutionists, Caron, Berg and Hanson, [who] were killed by [an] explosion of dynamite – sacrificed because of their willingness to risk life for their convictions.' But Emma Goldman, a regular contributor, was enthusiastic. She wrote Margaret that it was 'the best seller we've got'.[12] The first issue sold 500 copies in Los Angeles alone: the monthly circulation soon reached 2,000 copies. 'The thing is nauseating,' the *Pittsburgh Sun* commented.

However, it was soon plain that *The Woman Rebel*, if it was to continue at all – and there would hardly be much point in having it shut down immediately – would not be able to carry the sort of detailed information about birth-control and sexual hygiene which had been planned originally. 'The Postmaster did not like the first number of the *Woman Rebel*,' observed the second number. 'He advised her not to send any more copies through the U.S. mails. He said the *Woman Rebel* was unmailable under Section 211 of the Criminal Code, as amended by the Act of March 4, 1911. . . . In order to comply with the rules and regulations of the government, the *Woman Rebel* may be forced to become indecent and to advocate a total ignorance of Sexual Hygiene for women . . . This suppression may not be as important to you as it is to us, for you are not suppressed. Do not forget that you have a voice to protest and fight against a censorship that is busy suppressing scientific truths that the working people are demanding.' But all was not lost. The resourceful Margaret sat down and wrote a book, *Family Limitation*, which gave the kind of detailed information the paper could not provide. She had, however, the greatest difficulty in finding a printer. The thing was so obviously illegal that all the regular printers refused her. Eventually a man was found – not a firm, but just a lone man with a printing machine in a cellar. The original print run was planned at 10,000, but requests from trades union leaders led to this being increased to 100,000. When the copies were ready they were packed up and sent clandestinely to different centres throughout the States, to await the right moment for distribution. (In the next few years this work was to be translated into thirteen languages and ten million copies printed.)

On 25 August 1914, the inevitable indictment was served on Margaret Sanger. She was indicted on nine counts; if she were convicted on all of them, she might be liable to a sentence of forty-five years in prison. The Assistant District Attorney, Harold Content, argued for the trial to take place immediately, but a sympathetic judge, Judge Hazel, agreed to adjourn the case for six weeks.

Margaret took the threat of prison seriously. She made arrangements for the children's schooling, rushed to complete the September and October issues of *The Woman Rebel* (which were to be its last), and learned dances and exercises to keep herself fit in her cell. Lawyers explained to her that all this was unnecessary. There was no need to go to prison: they could get her off on a technicality if she co-operated with the court. But since the whole point of everything she had done was precisely that she would *not* co-operate with the court or any other authority, Margaret rejected this advice. As the *New York Mail* put it, 'She sees a distinct value in stirring up public sentiment by means of an act of voluntary martyrdom.'[13]

The case was called on 20 October, but Margaret was unaware of it and unprepared. She had no lawyer. In court, she asked for a month's adjournment, but this was refused. Judge Hazel ordered her to get a lawyer at once – the case would be heard after the noon recess. A lawyer was found; he pleaded for another extension, but this was refused. The case would be heard at ten o'clock in the morning of 21 October, the next day.

The lawyer, Simon Pollock, advised Margaret to enter a guilty plea, in which case she would get off with a fine. Bill Sanger, who had just returned from Paris, urged her to follow the lawyer's advice, and so did some other friends. Margaret rushed off to a small hotel downtown to sit quietly and think. She was quite sure that she would not, at any rate, follow Pollock's advice, which, as she saw it, would destroy her whole position. The question was whether it would be more valuable to leave the country for a few months and get some facts together than to waste time sitting in jail. She might go to Holland and to England, where there were active birth-control groups. She rang the railroad and learned that a train would be leaving for Montreal in a few hours. 'About half an hour before the train time I knew that I *must* go. I wrote two letters, one to the judge, one to the District Attorney. I informed them both that I would not be in court at ten o'clock the following day, and reminded them that I had asked for a reasonable time to prepare my case . . . I had asked for a month's postponement, and their reluctance had compelled me to take a year!'[14] The children would live with their father, and Margaret's sister Nan, who was working as an interpreter in New York, would look after them in the evenings and at weekends.

Travelling under the name of Bertha Watson she boarded the Montreal train, and from Canada found a berth in the RMS *Virginian*, sailing for Liverpool.

2

The *Virginian* arrived at Liverpool on 13 November 1914. Margaret, travelling as Bertha Watson, somewhat dreaded the arrival as she had no passport. But with her usual resourcefulness she had struck up a friendship during the voyage with an official of the American Embassy in London who took her under his wing, so that she was able to record, '*No trouble* at Customs as I had only one bag. Mr Girling helped me to a cab and I found myself winding through city streets greatly like all streets surrounding docks in all cities.'[15] The cab took her to the Adelphi hotel, 'a palace fairy like plus exceeding comfort', but the rain rained and the wind howled and homesickness set in. 'I knew it would not do to "set and think" as the Quakers say so I set off to find the Clarion café – advertized in Blatchford's *Clarion*.' (The *Clarion* was a popular socialist paper.) But she found that nobody would be at the café until six o'clock, so she spent the intervening time wandering round Liverpool looking at clothing prices in the shops, to get an idea of the value of the dollar.

Margaret made several friends among the Liverpool socialists gathered at the Clarion, including one, Lorenzo Portet, the Catalan radical educationalist, then teaching at Liverpool University, to whom she would be close for the rest of his tragically short life. Then, on 25 November, she moved on to London, where once again she was met by socialist friends among whom she soon felt at home. On 10 December she called at the Malthusian League where she met Dr and Mrs C.V. Drysdale, the leading advocates of birth-control in Britain. 'We had tea together,' she recorded. 'Mrs Drysdale is charming. It did seem to me I had known them both and seen them often.'

She was, naturally, missing her children – especially as Christmas approached. But in other ways she found the solitude almost rewarding after the perpetual action of the past few years. 'It seems almost good to be alone,' she recorded. 'There is time to get acquainted with oneself, to reflect, to meditate, to dream . . . it's a luxury to have time for anything but work.' A few days later, this pause for thought began to bear fruit. December 16 was a momentous day: 'I have this day cast the dye. I have written Bill a letter ending a relationship of nearly or over 12 years. I cannot seem to write or think connectedly yet. However it will come later. How lonely it all is – Could any prison be more isolated. Could one be more alone or more lonely in "solitary" than wandering about the world – separated from the little ones you love, from their childish prattle, caresses, whimpering and quarrels – and also from other men and things and friends one has and one understands it is not only the language which separates "comrades" it is psychology.' This, of course, is an observation made before and since by both Americans and British stranded on the wrong side of the Atlantic: the expectations raised by the common language being such that the 'separation' of outlook comes as a particularly rude shock. But Margaret was feeling isolated not only from home but from the whole of her adult life up till then. 'Yesterday I sent a letter to Bill S. parting the ways of our life together. He will not be surprised I know, for the past year he has been prepared for it. Only I am very slow in my decisions – I cannot separate myself from my past emotions quickly, all breeches [sic] must come gradually for me.'

On the same day she records: 'A very cordial letter from Mr Havelock Ellis today inviting me to call – I look forward to it with interest.'

Ellis, too, was feeling particularly lonely at this point. Edith was away, not just for a few days or weeks, which they were both used to, within easy reach of letters and trains, but for some months, on the other side of the Atlantic. She had decided to revive her flagging financial fortunes with an American lecture-tour, and had arrived in New York not long after Margaret Sanger had left that city. The war was making Atlantic crossings dangerous and mails uncertain, and Havelock was consumed with anxiety about her. She was not well;

she had diabetes and angina and had become physically rather frail, and there was a daunting programme of travel and lecturing to fulfil if she was to make enough to free herself, according to plan, from financial anxiety. For his part, the war made him miserable, the weather was suddenly very cold, and Mneme, who was still, despite her own marriage, his *petite amie*, was taken up with her own affairs and saw him rarely at this time.

Havelock and Margaret first met on 22 December. Her diary recorded:

Today I went to Brixton to call on Havelock Ellis. Tall, lovely simple man with the most wonderful head and face and smile. He opened the door in answer to my knock. We had no difficulty in feeling comfortable. It was four o'clock and he lighted two candles on the mantle. These threw a soft light onto his features which gave him the look of a seer. We had tea which he prepared and carried into the room, his workshop where we sat by the open fire and talked.

Wonderful mind, . . . easy, not in a hurry rush at all, such a relief to find. It seems to be the men who do the most creative and productive [*sic*] who are the simplest and easiest to meet and understand. He talked of the trial on his book Inversions . . . Spoke fully on the subject which was a relief.

There is a shyness and reticence about him of the student and simplicity of a great soul and mind.

I count this a glorious day to have conversed with the one man who has done more than anyone in this century toward giving women and men a clean and sane understanding of their sex lives and of all life.

Clearly Margaret was much taken with Havelock; and clearly he returned her feeling. On 26 December he wrote to her: 'Dear Woman Rebel, A line . . . to say that if nothing prevents, I expect to be at the Reading Room on Monday between 11 and 1 and if I do not arrive . . . I hope you will call at 9 o'clock or 10 or thereabouts . . . I was wondering if you had many friends here but in any cases it is lonely to be in a strange city and away from all those you care for most, and especially at Xmas – always a hateful time, *I* think.'[16]

In fact Margaret, never wanting for eager male company, spent Christmas Eve with Lorenzo Portet, until his train left for Liverpool. But her friendship with Havelock quickly ripened. Between the British Museum (still fulfilling its traditional function as club and meeting-place for advanced thinkers) and Havelock's flat in Brixton, the pair met two or three times a week.

'I have begun this new year at the stroke of midnight with a new kiss,' wrote Havelock on 1 January 1915;[17] and, as anyone who knew the usual snail's-pace of his reactions and commitments would have confirmed, this indicated for him dazzling speed and intensity of response. For like everybody else he had fallen headlong in love with the quicksilver Margaret, who responded in her usual eager fashion.

At first, it was Margaret who made the pace. 'She was quicker, more daring and impulsive, than it is my nature to be,' he wrote.[18] It seems clear that, as was only natural (on that she could be sure they both agreed!) and as she liked to do, she wanted to go to bed with him, while he, for his usual reasons, hung back. Soon after that first kiss he wrote: 'What I . . . feel, is that by just being your natural spontaneous self you are giving me so much more than I can hope to give you. You see, I am an extremely odd, reserved, slow, undemonstrative person whom it takes years and years to know. . . . I'm not the least good for gobbling up rapidly – really don't repay the trouble! And I don't feel a bit anxious to be gobbled up, while the gobbler is ahead unwinding the scarf to wave to someone else!'[19]

But these reservations did not last long. He was soon concerned not with holding Margaret back but with anxiously justifying his own position, evidently terrified lest he should have put her off: 'I think we should agree, dear Twin, on the subject of Love. I think that *passion* is mostly a disastrous thing, and certainly ruinous to work for it makes the work seem of less than no account. And then, too, it's always felt for the wrong person . . . But I cannot say that I think that *love* is anything but good, and good for everything, including work. I mean by "love" something that is based on a true relationship and that has succeeded in avoiding the blind volcano of passion . . . As you say, the average man and woman would only know passion – and not so very often at that!'[20] But if Havelock was not by now feeling passion, it is hard to know what he was feeling. On 2 February, his birthday,

he received a present from Margaret: 'Oh, you darling Woman,' he
wrote ecstatically, 'how wicked of you to send me that lovely present
– the most beautiful present I have ever received, and the precious
rose, which is now before me in a little vase and has almost as delicious
a fragrance as the woman it comes from, and which I mean to preserve
for *always*, and the dear message – oh you darling woman.'[21]

By now Havelock and Margaret were on terms of what was, for
him, the most complete intimacy. So much may be inferred from
the coy tone of a couple of notes referring to his own peculiar sexual
preference: 'I am glad my picture looks at you. *When* is a time, I
wonder, when "just it shouldn't"? I expect, however, it's a faithful
portrait and resembles the original. I only wish it was the original!'
And three weeks later: 'The sacred J.A.R. longs to be filled with
sacramental wine.'[22]

From this time on, Havelock abandoned all pretence. He was
obsessed by Margaret – the more so as she was clearly not obsessed
by him. For him this excitement was something that had happened
only once before, thirty years earlier with Olive, while for Margaret
this was just one of many such affairs with ardent cavaliers, though
certainly one of the most important.

It is worth noting an almost symbolic meeting arranged by Havelock
at this time between his old love and his new. It will be remembered
that Olive was in London throughout the war, feeling harried and
miserable. She often saw Havelock, and Margaret, an enthusiastic
reader of *The Story of an African Farm* and of *Woman and Labour*,
was delighted at the chance to meet their author. 'Knowing Havelock
to be a philosopher, I had expected him to be an elderly man, but,
despite his white hair, had found him young, physically and mentally.
Olive Schreiner's writings were so alive that I had visualized a young
woman. Instead, although her hair was black, her square and stout
body was old and spread. She had, perhaps, been partly aged by the
frightful asthma from which she had suffered for so many years.'[23]
Olive was, of course, a little older than Havelock. But even had she
been in the best of health and shape it is hard to imagine that, at the
age of sixty, she would have been blithely embarking upon a new love
affair, as Havelock was doing at the age of fifty-six (and it was not by
any means to be his last). It could be said that one of the male sex's
chief natural advantages in this respect was literally personified at this

meeting. Olive was an old woman, out of the sexual reckoning; her lover of thirty years before still an object of lively interest to young and attractive members of the opposite sex . . .

Lively interest; but not consuming. While Havelock was posting off impassioned letters almost every day, and looking for her (often vainly) every time he visited the British Museum, Margaret's thoughts were often elsewhere. She was receiving love letters from America, and she was also seeing Portet: her diary for early February, when Ellis so often, and so often vainly, sought her company, reveals that she was 'very busy all these days. Portet was in London on his way to Barcelona and I saw much of him.'24 The upshot of this was that she, too, arranged to leave London. She would visit The Hague, where Dr Aletta Jacobs led an important birth-control movement, and then go on to Barcelona, where Portet was to take over the directorship of an experimental school run along radical lines. Havelock was heart-broken. 'You said in your last letter, before leaving, that I was to *miss* you. But I began to miss you before you had left, I wandered off to Victoria Station on Saturday morning, but the trains were all altered and you had not told me which you were going by, so I just had to wander sadly back again,' he wrote.25

He had no real idea what her movements were to be (nor, probably, did she) so his letters followed her sadly round Europe, from Holland to Paris and eventually to Barcelona, always hoping that she was just on her way back. 'I feel like threatening to come along with you!' he wrote on 18 March. 'And it is sad to realise that you will scarcely be in England at all any more, when there are so many millions of things we have to say and do together.' On 30 March he had heard she was in Barcelona: 'I felt sad you should be in Barcelona without me, and longed to go over all the old places with you. It's an awful shame, but can't be helped now.' She had said she would be back the first week in April, so (on 1 April): 'I hope to see you *often* this month . . . for after this month my movements are a little uncertain for a while.'26

The reason for this was that most banal of circumstances, the return of the absent wife. Edith was expected back from her American tour in May.

When Ellis's autobiography was published after his death in 1940, Margaret Sanger was extremely hurt by it. The assumption of Ellis's companion for the last twenty years of his life, Françoise Lafitte-Cyon, was that this was because he had barely mentioned Margaret's great financial generosity to him in later years when she was rich and he, as ever, was not. However, it seems more likely that the hurt was caused by the enormous discrepancy between Havelock's account of their affair in the book and the reality, as disclosed by his letters to her at the time and as, no doubt, it remained in her memory. Havelock had his reasons for this, and they were entirely discreditable, if understandable. For the truth was that it was the affair with Margaret that set Edith off on the downward slope which led to her death eighteen months later; and this was a truth which Havelock could scarcely bear to admit to himself, let alone share, in its unvarnished state, with his readers. This is his account of what happened:

The relationship – I speak more especially concerning my own attitude in it and she showed herself beautifully willing to accept my attitude – was one of calm friendship, even though there was a sweet touch of intimacy about it. There was thus no trace of guilty consciousness to spoil its delight. It was not my habit to practise deceit, but here I never even felt the need of secrecy. Yet it was some weeks before I mentioned my new friend in my letters to Edith. The reason was that I wished to feel sure first about my new friendship. To form a friendship so quickly was such a novel experience in my life . . . that I needed to know first exactly where I stood. That this new friendship could prove a shock to Edith, who herself was constantly forming vivid new friendships, I innocently failed to recognise even as a possibility. It had come so naturally, so charmingly, so unsought, at a moment when in my loneliness I needed it so much, without even realising that I needed it, and it had come by so strange a chance in the person of one who combined the qualities of two lands both so congenial to Edith, that it seemed to me I was forming a new bond with her rather than breaking an old one. It thus came about that when I once began to write about my new friend, I wrote about her in every letter, so that it seemed to Edith my letters were all full of this new friend. [Rubbing salt in the wound he added:] Beautiful as my new friend was to me, and continues to be to this day, I have sometimes been tempted to wish that I had not met her.[27]

In addition to this delay in writing at all, the mails between America and England were at this time unusually slow and uncertain owing to the war; so that by the time Ellis was able to realize the effect of his first letter mentioning Margaret he had already sent at least six more in the same vein.

This account of the affair is of course very misleading. It is also highly disingenuous. There were several reasons why Edith might quite reasonably feel alarmed when, after so long, she received the letter in which Havelock first mentioned Margaret. The first was, precisely, the length of time he had waited before telling her about it. It should be remembered that these two were in the habit of maintaining a daily intimate correspondence when they were not together. Part of their arrangement was that, if they were often separated, they kept nothing hidden one from the other; so that if, so contrary to their usual habit, Havelock had not mentioned Margaret, there were only two possible conclusions to be drawn. One was that meeting her was a matter so trivial that it was not worth mentioning; the other was that it was so unusually significant that he had not been able to bring himself to do so. Since the first possibility clearly did not obtain, it was reasonable to assume that the second applied.

Then there was the question of there being no need for Havelock to feel guilty, since no physical intimacy had taken place. But in fact the arrangement at which they had so painfully arrived was quite the opposite. The basis of their marriage was that it was only physically that they did not fulfil each other, so that physical relationships with others were permissible. The unspoken corollary was that these relationships did not impinge on the emotional intimacy shared between Havelock and Edith alone. But Margaret, it was clear, was a threat at a level far deeper than that of, say, Mneme. Indeed, as we have seen, the only comparable relationship in Havelock's life had been that with Olive, who was already, in that respect, an extinct volcano before Havelock met Edith.

Consciously or unconsciously, Edith, when on 4 February she at last received her first inklings of Margaret, registered these cues and responded to them. She was in Chicago at the time: it was the climax of her tour. A large meeting was planned to be held at the Orchestral Hall in the centre of the city, at which Edith would read a paper Havelock had written specially for the occasion on *Masculinism and*

Feminism, together with a lecture of her own. She had been having an exhausting, exciting time, travelling up and down the country, meeting people, arranging for publication of her books and plays. Now, at her crowning moment, came news of Margaret. She wrote: 'My Darling Boy, Here on the great day of my public life I awake at five and write my English letters, for never am I alone now. I got all three of your letters and read them when resting after my Turkish bath. Of course I got a fearful jump when I realised there is another ---. [Ellis, when he reproduced this letter in his autobiography, felt it necessary to censor this word.] If it makes you happy I am glad, but somehow it is a kind of strange realization which makes it still easier for me to die. I *want* to die, and yet I am at my zenith, and if I can only live two more months I shall not die in debt . . . I lectured on Olive at the smartest Club here on Tuesday and they went crazy over me; they have given me the run of their beautiful Club: it is close by here and a great rest . . . I am terrified of tonight. It is a huge hall, but my voice carries, even in a whisper, almost all over it. They are all crazy over my voice . . . I wonder how you spent your birthday, Dear One? Which of the --- came, or did they come in relays? Now I must have my bath and my breakfast, go through my lecture, and then dictate to my typist. After lunch I mean to cut off the telephone and sleep. People say I look splendid. With my dearest love and all tender hope for your happiness, Your Wifie. P.S. – I drank to you and your new --- in a cocktail last night.'28

After this outburst Edith pulled herself together: she had to, if she was to go on with her lecturing. But an added strain was the fact that the topic of all her lectures, so far from being some outside subject in which she might for a while distract herself from her worries, was the structure and philosophy of that very domestic life which now seeemed to have gone so disastrously wrong. One was on 'Semi-Detached Marriage', in which her illustrations were drawn directly from life: 'Twenty-five years ago two writers of unusually sensitive temperaments, when entering that bond of matrimony which so often ends in disaster, decided, like Godwin and Mary Wollstonecraft, that they would not always dwell together in the same house, in order to escape the usual fate of boredom or indifference observed amongst so many of their friends . . . The man and woman are economically independent of one another, and in all external matters have behaved as true comrades or business partners would do. In their approaching old age they contemplate living side by side as a natural outcome of their experiment.'[29] In another, on 'Havelock Ellis', written expressly for this tour, she observed: 'He is literally always working, but his work is a radiant play, as he can never do anything he does not enjoy. He declares that he has never done an unselfish thing in his life.'[30] – a sentiment with which she was beginning now heartily to concur. To the subject of this lecture she now wrote: 'I always speak nicely of you, but I shall cease saying some things, as I've no wish to pose in America as a deluded *wife*.'[31] However, all pretensions to calm were once again destroyed when some friend showed her a newspaper cutting which described how Margaret Sanger was in London 'working with Havelock Ellis'. 'Yesterday morning when I woke I wrote long letters to you and to Y [her chief woman friend], and later thought it wiser to burn them and all the letters you both have sent me,' she wrote on 17 March. 'The thing I have dreaded ever since you wrote of M. has come. I have never been well since you told me, but thank heaven you did. . . . You have probably been hurt at what you think is my jealousy. It is not that – it is soul and heart and body weariness of perpetual everlasting crucifixion.'[32] When he received this Ellis wrote to Margaret, who was then in Barcelona: 'I trust, dear, you will agree with me that it is better *not* to mention me in your letters home, as everything you may chance to say becomes public property at once, and makes mischief.'[33]

To Edith's distraught brain, almost anything could now be registered as an attack, while the interest in her personal life, which the topics of her lectures inevitably engendered, became acutely painful. 'The Socialists have got hold of your helping M., and Mrs Ward even asked me if I'd show her just one of your letters. You see, we're both thought to be free-lovers, and she wanted to see if you really cared for me!!' she wrote from New York on 22 March, adding, 'If, as I shall be, I am badgered by interviewers, I shall say my work is not in that range and that I believe in free speech, but I do not believe in defying laws, except by trying to alter bad ones into good ones.'[34] It was clear that such calm as she was able to assume was achieved only with great effort, and the inevitable crack-up soon followed. At the beginning of April she went down with an ulcerated throat, which kept her ill in New York for most of the remainder of the month. Then some friends took her to convalesce at Brookline, near Boston, whence they and Edith urged Havelock to come over in order to look after her on the return voyage: she proposed to sail on 8 May. 'But I suppose you can't,' Edith added; and indeed nothing could have been further from Havelock's mind, which was, work apart, almost entirely occupied at this time with thoughts of the absent Margaret. 'I regarded [the invitation] as a kind formality on the part of Edith's hostesses and in my replies I seem not even to have mentioned it,' he wrote in his memoirs.35 For Margaret was expected back in London at any moment, and the thought of going to America, for which he had at the best of times no enthusiasm, just at the moment when he might see her again, was too appalling to contemplate. 'I am horrified to hear you are still in Barcelona and that you are even talking of not reaching London until 1st May!' he wrote to her on 21 April. 'When you *do* arrive I shall be eating *you* up if you aren't careful, I shall be so hungry.' On 8 May, the day Edith was due to sail, they finally met again. 'Lovely to see you again – though you were so shy,' he wrote. 'I was [illegible] for hours thinking of you and of little fascinating details. I look forward to seeing you tomorrow. Suppose we went to Hampton Court Tuesday? May is just the time for it.'36 The same day he wrote to Edith in America (for he had received no cable to tell him she had sailed, as actually she had): 'My ever darling Wifie, I have been restlessly awaiting cable to say you sailed . . . The *Lusitania* came as a great shock to me, more than anything that has happened in the war, and all the more as the news came on the very day you were to sail . . . I had your sweet and pathetic letter of the 29th yesterday . . . Of course you need not feel depressed; you have had great success, not "failure". In the same way it is of course quite ridiculous to refer to me as "merged in someone else"; I can't think what I can have said to put so silly an idea in your head. M. is quite nice and a very pleasant companion, but she has no power to help or comfort me; I should never dream of telling her I *needed* help or comfort. It will make no difference to me when she goes away.'37

This particular letter missed Edith and eventually followed her back to London. When she finally disembarked into her husband's waiting arms her first words were: 'Are you alone?'

3

When Havelock met Edith off the boat they went at once to the
Adelphi, that 'fairy palace' of comfort and luxury which had welcomed
Margaret on her arrival the previous November. Edith liked it and
wanted to spend a week resting there, but Havelock insisted on
returning to the Brixton flat. There, soon after, he was visited by
Mneme, and left the two women alone together for a short time while
he went out on some errand. When he got back he found that Mneme
had left and Edith had taken an overdose of morphia tablets. It was
more a gesture than a real suicide attempt, with, as far as he could
see, no cause: 'Nothing had happened to worry or upset her, only
the visit of [Mneme] for whom she had long had a genuine almost
affectionate regard.'[38]

That he could write this, in apparent genuine puzzlement, years
after the event (and without there being in this context any question
of that self-serving refusal to admit the real facts of the case so
evident in his description of the relationship with Margaret Sanger),
perhaps shows why Edith felt so helpless and depressed that she felt
only some dramatic gesture would bring the reality of the situation
home to Havelock. For the truth was that in their 'semi-detached
marriage' he remained, as he had always been, more detached than
she was. Edith had her lovers just as Havelock did – in fact more,
hers being a warmer nature – but, at the end of their marriage just
as at the beginning, there was always a sense in her letters that she
would like more of himself than he wanted or was able to give. And
even at this time it is clear from his letters, although the autobiography
never mentions the fact, that he was mostly taken up with Margaret.
He wrote to her nearly every day, letters generally bewailing the fact
that she seems oblivious to the arrangements for meeting with which
he showers her. On 27 May: 'What has become of you? In accordance
with my note of yesterday I went to the Museum this morning and
when you never came, I got desperate and had the impertinence to
call at your private residence where, of course, I . . . learned that
you were out.' On 2 June: 'Yesterday and again today I journeyed
to the Museum in the hope of seeing you, as opportunities . . . now
are so very few; but both times in vain. It is quite *possible* . . . that I
may go again on the same Mission tomorrow between 12 and 1.' And

on 3 June: 'I am just starting for Speen with Edith . . . not able to get away yesterday as intended. *Every* day this week including today, I have gone to the Museum about 12 in the hope of seeing you and carrying you off for lunch.'[39]

But Margaret's thoughts were turning elsewhere. Her work in Europe was done and she was feeling more and more insistently the need to return to America and her children. On 8 July Havelock writes that he is coming up to London as Edith is going to stay with a friend for a few days and reminding Margaret that she is to visit him at his flat. 'You will also, please, remember the dress . . . that is to be brought to the flat to be packed away in my big box until your return' – evidently a keepsake by which he will remember her.[40] And on 27 August there was a letter from Edith, written from Speen in the Buckinghamshire countryside where she and Havelock were spending that summer. It was couched in that tone of self-conscious restraint and goodwill with which she and Havelock were wont to address each other's lovers: 'I'm really angry with you for not coming here . . . I'm sure you have some subtle idea of not hurting me or something : . . Hope you two to be as much to each other as ever you care to be, and hope you care a little for me too.'[41]

That summer was a beautiful one, but Edith remained immovably depressed, despite the weather. Havelock's thoughts followed Margaret to America. Edith had thoughts of another lecture tour, but only if Havelock would accompany her – something he steadfastly held out against. He and Edith and Olive met and discussed the matter and Olive came down on Havelock's side: he must be left to decide such things for himself. 'Edith . . . says that if ever I *do* go to America, it would only be to see you,' Havelock wrote Margaret:[42] all of which was added to Edith's sense of grievance. It is hard to escape the feeling that Olive, although ostensibly the friend of them both, was much more on Havelock's side. Perhaps her own state of depression, which it will be remembered was so intense during these wartime years in London, was making her bitter and unsympathetic to the sufferings of others. Later on, when Edith became even more seriously depressed, she advised Havelock to leave her and go to Spain for six months, as company, in Olive's view, never did any good in those circumstances: a singularly harsh prescription.

Margaret, for her part, was beginning to feel it was time to go home.

Portet did not want her to think of it any more than Havelock did: he got his publisher to persuade her to sign a contract to remain in Paris. She agreed – but only if the date of the agreement was postponed till after 6 November. For some time she had been having vague fears and premonitions centred on the number six, and one day these solidified into a date: 6 November. She said to the publisher, 'All I know is that something is going to happen on that day that will affect my whole future.' Then they both laughed it off; nevertheless, the contract was dated 1 January 1916.[43]

But there were, besides this vague premonition, more concrete reasons for her to go back to America. One was the arrest of her husband, William Sanger.

Bill Sanger had been the victim of a set-up. In December 1914, just a month after Margaret's abrupt departure, a stranger introducing himself as Mr Heller had arrived at his studio on Fifteenth Street. Heller's story was that he was poor and had a large family and that he wanted a copy of *Family Limitation*. Bill said he was sorry: Mrs Sanger and he kept their work separate, and he had no idea where the pamphlets were stored. But the man pleaded pitifully, and at last Bill rummaged in a drawer and finally found a copy.

> I thought no more of it [he wrote to Margaret] until the same man called again last Tuesday and wanted to know where your books could be bought. I told him of a store on Grand Street. A few minutes later a grey-haired, side-whiskered, six-foot creature presented himself and said, "I am Mr Comstock. I have a warrant for your arrest." He was followed by that man, Heller, bearing a search warrant . . .
>
> He [Comstock] seemed anxious to enter into a discussion of the case, saying that any statement I made would not be used against me. I refused to discuss it, saying I wished to consult my attorney.
>
> He replied that lawyers are expensive and only aggravate the case; and, patting me on the shoulder, said he advised me like a brother, to plead guilty, and he would recommend to the court that I be given a suspended sentence.
>
> I refused to entertain any such plea. . . .
>
> I was arraigned and bail was fixed at $500. I was in that filthy

jail for 36 hours until bail was finally procured . . . There is every possibility of getting one year's imprisonment and $1000 fine . . . It was also mentioned that *if I would give your whereabouts, I would be acquitted*. I replied that they would wait until hell froze over before that would occur.44

The trial was postponed and postponed, and the case finally came up in September. Sanger remained defiant. He was quoted as saying, 'This pamphlet written by Mrs Sanger is nothing more than a clean, honest statement any doctor or trained nurse would give to their patients . . . The truth is never obscene.' And once in court, he began to read a typewritten statement: 'I admit that I broke the law, and yet I claim that in every real sense it is the law and not I that is on trial here today.'45 But the judge, Justice McInerney, an Irish Catholic, would have nothing of it. There was no doubt where his sympathies lay. 'In my opinion,' he declared, 'the pamphlet is not only indecent but immoral. It is not only contrary to the laws of the state but contrary to the laws of God. Any man or woman who would circulate literature of this kind is a menace to the community.' Sanger was offered the alternatives of a $150 fine or thirty days in jail. He declared, 'I want to say to the court that I would rather be in jail with my self-respect and manhood than be free without it.' 'At this,' the *New York Times* reported, 'the storm that had been gathering in the crowded courtroom broke. It began with a volley of handclapping and ended in a medley of shouts and cries. Men and women stood on the benches and waved their hats and handkerchiefs.'46

Sanger's trial had done two things. It had given focus to a growing public feeling in favour of what Margaret was trying to do; and it had left her children without either their mother or their father beside them. She sailed immediately, and was back in America on 4 October. Passing a newsstand on her way home the first thing that caught her eye was a headline: BIRTH CONTROL – the leading article in the *Pictorial Review*.

There were other strange omens to welcome her home. One was the death of Comstock, her chief tormentor. He had, with a curious appropriateness, caught a chill at Sanger's trial, and it had killed him.

Then her little daughter Peggy caught a chill in her turn. She seemed to be getting better: and then suddenly she had pneumonia. She kept saying to Margaret, 'Are you back? Are you really back?' as if she couldn't really believe it. But Peggy and her mother were not united for long. Two weeks later, on 6 November, the dread date of Margaret's dreams, she died.

It was the kind of awful, moral-pointing story that could have come out of a textbook written by Comstock himself – except that it was true. But not even Peggy's death – not even Comstock's – could prevent the wheels of justice turning. Now that Margaret was back, she was bound to come to trial, and in spite of everything she had to prepare herself for that. Otherwise, what use would all this sacrifice have been? Portet, from Barcelona, was urging her by telegram: KEEP COURAGE, HEALTH, HOPE REMEMBER EVEN YOURS WRITING PORTET. And again: GET CASE DISMISSED PREPARE RETURN EUROPE DEVOTEDLY PORTET.[47] But that was not the point. The point was to maintain the momentum of the birth-control snowball which was beginning to roll. Her trial would surely add to that momentum.

However, it became apparent that the New York authorities, who had been so anxious to arraign her a year earlier, were now doing everything they could to avoid the confrontation. But they could not delay for ever and there came a point when the trial date had to be set: 17 January 1916.

The night before the trial Margaret Sanger was given a dinner at the Brevoort Hotel, the guest list of which ranged from such liberal intellectuals as Walter Lippmann, John Reed and Herbert Croly, the editor of the *New Republic*, to socialites such as Mrs Willard Straight and Mrs Lewis Delafield. Many of these ladies had until now declared that, although they approved her aims, they could not condone her tactics; but now, it seemed, all respectable liberal opinion was for her.

The trial was scheduled for ten o'clock, and the courtroom and the surrounding streets were crowded. The congestion inside the building became so serious that the US Marshal had to order the doors closed. More importantly, there was a record number of pressmen present. The *Brooklyn Eagle* reported that 'The defendant was dressed in somber black, but the severity of her costume was somewhat relieved by a pair of white "spats". She wore a black felt hat, a sort of semi-opera hat formerly worn by members of the other sex.'[48]

At ten-thirty Judge Clayton and Assistant District Attorneys Knox and Content finally arrived. Mr Knox immediately requested that the case be postponed for a week. Margaret, acting as her own lawyer, objected strongly, but her objection was overruled. Anticlimax reigned. On the street, she was given three resounding cheers; next day, the case was headlined coast to coast, competing successfully with the news of the German onslaught at Verdun. As the Chattanooga *News* put it, 'There is strong sentiment throughout the nation in favor of Mrs Sanger . . . However the case comes out in New York, the courts will not be able to stop talk of birth control.'[49]

The situation had now reached an impasse. Margaret was determined to be brought to trial; the authorities were determined 'that Mrs Sanger shouldn't be a martyr if we could help it,' as Assistant D.A. Content put it.[50] Yet the longer they postponed the trial the more publicity Margaret got. On 15 February the New York *Sun* reported that 'Mrs Margaret H. Sanger appeared at the Criminal Branch of the United States District Court yesterday to make her weekly demand that she be placed on trial.' Three days later the farce was ended. The government, through US District Attorney H. Snowden Marshall, issued a *nolle prosequi*, dismissing the case.

In law, nothing had been settled. As the New York *Globe* put it, 'the quashing of the indictment settles nothing. The right of American citizens to discuss sociological questions according to their convictions is just where it was before – subject to the mutton-headed restrictions of some post office clerk and the complaisant prosecution of a Federal district attorney.'[51] But things had changed, and they had changed because of the remarkable and courageous figure of Margaret Sanger. The fact that she had fought on even after Peggy's death, the fact that she had forced the government into a position where it could only retreat, meant that it was no longer possible to sideline the issue of birth-control, and women's right to discuss it, as a trivial obscenity to be dealt with by men who, as a matter of course, knew better. There was now a national movement centred around a national figure. The genie was out of the bottle and could not be pushed back.

For Margaret, even with the calamity of Peggy's death, it seemed that life, in many respects, was just beginning. But for Havelock and Edith it was beginning to be clear that nothing would ever be the same again. Havelock, in his memoirs, describes Edith's continual depression; yet it seems clear that, with Margaret's departure, he was in not much better state. Indeed, on 7 November – the day after Peggy's death, though of course they did not yet know of that – we find Edith writing to Havelock: 'Well, darling – take care. Your letters make me ache for you, for none of us except M. and she is away, seem much good to you.'[52]

In fact, Margaret's departure seems to have led to a slight respite for Edith. She went down to Cornwall, first with her lover Y. and later joined by Havelock, and for a few months was more or less happy living quietly there. Then, early in 1916, this fragile equilibrium was shattered by a quarrel with a servant. Edith spiralled into deep depression, and finally agreed to enter a convent nursing home nearby. She always had a soft spot for nuns: the only happy times of her childhood had been at a convent, from which her father had summarily removed her when she voiced a desire to become a nun. Here, on doctor's orders, she was to be kept completely sequestered from the world. No visitors, no letters: only Havelock was allowed to see her.

For a while she seemed to be recovering. Then came catastrophe. Havelock wrote to Y. suggesting that she might send a parcel of flowers or fruit without a letter. When this arrived (it later transpired) Edith remarked: 'So she has found me, has she?' and an hour later tried to commit suicide by throwing herself from a lavatory window.[53] In fact she only injured her foot: but the Mother Superior was so alarmed by this behaviour that she demanded that Edith be removed from the nursing home.

Another home was now found at Sydenham in south London, not very far from Havelock's flat in Brixton, and here for a while the patient was once again satisfactorily settled. The suicide attempt proved to be the climax of the depressive stage of her behaviour, and from now on she regained more and more energy until, at the end, her life was a whirl of perpetual activity, feverish and unreal. She stayed at Sydenham until an incident concerning an American visitor caused her to take offence; she left the home abruptly and, to Havelock's consternation, announced that she wanted a legal separation from him. 'What she had come in her disturbed mental state to think was that, owing to some strange and altogether unexpected perversity or weakness on my part, I had become a menace to her personal freedom,' he observed in his memoirs.[54]

Havelock dismisses this notion as an absurdity, which no doubt it was in the lofty terms in which, throughout their marriage, he had been accustomed to interpret the idea of 'personal freedom'. But the wording of the Deed of Separation which they both signed at her lawyer's (and then went out to lunch together) makes it clear that what Edith had primarily in mind were the two incarcerations she had just endured in nursing homes. However much they had been for her own good, she never wanted to be subjected to such a thing again, and specifically not by Havelock.

One might also note here the ironic commentary on that theme of personal freedom which had run, overtly in accord, but so fraught beneath the surface, all through this marriage. From the first it had been Havelock who had insisted on this independence and Edith who had gone along with it. All her attempts to draw nearer had been, ever so kindly, rebuffed. Even at the very end she had continued to talk about the old age they would spend together: remarks upon which he does not comment, as habitually he did not comment. But now the boot was on the other foot: it was Edith who was throwing him off.

Edith took a flat in Maida Vale, and although Havelock thought it was far too expensive for her there was nothing he could say, since the Deed of Separation specifically indemnified him against all her debts. There was to be a room there for him, but he never used it, since 'it seemed to me a little ridiculous for a man to share rooms with a wife who had just received a legal separation from him'.[55] Nevertheless, Edith insisted that he accompany her on visits to agents and upholsterers; it was only later that he realized that this was probably because such people generally preferred the guarantee of a husband before they entered into business arrangements with a wife. So Edith's mental illness, or new view of reality, took the form of punishing Havelock.

Through the unhappy summer of 1916 Edith lived in Maida Vale in a state of furious activity. She gave almost daily lectures and readings in her own rooms (to what absent audiences may be imagined), and even tried to take the Wigmore Hall for one such. She started a publishing company and had a large edition of her own stories printed: she even enticed the popular novelist Marie Corelli onto her list, until Corelli's agent vetoed the deal. She rented cars and typists, and failed to pay them. She started a film production company with which she planned to raise the level of screen entertainment, and proposed to write some scenarios. She finished her book on James Hinton, which had long been under preparation. Occasionally she would visit Havelock in Brixton, unannounced, always with a friend; the visits would almost always end in acrimony.

On Sunday 3 September, the first Zeppelin was brought down in flames over north London. Edith was out watching it at three in the morning. It was a cool night, and in her usual impulsive way she lent her cloak to another watcher who complained of feeling cold. On the Monday Havelock failed to lunch with her; on the Wednesday she was to meet him, but sent a note to say she had a chill and could not go out. On the Thursday a friend sent a note to say she had a high temperature, but would write when she could. Then there was no more word. Havelock, who had been preparing to spend some days in Suffolk, was worried at having heard nothing of Edith, and came round to her flat unannounced, to find her lying in bed there with a nurse at her side, apparently recovering from pleurisy. That was on Saturday. She urged him to go to Suffolk as he had arranged: she was getting better. He received two letters there to that effect, written at her dictation by a friend. He had been half meaning to return to London on Tuesday, but, now reassured, put that off until Wednesday. But on Wednesday, when he returned to Brixton, he found a telegram: MRS ELLIS DYING. COME AT ONCE.

At Maida Vale Edith was in a coma. Nothing could help her. She lasted a few more hours. After she died, Havelock observed how strange it was that in the course of a long life, partly spent practising as a doctor, he should have seen just two people die: his mother and his wife.

4

The marriage of Havelock and Edith Ellis was a very odd affair. Not the least peculiar aspect of it was that Edith was so absolutely not the kind of woman to whom Havelock was attracted, and yet was so deliberately chosen by him – for it seems clear that it was he who did the choosing and set the form of the marriage throughout, just as much as if it had been the most old-fashioned of arrangements instead of the most self-consciously modern. It also seems clear from the steady stream of fulsome love-letters Edith wrote him throughout her married life that the same was not true of her. The gentle, passive Havelock, who was yet so firm in his opinions and decisions, was perhaps the only man she, with her terror of being bullied, could contemplate living with. She was even, despite her sexual preferences, in love with him to the extent that she proposed an exclusive sexual union with him – which he rejected. As soon as he was given a chance – by the relationship with Claire, which began little more than a year after the marriage – he pronounced Edith 'ineradicably' (his word) lesbian and slid out of any sexual commitment to her. After that she had little choice, if she wanted any sex-life at all, but to be lesbian, which was not contentious since to the public eye she merely had a succession of close friendships with women, which were perfectly normal and permissible.

That there was a type of woman he found particularly attractive is apparent. The three women with whom he fell seriously in love – Olive Schreiner, Margaret Sanger and, after Edith's death, Françoise Lafitte-Cyon, had a lot in common. They were all *intrepid*. Nothing frightened them – nothing about sex, nothing about any other aspect of life. Or perhaps one should say that nothing *appeared* to frighten them – for Olive's asthma was surely a manifestation of the conflict between what she felt she must do and what she felt able to do. With her character and Margaret's the reader is acquainted. As for Françoise, whom he met while clearing up Edith's affairs – she was translating some of Edith's work into French – by the time she met him she, the daughter of a respectable French family, had two young children and was ostensibly married to an unreliable Russian she had met during the war, who had now returned to his newly socialist homeland. She was eking out a living by occasional writing, teaching and translations. Before the war she had been living in London, sharing a flat with another independently-minded young woman, from whose diary a picture emerges of a brave, buoyant, tough-minded survivor. In this shared flat Françoise gave birth to her first child. Françoise's flat-mate's friend described the scene:

Françoise has a baby boy! Such a terrible confinement – she was in agony and then four hours under chloroform – room in a terrible condition, and the Doctor almost in despair. Terrible as it all was, there were some touches of humour. Madame Lafitte (who arrived on Thursday with an ocean of luggage, three umbrellas, three parasols, six costumes, blouses, etc., and without being able to speak a word of English) rushed about the room whilst Françoise was in labour, clapping her hands and crying, 'Ma pauvre Françoise, ma pauvre Françoise!' then seating herself she would scribble upon paper, 'Sacrifice the child, but spare the Mother!' At last the Doctor turned her out of the room! Just as the nurse was about to plunge the baby into the bath, in rushed the dog, whereupon the nurse waved the baby at him in such a frantic manner that the dog turned and fled!

I think her friend Mrs Camebus has been exceedingly good to Françoise – it has been a big undertaking to see her through this trouble. Dr Eder and the Doctor who attended Françoise have both offered from sympathy to become responsible for the expense of the child for the first year of its life: I do not know if Françoise will accept – it is all so wonderful! I am afraid I feel somewhat envious; so many girls suffer in loneliness. Help and friendship has just poured in upon Françoise – is it all, however, good for her? She seems already inconsiderate and almost to demand things as her right!'[56]

This quality of unashamed delight in living on her own terms, together with the mixed reactions it evoked in more timid souls and the bonuses it brought in the shape of help from admiring men friends, will strike a chord with everyone familiar with Olive Schreiner's early London years (when Havelock was in love with her) and with the story of Margaret Sanger. It was a quality which brought Havelock to his knees, and it was entirely absent from Edith.

Why, then, did he decide so arbitrarily to marry her? Françoise herself was in no doubt. In her opinion Havelock, consciously or not, saw Edith primarily as a case to be studied.

She explained this view of their marriage in a series of letters to Margaret Sanger in which Françoise tried to explain Havelock's position when Margaret, who had shown exceptional goodness and generosity to Havelock throughout his life, was distressed by his treatment of her in his memoirs. 'I have always taken *My Life* far more as the record of a sexological case than as a work of art,' Françoise wrote. Unlike Freud, who thought that Havelock was interested in studying sexual abnormalities because of his own abnormality, Françoise put it the other way about: 'As a sexologist could he but wish to dwell on this sort of unions [sic] as lived by himself . . . Havelock chiefly related a case (his case) using himself and others as symbols.' In another letter she wrote (also to Margaret): 'I always considered that Havelock was doomed to marry an invert, the better to understand inversion.'57

This view of the marriage (though it seems highly unlikely that this was ever Havelock's intention on a conscious level) makes a lot of sense. But it is hard to reconcile with Françoise's equally strong conviction that he did not know Edith was a lesbian before they married. Of this she was quite sure: 'Havelock went to [the Fellowship House] not to seek Edith but as an outcome of his interest in the Fabians. Edith may have sought out, among these people, those of her type. But she also sought Havelock. This, surely, shows that she herself was not clearly aware of her sexual temperament . . . Havelock became aware of their blindness over all this in later years.'58 Françoise's view was that, having married Edith in all ignorance, when Havelock found out her real preferences he felt bound to stay with her to protect her from the kind of scandal which was just then engulfing Oscar Wilde, after which a witch-hunt was declared against all homosexuals.

This seems rather improbable. But there are other possibilities. One we have already considered, which is that Edith was bisexual, but that Havelock, as soon as her lesbian side reasserted itself during those long periods when they were, as per their agreement, separated, refused any longer to recognize her heterosexual side. If indeed he had not known of her lesbianism before their marriage, this revelation of it might have come as a terrible shock to him and finally extinguished any sexual desire he felt for her. Such a reaction would be understandable, although considering his profession it seems unlikely.

But in fact it makes much more sense to assume that, when they married, Havelock was *not* ignorant of Edith's lesbianism. According to his case history of her in *The Psychology of Sex* she had had several passionate affairs with women before she married, and it seems inconceivable that, given Havelock's special interest in sexual openness, she should not have told him something about these while they were getting to know each other. It seems equally inconceivable that, having had these experiences, she should not be aware of her own sexual temperament. Edith, after all, was no prudish Victorian Miss. And from his point of view such a marriage would have many advantages. For one thing it would let him off the hook sexually. His experiences with Olive had taught him that he was impotent, and if he married Edith, who anyway preferred women, there would be no more worries for him in that direction. (There is some question as to whether he did, in the end, actually achieve sexual intercourse with Françoise. But from what she wrote to Margaret it seems unlikely: 'You must not think, Margaret, that the hurt which came to Havelock as a result of this unnatural union, was a neurosis with roots in his infancy, a sort of arrested development. But he was hurt in his manhood, he was maimed.'59) We have already seen how insistent he was that there should be no children, and how the initiative in this came wholly from his side: she acquiesced, but unwillingly. He liked and admired Edith, he enjoyed her company and she clearly enjoyed his. The marriage would be good for both of them: giving each of them the secure base they otherwise lacked, while making none of the usual awkward demands of marriage – demands which, as Havelock made clear from the outset, he was not prepared to tolerate.

In Françoise's view, any sacrifice entailed in this union was all, or almost all, on Havelock's side. 'Such unions are always, in part, martyrdom for the heterosexual partner; perhaps for both,' she wrote. 'And the martyrdom is greater if the incompatible sexual partner is a person of beautiful personality (as was Edith in my eyes) whom the other wants to *protect* . . . Havelock, by the side of Edith, might have grown beyond the hurt which resulted from such marriage could he and Edith have parted. But how could he let her court the dangers which might follow?'60

There can be no doubt that most of the Ellises' acquaintance would have shared this view if they had been aware of the circumstances (which it seems they mostly were not: Edith became extremely worried when once, on account of some friend's indiscretion, it seemed as though gossip to the effect that she was a lesbian might be going around London). But the facts of the case do not bear it out. It was, after all, not Havelock who tried to commit suicide and spent the last two years of his life wishing he might die. It was Edith.

Strange as her marital set-up was, it was not unique, and nor was her reaction to it. Françoise herself says, 'How could he help but be haunted, he who followed so many other cases similar to his own, and saw them often end in tragedy? I witnessed one at close quarters, which ended in suicide.'[61]

Indeed, there was one such case which must have been well-known to all members of 'advanced' circles at this time: that of the Salts.

Henry Salt was a young master at Eton when he became a convert to socialism in the early 1880s. No more unlikely convert could have been imagined. Educated at Eton and later at King's College, Cambridge, he seemed destined to pass his life within that unbroken charmed circle. But he and his fellow Eton master, Jim Joynes, were carried away by the eloquence of Henry George, the Land Tax reforming economist – Joynes to the extent that he went over to Ireland to accompany George on a speaking tour there: an act which cost him his mastership after it came to the authorities' attention that he and George had both had to spend a night in some obscure Celtic jail. Salt married Joynes' sister Kate, and this couple, too, soon attracted unfavourable attention on account of their vegetarianism – 'a thing almost unheard of at Eton except in the dubious connection of Shelley'.[62]

The Salts soon realized that, if Eton disapproved of them, it was not half so much as they disapproved of Eton. They disliked the luxury and indulgence of its life, and (even more) the favoured pastimes of both boys and masters, such as hare-coursing and shooting birds. It became clear that they could not continue to live and work in such uncongenial surroundings. Henry had always intended to leave Eton as soon as he had saved enough to guarantee him a small income on which he could live. Now they decided that he would leave anyway, and they would adapt their lives to the meagre income available from what he already had. They bought a small cottage in Tilford, Surrey, and became apostles of the simple life.

The Tilford cottage became a social centre for the New Lifers and Fabians in the 1880s and 90s. The Salts were, of course, enthusiastic Shelleyans, and were visited on this account by the Avelings: Edward reduced himself to tears on one occasion by the reading aloud of *Prometheus Unbound*, after which he contrived to borrow some money from the completely impecunious Kate. They were also militant vegetarians, and became great friends of Bernard Shaw and Edward Carpenter, who were attracted both by the Salts' simple life and also by their music, for which Kate had a great talent: Shaw and Carpenter both enjoyed playing piano duets with her. And between Carpenter and Kate there was also another bond: both were homosexuals.

Kate's predilections were well-known to her friends. The fact that he was perfectly safe from her attentions made Shaw feel particularly at home in Kate's company: the Salts became one of the several couples to whom he was playing 'Sunday husband' at this time. 'Salt's tragedy,' wrote Shaw, 'was that his wife . . . would not consummate their marriage, calling herself an Urning. She got it from her close friend Edward Carpenter who taught Kate that Urnings are a chosen race. [Carpenter derived Urning from Uranus – Urning = child of Uranus; he referred to 'the Uranian temperament'.] Carpenter and I used to meet at Salt's cottage in Tilford. We all called him "The Noble Savage" and wore the sandals he made. He and I played piano duets with Kate, making a fearful noise with Wagner's *Kaisermarch* and *The Ring*, and shared her friendship about equally. We were "Sunday husbands" to her. Salt was quite in the friendship.

'Though Kate would not sleep with Salt she was always falling in love with some woman . . . Such escapades were bad for her, as what she really needed was children; and I told her to get a job in a factory to bring her to her senses. To my surprise she actually did so, and became an employee in my friend Emery Walker's engraving works. But as she could not engrave she was set to work in the office. She soon left it and worked for me as unpaid typist secretary until my marriage. Finally she went back to Salt and lived with him until she faded out mentally and died.'[63]

Such, in brief outline, was Kate Salt's life; and Shaw's manner of telling it perhaps reveals, as much as anything could, why Kate gravitated towards Edward Carpenter. For it is clear from these few sentences that Shaw made two assumptions with regard to Kate. One was that (like Françoise) he assumed that, in such a union, it was the heterosexual partner who suffered most. The other was that homosexuality was reprehensible and unnatural.

It was perhaps not surprising to find that Shaw, who had a puritanical aversion to all forms of sex, felt this way; but it is clear that this was the general sentiment even in the most enlightened circles. For Havelock Ellis – and no one at that time could possibly have been more enlightened than he – made it clear that, although he might tolerate homosexuality, he too thought it was unnatural. For example, in the last sentence of Edith's case history in *The Psychology of Sex* he writes of her: 'the inverted instinct is too deeply rooted to eradicate, but it is well under control.'[64] What this of course meant was that, even among their closest friends, people like Kate and Edith could never escape the perception that they were regarded as pathological cases, to be tolerated if it were not possible to cure them.

However enlightened one's partner, it can hardly be doubted that the consciousness of always being so regarded must be a strain – which can only be compounded by the bracing instruction that what you really need is children. So it is not surprising that both Kate and Edith turned towards Edward Carpenter as a confidant. For Carpenter was not merely homosexual: he was convinced that this was as normal – for homosexuals – as heterosexuality was for heterosexuals, and was determined to do what he could to open the closet doors and let everybody out. This was at that time – the time of the Wilde trial with its hysterical anti-homosexual backlash – an act of the greatest courage.

Carpenter did not publish his main book on these matters, *The Intermediate Sex*, until 1912. But he had earlier given a fairly clear indication of his position in his Whitmanesque cycle of poems *Towards Democracy*; and he acted upon his views by going and living perfectly openly with a succession of lovers in a cottage near Sheffield, where he grew his own vegetables (he, too, was of course a vegetarian) and made sandals which, he assured all his friends, were the perfect footwear. (Shaw abandoned his after one trial.)

To Carpenter, both Kate and Edith could write openly in a way that was quite impossible with anyone else. Thus, after the death of the great love of her life, a woman called Lily, Edith wrote to Edward about her feeling of sexual frustration: 'Dear – I wondered *why* I got headaches a bit – a thing I've not had for years and began to think the need of the lusts of the flesh – like mine – was the reason! . . . A *very* good person like your sister could not really heal me – it is the sinner in you as well as the saint . . . that touch the spot. I used to worry horribly about my sins – dear old pals that have taught me all

I know, I believe.'[65] It was to Carpenter, too, that she revealed her worry about her inversion being ' "the talk" in the higher thought' later on.

But if Edith was close to Carpenter, Kate Salt was even closer. She was a much freer writer than Edith, who could never lose a certain self-consciousness, and much less worried about being loyal to her husband. To Carpenter she poured out grumbles about Shaw and Henry Salt in a way that Edith never would have spoken about Havelock or any other close friend, even if she had felt like doing so.

Kate felt very ambivalent about Shaw and his power to weave tangles of words around her. 'That blessed Shaw turns up here two or three times a week,' she wrote to Carpenter in 1896. 'Sometimes we have rapturous music – mounting on clouds till we touch high heavens – but sometimes bewildering whirlpools of talk – when I lose all hold, and feel myself being dragged down into abysses.' What worried her about Shaw – among other things – was that he did not, or would not, understand or believe that she was truly homosexual, just as he was heterosexual: 'I remember telling Shaw once that the shuddering horror felt by him (or any normal man) at the thought of being touched or fondled by one of his own sex, is no stranger than my own feeling with regard to the touch of the opposite sex. (Whereupon doubting Thomas went and wrote a play called "You never can Tell"!)'[66]

About her husband, too, she had reservations, though she tried to persuade herself that she did not: 'Your letter to Henry (the "business" one) he felt a good deal, I think, – in that hidden way of his. He *is* a good and wonderful thing; I realise that more and more – even though I see him in an outside way only, and not at all in the right sort of way for really understanding anyone. – And more and more thankful am I, year by year, in spite of everything, that no waves have washed us two shipwrecked mariners apart and away from the old raft we both cling to!'[67]

In the sea of sexual uncertainty the quietly confident Carpenter was a rock, and people like Kate and Edith clung to it. So did Olive Schreiner, who told Pearson that part of his attraction for her was that he and Edward Carpenter were the only men she knew capable of regarding a woman 'as a worker and not as a woman'.[68] But the help he could give them was strictly limited. For all the attraction of his bold stance, and the reassurance provided by his steady convictions, he was Englishly dry and limited when it came to personal relations with people like Kate and Edith and Olive. Strong emotions did not please him – and yet he was someone people turned to when they were in emotional trouble. It was a paradox that did not escape Kate. She had been enraptured by *Towards Democracy*, and often addressed Carpenter as 'Dear T.D.' – an indication, perhaps, that the persona she was addressing was the intellect rather than the man. 'I wonder if you will understand when I tell you that I feel nearer to you when you are away than when you are near,' she wrote him in 1892. 'I *do* feel the "apartness" when you are near; but that all drops away when you are far off, and then I feel myself hand in hand with the real you – the better you – which is hidden from me when you are here, because – well, you know why!'[69]

But it is not always enough to commune with a far-off soul, however sympathetic; and when anything more was demanded, Carpenter ran away. When Olive broke with Pearson he supported her with his letters and even went to see her in her exile at Alassio for a few days in 1888; but by then she was over the worst of her trouble and he was suffering on his own account. But when she came to visit him at Millthorpe he ran off to London almost at once, and left her to spend three weeks there without him. As for Kate, to his horror he became something of a fixation with her: 'Please dear Only One don't think it very bad of me to bother you,' she wrote in 1897. 'I find there's only You in all the world – so you see it *is* rather important for me – Edward! Don't leave me altogether if you can help it. I have really tried hard – but it is *so* hard – and sometimes I feel as if I shall go down.'[70] This was the time when Shaw was advising her to have children or find work in a factory. Carpenter's reaction to this kind of effusion was just as bracing, if less practically detailed: 'I wonder if these complications of your life will unravel themselves – perhaps not. Is it rather that they want to be *cut* by Necessity, or a fixed resolve? What a blessing Necessity is'[71] – a response calculated to bring little comfort to a soul in torment.

Carpenter, then, was a source of comfort and inspiration for those women of his circle who were troubled by their sexuality, either because it obtruded itself when they would have preferred it to be ignored – like Olive – and Edward, of all men, could be relied on to ignore a woman's sexuality; or because, as with Kate and Edith, it put them in a position with which only he, of all the men they knew, could really empathize. He, at least, did not think of them as being fortunate beyond measure in their so self-abnegating, so self-sacrificingly sympathetic husbands. Up to a point, of course, they were indeed fortunate; but such a relationship is not a solid foundation upon which to build a satisfactory life. It implies a giver and a receiver, a sense of dependency – a sense of being a 'case' – which it is not, in the end, possible to endure. Kate, for all Henry's understanding and devotion, lapsed into madness and death. (As, in not wholly dissimilar circumstances, did Virginia Woolf.)

Edith's case was slightly different. Her marriage *was*, she thought, established upon an equal footing. After they had sorted out their physical arrangements they had arrived at a plateau of what Havelock called 'the triumph of a deeper passionate love over physical passion'.[72] The importance attached to this by Edith can be seen in the insistent iteration in her letters throughout their years together of the necessity and permanence of this love. 'Thank God you love me – I love you and know that neither of us could live long without one another,' she wrote, in a letter typical of hundreds written during their marriage.[73] What the affair with Margaret destroyed was this confidence in the uniqueness of Havelock's love for her. Without that their marriage was a farce, which is clearly what, after Margaret's advent, she felt it to be. Her insistence on a legal separation followed logically from that. Her eventual death was not, as it happened, suicide; but when, for the past two years, she had been stating at every opportunity that she wanted to die, she would die soon, she could not last long and would not be sorry to go, there was no reason to disbelieve her, nor to think that death, when it came, was in any way unwelcome to her.

Conclusion

THE NEW WOMEN
AND THE OLD MEN

Twenty years after her passionate fling with H.G. Wells, Rosamund Sharp wrote to him: 'I was ill in bed, and . . . I re-read your earlier books – all that I read at nineteen or twenty. I found that what I had, for years, thought of as "Rosamund" was simply something made up of bits of H.G. Wells . . . It put me on the track of myself and by going further back still, and then following the scent later, up to the present-day, I discovered that I was simply a conglomeration of about five different men.'[1]

Most people, men and women, could probably make the same observation; and yet it was less true of the women who figure in this book than of most. Nevertheless it is remarkable how few of these brilliant, forceful, ambitious women – and nearly all of them were that – managed to avoid living their lives on the terms of a male lover or husband. Eleanor Marx, Edith Ellis, Amber Reeves, even such obviously successful women as Beatrice Webb and Rebecca West – none of them managed to live their lives as they would have done had they been entirely free agents. And if it is argued that none of us are free agents, then one need only compare their lives with those of the men they were involved with.

H.G. Wells, Havelock Ellis, Edward Carpenter, even Edward Aveling, lived according to their own plans. That was the essence of their lives. They saw themselves as the architects of a new social order, and as such their job was twofold: to expound and, as far as possible, to demonstrate. Since it seemed most unlikely that they would ever be in a position to legislate for the kind of behaviour they felt to be desirable, the first necessity was to persuade. Once enough people were persuaded, then legislation might become possible, or even unnecessary. In those circumstances, the least – and the most – they could do, apart from arguing, writing and speaking, was to live out their lives according to their newly forged ideals. Their personal lives were as much a political statement as anything they wrote.

This was as true of the women as of the men. Yet their personal fates were very different. Given that all human beings have to make compromises, it could fairly be said that the men of this circle made very few sacrifices that they felt as painful. Their great achievement was to live, to a very great extent, lives freed from compromise. In this venture, which was generally a joint venture, the women were their more than willing partners. But *their* lives, on the contrary, were notable for the enormous compromises they put up with in the cause of the ideal. In almost every case something very important to them was given up as a consequence of their accepting the kinds of lives they did. Edith Ellis gave up children and that unquestioning interdependence which is for many – for most, perhaps – the great blessing of marriage, and which she so obviously and sometimes demeaningly sought. Beatrice Webb gave up children and the pleasures of the senses, since she could not reconcile them with the kind of life she intended to live with Sidney – there being only one kind of life it was possible for her to live with Sidney. When they were engaged and he sent her a full-length photograph of himself, she returned it with the comment that it was 'hideous', and requested one which showed only his head – 'it is the head only that I am marrying!'[2] Amber gave up her intellectual life. Rebecca West gave up that glittering life at the centre of the London literary world, which she would so much have enjoyed, for an almost furtive existence until her son was old enough to be sent away to school. Eleanor Marx made the greatest sacrifice of all, and for the most worthless man: she gave up her life.

So a picture emerges of men who were free and women who were, to a large extent, unfree. Yet, except in the case of Olive Schreiner and the impossibility of her following her natural bent and becoming a politician, there was no very obvious reason for this. No external factor compelled these women to subordinate their lives to the demands and convenience of the men – least of all, on the face of it, the men themselves. For these particular men the equality of women was a given of the new way of life to which they all aspired. There was some less visible force at work.

That force, it seems to me, was guilt. Guilt, its uses, its effects, and the uses and effects of its intimate ally, principle, have in a way been the subject of this book. Those of the book's protagonists who achieved freedom – that is to say, those who led the lives they wished rather than lives which were imposed upon them – abjured guilt. At the same time they used principle, firstly to free themselves from any feelings of guilt, and secondly, to displace guilt – that guilt which they would otherwise be forced to assume – on to others.

This should not be taken to imply that the members of this group were irresponsible. Nothing could be further from the truth. What distinguished them was, on the contrary, their attempt to construct a new system of ethics which would be the basis for a better, freer, more modern world. The irony, from the women's point of view, was how very traditional, when it came down to it, all the modernity was – a fact which was disguised from everybody, none more so than the protagonists themselves, by the theorists' public personae as the embodiment of the New Thought.

The philosopher William James (whose time this also was) had a blinding revelation one night in a dream, and, mindful of the way these things can slip into oblivion (witness *Kubla Khan*), he roused himself and wrote it down. When he awoke next morning he found:

> Hogamus, higamus,
> men are polygamous,
> Higamus, hogamus
> women are monogamous.

This, of course, *was* old-fashioned – profoundly; and it was one of the aims of men such as H.G. Wells and Havelock Ellis to abolish such thinking. Wells wanted to make everyone polygamous, while Havelock Ellis was concerned that everyone should be entitled to find unashamed pleasure in his or her own particular way. Each devoted acres of paper to his particular preoccupation, and each considered himself to be in the vanguard of social thinking. Yet at the core of each of their philosophies the most old-fashioned thinking of all remained untouched. For each of them Woman the Mother reigned supreme. For Wells, the raising of 'ripping' children was woman's highest duty to the State, while for Ellis motherhood was woman's supreme physical and emotional fulfilment, and 'the primary end of marriage is to beget and bear children'.[3]

This differentiation of male and female roles was a fundamental part of that Darwinian thinking which so influenced Wells and Ellis and which represented for them and their generation the break with the medieval past. Darwin himself defined the 'natural' differences between men and women in *The Descent of Man*; his ideas were developed by Herbert Spencer and formed the basis of the most advanced thinking in both biology and psychology. As Henry Maudsley, one of the leading psychiatrists of this time, put it: 'There is sex in mind as distinctly as there is sex in body.'[4]

This brought with it certain implications for the behaviour of men as well as women. Obviously, if men really believe that women's highest destiny is mothering and that this is the world's most creative and important activity, then it follows (at a conscious or unconscious level) that, since women alone are able to enjoy this activity, they should concentrate on that and leave the rest of the field free for men. This (or the reaction against it) has of course become a founding cliché of feminism. It underlay the thought (and therefore the behaviour) of the rationalist New Men just as much as it had underlain (with different authority) that of their religion-bound forebears.

Maudsley enunciated with unusual honesty and clarity what most men really felt about the glorious task of motherhood. Women, he explained, 'are manifestly endowed with the qualities of mind which specially fit them to stimulate and foster the first growths of intelligence in children,' while men were not so endowed. 'If the nursing of babies were given over to men for a generation or two, they would abandon the task in despair or in disgust, and conclude it to be not worth while that mankind continue on earth.'[5]

This view was not confined to Henry Maudsley alone. It was clearly shared, for two at least, by H.G. Wells and Havelock Ellis. While both extolled motherhood, neither of them showed the slightest inclination to share their life with babies. Ellis made it a condition of his marriage that it would not be interrupted by children, while Wells, as soon as babies actually arrived, skedaddled. Where Amber and Rebecca went wrong was in fulfilling what was in Wells's eyes woman's highest calling, that is to say in having babies. Wells liked the thought of babies, hugely enjoyed the sensation of having made them, but found prolonged contact with them and the discomforts they brought in their train boring and annoying. The presence of the child, as he made only too clear to Rebecca, interfered with his enjoyment of its mother; while, as we have seen, he regarded Amber's baby as nothing more than an irrelevance and a nuisance. As his boys Gip and Frank grew up, and as Jane blossomed in the expansive and comfortable atmosphere of Easton Glebe, which was her creation and which Wells so enjoyed, so he grew closer to her again – which is not to say that he was any the less inclined to take mistresses; indeed, it was while he was with one of these in the south of France that he received a telegram telling him Jane was fatally ill with cancer; a circumstance which, once she was actually dead, filled *him*, for once, with guilt, as his autobiographical account of that time shows. It may be noted that one of the uses of autobiography among this group was to portray their behaviour in the justifying and guilt-deflecting light of principle. This was certainly true, for instance, of Havelock Ellis's autobiography, *My Life*, which is very largely an exercise in self-justification vis-à-vis the débâcle of his marriage to Edith. But whatever his feelings after Jane's death, while she was alive principle had enabled Wells to avoid the exigencies of Gip and Frank's babyhood, just as principle enabled him to hand the boredom of his daughter's babyhood over to the obliging Blanco-White, while Anthony, as a young child, was (with brief Wellsian interludes) entirely Rebecca's responsibility.

If we look at the careers of the women who appear in this book, it is clear that only two of them succeeded in living their lives as freely, in a psychological as well as a material sense – the psychological, of course, being the key to all the rest – as if they had been men: Olive Schreiner and Margaret Sanger. All the rest were in some degree kept from fulfilment. It was not merely a question of whether or not they had children – some did and some did not: Margaret did and Olive did not. It was a question of expectations.

While the men of this group got on with their task of setting the world to rights, and the women, to a greater or lesser extent, adjusted their lives to fit and did what they could to help, Olive and Margaret flashed on and off the scene unpredictably, following their own star. They enthralled everyone they met, and a large part of their magnetism was undoubtedly the sense that, like the men, they held themselves accountable only to themselves. This did not mean that they led lives of unusual happiness – this was certainly not true in Olive's case. And although it would be true to say that both were able genuinely not to care what the world thought of them, this statement, too, must be qualified in Olive's case. The thinness of her skin when it came to gossip about the petty details of her life – the kind of gossip which her life rendered virtually inevitable – was a source of constant agony to her. But on the larger stage she, like Margaret, was her own woman. How did they achieve this?

To begin with, of course, neither of them was European.

This may sound banal, but its importance can perhaps be shown if we contrast the careers of Margaret Sanger and of Eleanor Marx.

Eleanor grew up in a household where everything about society was to be questioned – except the family. She believed everything her adored father taught her – including what he taught her by example: and Marx, as we have seen, was in every way the European bourgeois paterfamilias.

But one of the specifically American things about the New York socialists among whom Margaret found herself was their rejection of this view of the family. The German émigrés (and not only them, as Beatrice Webb's remarks about how the Wellses were accepted *in spite of* his divorce, show) rejected only the capitalist system; the American socialists rejected, too, its offshoot, bourgeois family values.

By the time she came to New York, Margaret had already begun this rejection. Her breakdown during her first pregnancy and after the birth of her eldest child was, it may be assumed, the result of recognizing, consciously or subconsciously, that she was apparently, despite everything, doomed to repeat the experience of her mother, buried in domesticity and in the end killed by it; and she wanted no part of this.

As it happened, her breakdown in this respect echoed the experience of another pioneering American feminist, who articulated the course of these events with exceptional clarity: Charlotte Perkins Gilman.

Both Margaret and Charlotte married delightful and talented young men who loved them dearly. Both soon got pregnant. Both drifted into a depression so deep that they very soon turned their faces to the wall and lost the will to live.

Mental illness has for centuries been associated with the reactions of women to a society whose shape is dictated by men. In the nineteenth century, the women sometimes responded to the impossible role assigned to them by retreating into 'hysteria'. This was the case with many unmarried women stuck in a relative's house without occupation or status. Florence Nightingale, before she so spectacularly broke the bonds of her stifling home life, wrote an autobiographical novel about this experience, called *Cassandra*. Elizabeth Barrett Browning, mysteriously immobilized with an unnamed sickness before Robert Browning whisked her away to love, health and creative life, would seem to be another example of the same syndrome. It was a way in which such women, otherwise powerless, could exercise control over a household in which there was only too obviously no useful place for them and nothing they could decently do to occupy themselves.[6]

In the case of women in Margaret's or Charlotte's position, the situation was reversed. They did not call themselves ill because they found their situation intolerable; rather, they found their situation intolerable, and society concluded that they must therefore be ill. No sane woman could find the role of a happy wife and mother insupportable.

In Charlotte's case, the situation could not have been clearer. It was decided when the baby was five months old and Charlotte, who before her marriage had been a compulsive worker, was incapable of the slightest effort, that she should go away to California for a change. The change indeed did her good: 'I recovered so fast . . . that I was taken for a vigorous young girl. Hope came back, love came back, I was eager to get back to husband and child, life was bright again. I reached home . . . the dark fog rose again in my mind, the miserable weakness – within a month I was as low as before leaving.'[7] Her physician, the famous Dr Weir Mitchell, confined her to bed for a month, the notorious 'rest cure' which he described as 'a combination of entire rest and excessive feeding'. Mitchell ordered Charlotte, on her return home to husband and baby, to: 'Live as domestic a life as possible. Have your child with you all the time . . . Lie down for an hour after each meal. Have but two hours intellectual life a day. And never touch pen, brush or pencil as long as you live.'[8]

It was an instant recipe for relapse. 'I returned home,' she wrote, 'and obeyed these directions for some three months, and came so near the borderline of utter mental ruin that I could not see over. Then, using the remnants of intelligence that remained . . . I cast the noted specialist's advice to the winds and went to work again – work, the normal life of every human being . . . ultimately recovering some measure of power.'⁹ It was at this point that she wrote *The Yellow Wallpaper*, a powerful story in which it is the treatment – confinement alone in a room called 'the nursery at the top of the house' – which finally, literally, drives the woman out of her mind.

What had almost driven Charlotte out of her mind was the confinement of family life, for which the 'nursery at the top of the house' is such a terrifying metaphor. The fact that she recovered when she lived away from her husband and became ill again as soon as she returned showed her, if not the doctor, what was wrong, and she got a divorce and went to live with her little daughter (then aged two) in California.

Margaret, like Charlotte, was rejecting not just her child, but a whole domestic scenario. She was worn out from her nursing work, and she was confined, before and after her baby, Stuart, was born, to a sanatorium in the Adirondacks. But the treatment did not seem to be doing her good: 'at the end of eight months I was worse instead of better, and had no interest in living.'¹⁰

Charlotte had diagnosed her own illness and its cure, but Margaret was jolted out of her state by a doctor. His professional diagnosis was that the baby (who had been living with her) should go to her brother or mother-in-law, and that she should be separated from all responsibilities. But, having delivered this prescription in the company of a colleague, the doctor came back and urged her to 'Do something! Want something! You'll never get well if you keep on in this way!' Thus jolted by the awareness that she was considered to be a possibly terminal case, Margaret returned to New York and Bill: she would rather die with her family than in hospital. A slow recovery began. But her heart was never really in domestic life. When their dream house burned down she was 'conscious of a certain relief, of a burden lifted'.¹¹ And, as with Charlotte, the moment when she really found herself was when, alone in London, she finally decided that she must divorce her loving husband. After that she could resume the business, begun when she left her father's house and interrupted during the years with Bill Sanger, of being herself. The point was that, contrary to received values, only one part of this person was the mother of Stuart, Grant and Peggy. It was an important part, but it did not automatically take precedence over everything else.

She had begun to overcome guilt when she admitted her relief at

losing the beautiful house and all its prized contents; and this process
was reinforced by contact with the socialist group whose values echoed
this very relief. They were thus able doubly to reinforce her new
strength: firstly by supporting her attitudes vis-à-vis family life, and
second by setting these new values firmly within a system of ethics:
socialism. The Marx girls had been able to benefit from the same
ethical system. It was the great strength conferred upon her by this
intellectual confidence which imparts such a particular note of tragedy
to Eleanor Marx's death, for it seems almost certain that if only things
had turned out a little differently – if she had had a child to hold her
to life, or if Aveling had died a little earlier and thus not been able to
push her finally over the brink – she would have survived to make a
great political mark in her own right. In the end it was the unbreakable
sense of family loyalty implanted in her which killed her. But Margaret
was able to escape from this, with the result that she was able to use
her life constructively and without it being marred by useless guilt.

The proof of this, if proof were needed, was in her reaction to the
tragic death of her little daughter. She always remembered this – as
any parent would – as the most awful thing that had ever happened to
her. It happened, of course, at a time – 1915, during the First World
War – when millions of parents were having to face the same frightful
situation. Her friends Dr and Mrs Drysdale, like so many others,
had just lost their son, and Mrs Drysdale wrote her heart-rending
letters of commiseration. But the fact that many similar tragedies are
taking place does not make each individual one easier to bear; and the
circumstances of this one, taking place as it did just when she had
been absent from her children for almost a year, must have made it
particularly hard for Margaret (though not quite so bad as if she had
been absent for the death itself). It could have been seen – must have
been seen by many – as a just punishment for her behaviour over the
past two years, and it seems impossible to imagine that nobody tried
to point this moral to her, or that a hint of such a feeling did not
ever creep into her heart.

But what would have been the point of it? To repine would not bring
Peggy back, nor undo her own months of absence. And Margaret did
not want to repine, because that would have nullified everything she
was trying to do. So she went forward, and if she had sacrificed a year
of Peggy's company, that sacrifice had not been a pointless one; nor

did Peggy's death embitter her, as it must have done had she assumed the mantle of guilt which conventional society would so eagerly have held out to her.

Olive Schreiner's was a different case. She had no need to reject her family: they pre-empted this by rejecting her. As a result her problem was not one of escape, but of searching. She had to create her image of an acceptable life entirely for herself, and then she had to find somewhere for that self to live. The effort involved in all this was very great. One consequence of it was that she was constitutionally unable to be happy – literally so: her asthma prevented it. She was also – as that same asthma continually underlined – riddled with guilt. But her guilts were not the usual female guilts, which were, after all, themselves products of a society she had not so much rejected as never known. Olive – as she often pointed out – never even went to school. So her constant and pervading sense of guilt – and perhaps no one influenced by a Protestant household, let alone a missionary one, can escape guilt of some sort – was that she was failing *herself*. That ideal self was the flag constantly waving before her, was the subject of all her work, the goal of her life. Her constant wanderings were a reflection of her psychological wanderings, forever in search of this self and the place where it could blossom.

Both Olive and Margaret – and here, too, is where not being European was important – were helped by the extremely crude and obvious nature of the forces opposing them. They were both in a sense fortunate in coming from societies where great extremes – not only economic but psychological – were so unblurred. It was clear to them both very early on what they must react against. The European gauze curtain of ancient tradition had not fallen to obscure black and white with shades of misty grey. The life of the women Olive met in her youth was so extraordinarily trammelled, so hard, so narrow, its intellectual horizons so confined, that it was quite clearly unsupportable as far as she was concerned; what was more, it had always to bear the contrast with the hugeness of the physical horizon, the vastness of Africa. And this intolerable narrowness was echoed by the extreme Calvinism from which she had so early turned away. For Olive, there was never a time when it was not clear what she must escape from. As for Margaret, it is hard to imagine a more grotesque – or more quintessentially American – embodiment of reaction than Anthony Comstock with his appalling

powers – a forerunner, it could be said, of the TV preachers whose
bizarre antics seem so alien to European eyes, and whose political
power is so enormous.

Both Margaret and Olive, then, descended upon Europe untram-
melled; and this, allied to their energy and intelligence, was the secret
of their immense charm, just as it was the secret of the charm of Wells,
Shaw, even Havelock Ellis. For one of the undeniable bonuses of
shedding guilt is that the guilt-free state is a highly attractive one.
To him (or her) that hath shall be given; and, when guilt returns,
the magnetism is shed. How dramatically this may happen is shown
by the story of Olive and Pearson. For what Pearson did is clear:
he used the force of the peculiar principle he imposed upon Olive
and those other women (such as Elisabeth Cobb) whom he wanted
to keep at a distance, that is, the desirability of resisting emotion and
the culpability of strong feelings, to fill Olive with guilt at having
(what was after all, a perfectly natural thing) fallen in love with him.
Looked at objectively, the blame should not have been hers but his,
for acting in such a cowardly way. Here again is an example of the use
of principle to deflect guilt. As a result Olive was totally deprived of
that audacious charm which had so strongly marked her first impact
upon London, and was not to find it again until she shed the double
load of Pearson and his burden of guilt.

The insidious effects of this burden, or of the inability to deflect
it, could even be seen affecting the relations between mothers and
children. In conventional terms, Margaret Sanger behaved abominably
to her children, abandoning them and their father for months at a
time, putting her work before her family. But their affection for her
was unimpaired. They knew she was devoted to them, and that her
love was unmarred by any of the resentment of frustration or any care
for what 'people' might think. Having such a notorious mother was
not easy for them: the boys were sent to boarding schools where they
got black eyes through fighting those classmates who taunted them
about their mother having been to jail (she was imprisoned in 1917
for running a birth-control clinic in Brooklyn). When she said to them,
'But what did you say?' they told her they had said, 'That wasn't my
mother. That was another Margaret Sanger' – a response which must
have given her food for thought.[12] But their mutual loyalty was never
in question.

By contrast, the responses of Anthony West, the son of Wells and Rebecca West, to his upbringing were very different. It is clear from his life of his father, *Aspects of a Life*, and his novel about his mother, *Heritage*, that he entirely blamed his mother for what he saw as his unsatisfactory upbringing, feeling a deep resentment and even hatred for her which can be said to have dominated his life and marred hers, while for his father, whose inadequacies in respect of parenting were just as gross and who felt free to decline responsibility for Anthony whenever he chose to do so, the son felt little but admiration and affection.

On the face of it this seems very unfair. One can hardly blame him for being charmed, like all the rest of the world, by his father, but how can one explain his reaction to his mother? The answer seems to be that, even when he was with her (which, after he grew old enough to go to boarding school, was not that often) he could never feel sure that she was happy to be his mother, for the very good reason that she was always pretending *not* to be his mother. Indeed, he never called her mother, but knew her as 'Aunty Panther', an oddity which reflects her own equivocal feelings about her awkward maternal status. 'I had been brought up from the beginnings of my conscious awareness of such things to think and speak of my mother as my aunt,' he writes in his life of his father. 'My father had always been against this on realistic rather than other grounds. . . . He had told my mother that any nurse or ordinarily observant servant with the usual number of eyes in her head would only have to see us together to realise what we were to each other, and that the ploy would be bound to create more difficulties for her than it could possibly remove. He had been unable to turn her from the idea at the outset, and could not get her to change her mind later. . . . He, after all, had begun the deceptions by calling himself "Mr West," and he was still insisting that I should not know that he was my father.'[13] But of course such a game had resonances which went deeper than mere convenience, and Anthony felt them, as he could not fail to do.

In more ways than one, Rebecca West, when she became pregnant, found she was in the same boat as Amber Reeves. It was not only that both were very young (Rebecca was only nineteen), very brilliant, and pregnant by H.G. Wells without being married to him. It was also that they both found themselves confronted by a situation with which, despite all the brave words, they could not really cope. In the end, society and the threat of its disapprobation was too much for them. Amber took one way out, and, because Blanco-White loved her, it succeeded in the sense that they then went on to have a happy and united family life. Amber accepted what seemed to be inevitable, namely, that the baby would force her to limit her horizons.

Rebecca did not accept this. Her affair with H.G. had really begun (after an earlier, unsuccessful attempt) when she wrote a review of *The Passionate Friends*, one of the many novels he devoted to justifying his relations with Amber, saying that they had failed their own brave standards in this respect. Ann Veronica had said, 'Once you begin with love you have to see it through,' but Amber and H.G. had not done this.

But Rebecca, when it came to the point, found that she could not do so, either. One point of the 'Aunty Panther' pretence was that she, too, found that she could not outface society (in the person of the servants on whom, if she wanted to be able to do any work, she had to rely to run the house and mind the child). This, as Wells predicted, made her life much more unpleasant and difficult than if she had made no such pretences. But it also clearly meant that she did not accept her situation. Unlike Amber, she preferred the freedom she had enjoyed before Anthony's arrival, and did all she could to minimize his effect on her life. She was not able to accept her new self either in Amber's more limited way or in Margaret Sanger's more radical and thoroughgoing style, and Anthony suffered for it. As a result he was among the few people never to have been charmed by Rebecca West, who was so magnetically guilt-free in all other aspects of her life.

What the New Women in their moments of success learned, was what the New Men never needed teaching – namely, that the world will always give you what you claim as of right. When they were able most truly to be buccaneers, they found themselves. But this was not easy, and many quailed at its implications, which seemed to posit the rejection of precisely those family priorities in which women, according to even the most advanced of new thinkers, were supposed to find their deepest satisfaction. It is hardly surprising that many of them found this step too difficult to take. It meant rejecting, not merely conventional wisdom but the wisdom of those very men who embodied the new thought.

Perhaps it was inevitable that H.G. Wells and Margaret Sanger should have an affair. They had their first fling in England in 1920, when Margaret was over on a visit and clearly both available and not wishing involvement – a situation which suited H.G. perfectly. He expected it to go no further than this – a pleasant few meetings for both of them. Then in 1921 he undertook an American tour, and they met again; and H.G. found himself well and truly smitten. 'My plans in New York are ruled entirely by the wish to be with you as much as possible – and *as much as possible* without *other people* about. I don't mind paying thousands of dollars if I can get that – I'm really quite well off you know,' he told her.[14] And months later he was still signing himself 'ever glowingly, Yours H.G.'[15]

His feeling for Margaret in fact developed into a fondness which was to last for the rest of his life. And there was nothing so very surprising in that. For in Margaret Sanger Wells in many respects met his true mate: not the adoring, sock-darning girl of his fantasies, into which mould so many intelligent, emancipated women had striven, with varying degrees of success, to cram themselves for his sake, but a tough-minded, independent woman who had as strong a sense of her own life's requirements as he had of his. And this sense very much matched his: plenty of sex, plenty of pleasure – including, but not overridingly, family pleasures – and, taking precedence over all of this, though never extinguishing it, a burning sense of work to be done.

But if Margaret's view of life so perfectly matched H.G.'s as far as sex went, it was because the real driving force of her life was elsewhere, just as his was. As she wrote to a friend at about this time, 'Where is the man to give me what the movement gives in joy and interest and freedom?'[16] And here, of course, was the paradox. It was only in such circumstances that a woman could respond to a man in the way Wells envisaged; and yet the genuine compelling interest in the non-sexual, non-emotional aspects of life which this attitude demands involved just what he did not like, her being 'the engine' rather than 'the petrol'. Wells and Sanger seemed a perfectly-matched pair; but, had it ever come to any more permanent relationship, it seems doubtful whether Wells could have borne to be as little the centre of any woman's world as any man had to be of Margaret's.

In fact, not many years after their liaison, Margaret did find such a man. He was called – improbably enough – J. Noah H. Slee. He was a millionaire from the Midwest, and he admired and loved her so absolutely that he was prepared to agree to any conditions she might set, so long as she would marry him and allow him to love and support her. After some hesitation, Margaret agreed. Wells was not amused. 'My dear Margaret Sanger, marry if you must, but don't expect me to be enthusiastic,' he wrote to her huffily.[17] For was she not, the Woman of the Future, doing the old-fashioned thing and tying herself down to one man (and that man not him)?

But in a way her marriage pointed up deeper differences between them – differences that lie at the bottom of much that has been described in this book. For, as with so many of the New Men, what Wells said and what he did in questions of relations between the sexes were two different things, and many of the muddles he got into arose on account of the moral acrobatics entailed by this disparity. But Margaret – truly a New Woman – was consistent. She married Mr Slee because she decided that to do so would be good for her and good for her work. In this she, too, was guided by principle. But her principle, unlike that of Wells or Ellis, was never a strait-jacket into which life must in some way be crammed, but was rather a determination to avoid all such artificial constrictions, whether of the old-fashioned or the newfangled variety. Pragmatic to the end, she was not about to allow the principle that marriage was not suitable for a woman like her to stand between her and the possibilities offered by Mr Slee. And, uniquely among the protagonists of this book, she did indeed live happily ever after.

NOTES

LIST OF ABBREVIATIONS

HRC   Harry Ransom Humanities Research Center, University of Texas at Austin

LC   Library of Congress

SCL   Sheffield County Library

SSC   Sophia Smith Collection, Smith College

UCL   University College, London (Pearson papers)

1: A DERBYSHIRE IDYLL

1 Havelock Ellis, 'Eleanor Marx', *The Adelphi*, Sept. 1935.
2 Havelock Ellis, *My Life*, p. 186.
3 W. B. Yeats, *Autobiographies*, p. 398.
4 Beatrice Webb, *The Diary of Beatrice Webb*, eds. N. and J. Mackenzie, vol. 2, 31 Jan. 1900.
5 'Old Nick' was one of Marx's many nicknames among members of his family.
6 Olive Schreiner, *The Story of an African Farm*, p. 236.
7 *Olive Schreiner – Letters*, vol. 1, ed. Richard Rive, p. 33, 15 August 1881.
8 Olive Schreiner, *Letters of Olive Schreiner*, ed. S. C. Cronwright-Schreiner, p. 56, 19 Jan. 1885.
9 Quoted R. First and A. Scott, *Olive Schreiner*, p. 119.
10 Ibid.
11 Ibid.
12 Ellis, *My Life*, pp. 182–3.
13 Ibid. p. 183.
14 Ibid. p. 44.
15 Ibid. p. 48.
16 Ibid. p. 117.
17 Ibid. p. 119.

18 Ibid.
19 Ibid. pp. 125–6.
20 Havelock Ellis, *The Dance of Life*, p. 199.
21 Havelock Ellis's journal, now in Mitchell Library, State Library of New South Wales, quoted P. Grosskurth, *Havelock Ellis*, pp. 44–5.
22 Havelock Ellis, Introduction to James Hinton, *Life in Nature*, p. xviii.
23 Ellis, *My Life*, p. 131.
24 Ibid. p. 45.
25 Ibid. p. 316.
26 Havelock Ellis, 'Eleanor Marx', *The Adelphi*, Sept. 1935.
27 Schreiner, *The Story of an African Farm*, p. 187.
28 Marx to Paul Lafargue, quoted Yvonne Kapp, *Eleanor Marx*, vol. 1, *Family Life, 1855–1883*, pp. 298–299.
29 Eleanor Marx to Jenny Longuet, 15 Jan. 1882, *The Daughters of Karl Marx*, ed. O. Meier, pp. 147–8.
30 Eleanor Marx to Laura Lafargue, 28 March 1883, *The Daughters of Karl Marx*, ed. O. Meier, p. 167.
31 Beatrice Webb, *The Diary of Beatrice Webb*, vol. 1, pp. 87–8, 24 May 1883.
32 Havelock Ellis, 'Eleanor Marx', *The Adelphi*, Sept. 1935.
33 H. M. Hyndman, *Further Reminiscences*, p. 140.
34 Quoted Kapp, *Eleanor Marx*, vol. 1, p. 257.
35 Ibid.
36 Ibid. p. 258.
37 Quoted Tsuzuki, *The Life of Eleanor Marx, 1855–1898*, pp. 101–2.
38 Hyndman, *Further Reminiscences*, p. 142.
39 Aaron Rosebury, quoted First and Scott, *Olive Schreiner*, p. 204.
40 Hesketh Pearson, *Bernard Shaw*, p. 123.
41 Quoted Kapp, *Eleanor Marx*, vol. 2. *The Crowded Years*, pp. 19–20.
42 E. Bernstein, *My Years of Exile*, p. 162.
43 Havelock Ellis, 'Eleanor Marx', *The Adelphi*, Sept. 1935.
44 Quoted N. and J. Mackenzie, *The First Fabians*, pp. 95–6.
45 Kapp, vol. 1, p. 257.
46 18 June 1884, quoted Kapp, vol. 2, p. 15.
47 This and the previous letter quoted Kapp, vol. 2, pp. 16–17.
48 Schreiner, *Letters*, vol. 1, ed. Rive, p. 10, 30 April 1873.
49 Ibid. p. 19, 2 Nov. 1875.
50 Ibid. p. 22, 24 April 1878.
51 Ibid. p. 64, 17 May 1885.

52 Havelock Ellis, 'Notes on Olive Schreiner', 1884, manuscript at the Harry Ransom Humanities Research Center, University of Texas at Austin.
53 Schreiner, *Letters*, ed. Rive, p. 39, 2 May 1884.
54 Michel Foucault, *The History of Sexuality*, p. 145.
55 Schreiner, *Letters*, ed. Rive, p. 36, 28 March 1884.
56 Ibid. p. 37, 8 April 1884.
57 Ibid. pp. 36–7
58 Schreiner, *Letters 1876–1920*, ed. S. C. Cronwright-Schreiner, p. 20, 21 May 1884.
59 Foucault, *The History of Sexuality*, p. 71.
60 Ellis, *My Life*, p. 183.
61 Schreiner, *Letters 1876–1920*, ed. S. C. Cronwright-Schreiner, p. 19, 14 May 1884.
62 Havelock Ellis, 'Eleanor Marx', *The Adelphi*, Sept 1935.
63 Schreiner, *Letters*, ed. Rive, p. 43, 29 June 1884.
64 Ellis, *My Life*, p. 184.
65 Schreiner, *Letters 1876–1920*, ed. S. C. Cronwright-Schreiner, pp. 51–2, 16 July 1884.
66 Ibid. 29 July 1884.
67 Ibid. 8 July 1884.
68 Schreiner, *Letters*, ed. Rive, pp. 48–9.
69 Havelock Ellis's journal, annotated by Olive Schreiner, at Mitchell Library, quoted Grosskurth, pp. 84–86.
70 Havelock Ellis, 'Eleanor Marx', *The Adelphi*, Sept. 1935.
71 Ellis's journal, quoted Grosskurth, pp. 84–86.
72 Ellis, *My Life*, p. 185.
73 Schreiner, *Letters*, ed. Rive, pp. 51–2.
74 Olive Schreiner to Havelock Ellis, *Letters*, ed. Rive, 5 Nov 1884, Rive, p. 52.
75 Ellis's journal, quoted Grosskurth, p. 92.
76 Ellis, *My Life*, p. 186.
77 Schreiner, *Letters*, ed. Rive, p. 134, 24 Jan. 1888.
78 Ibid. p. 223, 11 Aug. 1893.
79 Quoted First and Scott, pp. 78–9.
80 Ibid.
81 Havelock Ellis, 'Eleanor Marx', *The Adelphi*, Sept 1935.
82 G. B. Shaw's diary, 24 August 1885, quoted Holroyd, *Bernard Shaw*, p. 155.

83 Havelock Ellis, 'Eleanor Marx', *The Adelphi*, Oct 1935.
84 Ibid.
85 Schreiner, *Letters*, ed. Rive, p. 53, 16 Nov. 1884.

2: OLIVE SCHREINER AND THE NEW MEN

1 Havelock Ellis to Olive Schreiner, HRC. None of these letters are
   dated exactly.
2 Ibid.
3 Ibid.
4 Ibid.
5 Ibid.
6 Ibid.
7 M. S. Pearson, 'Autobiographical Notes of the Men and Women's
   Club 1885–9', Pearson papers, UCL.
8 Olive Schreiner to Elisabeth Cobb, 12 Feb. 1885, UCL.
9 Olive Schreiner to Havelock Ellis, 14 May 1890, HRC, Schreiner,
   Letters, ed. Rive, p. 172.
10 Elisabeth Cobb to Karl Pearson, Spring 1885, UCL.
11 Elisabeth Cobb to Karl Pearson, 18 Feb. 1885, UCL.
12 Elisabeth Cobb to Karl Pearson, 26 June 1885, UCL.
13 Minutes of Men and Women's Club, UCL.
14 Quoted First and Scott, p. 147.
15 Olive Schreiner to Maria Sharpe, 23 March 1886, UCL.
16 Olive Schreiner to Karl Pearson, Oct. 1886, UCL, (Schreiner, *Letters*,
   ed. Rive, p. 109).
17 Havelock Ellis to Olive Schreiner, HRC.
18 Karl Pearson, 'The Woman's Question', *The Ethic of Freethought*,
   p. 361.
19 Ibid. p. 360.
20 Emma Brooke, 'Notes on a Man's View of the Woman's Question',
   p. 4, UCL.
21 Olive Schreiner to Karl Pearson, 14 July 1885, UCL.
22 Karl Pearson, quoted First and Scott p. 148.
23 Havelock Ellis to Olive Schreiner, HRC.
24 Olive Schreiner to Karl Pearson, 14 July 1885, UCL.
25 Olive Schreiner to Havelock Ellis, 29 March 1885, Schreiner, *Letters*,
   ed. Rive, p. 65.
26 Olive Schreiner to Havelock Ellis, 5 Jan. 1886 (ibid. p. 72).

27 Olive Schreiner to Karl Pearson, 6 Feb. 1886, UCL.
28 Olive Schreiner to Karl Pearson, 5 March 1886, UCL (Schreiner, *Letters*, ed. Rive, p. 73).
29 Karl Pearson to Maria Sharpe, 8 Sept. 1889, UCL.
30 Olive Schreiner to Karl Pearson, 14 Dec. 1886, UCL (Schreiner, *Letters*, ed. Rive, p. 116).
31 Olive Schreiner to Karl Pearson, 19 July 1885, UCL.
32 Schreiner, *Letters*, ed. Rive, pp. 70–71.
33 Olive Schreiner to Karl Pearson, 4 April 1886, UCL (Schreiner, *Letters*, ed. Rive, p. 74).
34 Olive Schreiner to Karl Pearson, 29 June 1886, UCL.
35 Olive Schreiner to Karl Pearson, 2 July 1886, UCL (Schreiner, *Letters*, ed. Rive, p. 87).
36 Olive Schreiner to Karl Pearson, 20 July 1886, UCL (Schreiner, *Letters*, ed. Rive, p. 98).
37 Olive Schreiner to Karl Pearson, 11 Oct. 1886, UCL (Schreiner, *Letters*, ed. Rive, p. 107).
38 Havelock Ellis to Olive Schreiner, HRC.
39 Emma Brooke to Karl Pearson, 4 Dec. 1885, UCL.
40 Olive Schreiner to Karl Pearson, 19 Dec. 1885, UCL (Schreiner, *Letters*, p. 69).
41 Olive Schreiner to Havelock Ellis, 25 April 1886, Schreiner, *Letters 1876–1920*, ed. S. C. Cronwright-Schreiner, p. 98.
42 Olive Schreiner to Karl Pearson, 31 Oct. 1886, UCL (Schreiner, *Letters*, ed. Rive, p. 112).
43 Elisabeth Cobb to Karl Pearson, 2 Nov. 1886, UCL.
44 Olive Schreiner to Karl Pearson, 11 Oct. 1886, UCL (Schreiner, *Letters*, ed. Rive, p. 107).
45 Olive Schreiner to Karl Pearson, 9 Nov. 1886, UCL (Schreiner, *Letters*, ed. Rive, p. 115).
46 Olive Schreiner to Karl Pearson, 10 and 11 Dec. 1886, UCL (Schreiner, *Letters*, ed. Rive, p. 115).
47 Olive Schreiner to Karl Pearson, 12 Dec. 1886, UCL.
48 Olive Schreiner to Karl Pearson, 20 July 1886, UCL (Schreiner, *Letters*, ed. Rive, p. 99).
49 H. B. Donkin to Karl Pearson, 15 Dec. 1886, UCL.
50 Olive Schreiner to Karl Pearson, 14 Dec. 1886, UCL (Schreiner, *Letters*, ed. Rive, p. 116).
51 Elisabeth Cobb to Karl Pearson, 14 Dec. 1886, UCL.

52 Elisabeth Cobb to Karl Pearson, 15 Dec. 1886, UCL.

53 Olive Schreiner, 'The Sunlight Lay Across My Bed', *Dreams*, p. 173.

54 Olive Schreiner to Havelock Ellis, 1 Feb. 1887, UCL (Schreiner, *Letters*, ed. Rive, p. 124).

55 Envelope with notes in Mrs Hacker's handwriting of a conversation with Pearson's former secretary at the Galton laboratory, E. G. Everton–Jones, in 1956, UCL.

56 Olive Schreiner to Karl Pearson, 30 Jan. 1887, UCL (Schreiner, *Letters*, ed. Rive, p. 122).

57 Olive Schreiner to Edward Carpenter, 13 Jan. 1887, Sheffield County Library (Schreiner, *Letters*, ed. Rive, p. 118).

58 Charlotte Wilson to Karl Pearson, 1889, Pearson UCL.

59 Notes on Olive Schreiner, 1884 – MS by Havelock Ellis at HRC.

60 Olive Schreiner to Karl Pearson, 30 Jan. 1887, UCL.

61 Elisabeth Cobb to Karl Pearson, 30 Dec. 1886, UCL.

62 Olive Schreiner to Havelock Ellis, 25 Feb. 1884, Schreiner, *Letters*, ed. Rive, p. 35.

63 Ibid.

64 Olive Schreiner to Havelock Ellis, 11 July 1884, Schreiner, *Letters*, ed. Rive, p. 46.

65 Olive Schreiner to Karl Pearson, 23 Oct. 1886, UCL (Schreiner, *Letters*, ed. Rive, p. 109).

66 Olive Schreiner, *From Man to Man*, p. 122.

67 Olive Schreiner to Ernest Rhys, early 1888, Schreiner, *Letters*, ed. Rive, p. 136.

68 Olive Schreiner to Edward Carpenter, 14 Sept. 1889, SCL.

69 Yeats, *Autobiographies*, pp. 204–5.

70 J.B.S. Haldane, from *KP: 1857–1957*, speeches delivered on the occasion of Pearson's centenary, privately issued, London 1958, p. 6.

71 Karl Pearson to Elisabeth Cobb, 12 April 1927, UCL.

72 Karl Pearson to Maria Sharpe, 14 Dec. 1886, UCL.

73 Beatrice Webb, *The Diary of Beatrice Webb*, vol. 1, p. 115, 22 April 1884.

74 Schreiner, *Letters*, ed. Rive, p. 165.

75 Olive Schreiner to Havelock Ellis, 22 June 1890, Schreiner, *Letters*, ed. Rive, p. 175.

76 Olive Schreiner to W. T. Stead, 21 July 1890, ibid.

77   Olive Schreiner to Havelock Ellis, 25 March 1890, Schreiner, *Letters*, *1876–1920*, ed. S. C. Cronwright-Schreiner.

78   Olive Schreiner to Mary Sauer, Jan. 1892, Schreiner, *Letters*, ed. Rive, p. 198.

79   Olive Schreiner to Will Schreiner, Jan. 1892, Schreiner, *Letters*, ed. Rive, p. 199.

80   Olive Schreiner, 'The Buddhist Priest's Wife', from *Stories, Dreams and Allegories*, p. 73.

81   Olive Schreiner to her mother, Rebecca Schreiner, Feb./March 1896, Schreiner, *Letters*, ed. Rive, p. 268.

82   Beatrice Webb, *The Diary of Beatrice Webb*, vol. 1, p. 371, 23 July 1892.

83   Olive Schreiner to Will Schreiner, 13 Sep. 1892, Schreiner, *Letters*, ed. Rive, p. 208.

84   Olive Schreiner to W. T. Stead, March 1892, Schreiner, *Letters*, ed. Rive, p. 202.

85   Olive Schreiner to Edward Carpenter, Christmas Day 1892, Schreiner, *Letters*, ed. Rive, p. 216.

86   Olive Schreiner to S. C. Cronwright-Schreiner, 27 April 1893, Schreiner, *Letters*, ed. Rive, p. 221.

87   Olive Schreiner to Edward Carpenter, 1 Aug. 1893, Schreiner, *Letters*, ed. Rive, p. 223.

88   Quoted D. L. Hobman, *Olive Schreiner. Her Friends and Times*, p. 100.

89   Olive Schreiner to S. C. Cronwright-Schreiner, quoted Hobman, p. 102.

90   Schreiner, *Letters*, ed. Rive, pp. 256–7.

91   Olive Schreiner to Will Schreiner, Nov. 1893, Schreiner, *Letters*, ed. Rive, p. 227.

92   Olive Schreiner to W. T. Stead, 10 Jan. 1896, Schreiner, *Letters*, ed. Rive, p. 262.

93   Olive Schreiner to J. X. Merriman, 29 June 1896, Schreiner, *Letters*, ed. Rive, p. 283.

94   Olive Schreiner to Mrs Isie Smuts, 24 Sept. 1899, Schreiner, *Letters*, ed. Rive, p. 378.

95   Olive Schreiner to Will Schreiner, 14 Sept. 1899, ibid.

96   Olive Schreiner to W. T. Stead, 26 Feb. 1892, Rive, pp. 200–201.

97   Olive Schreiner to Will Schreiner, 24 Sept. 1899, Rive, p. 382.

98   Olive Schreiner, *Woman and Labour*, pp. 18–19.

99   Olive Schreiner to S. C. Cronwright-Schreiner, quoted Hobman, p. 167.
100 S. C. Cronwright-Schreiner, quoted Hobman, p. 171.
101 Olive Schreiner, *Woman and Labour*, p. 258.
102 Ibid. pp. 201–2.
103 S. C. Cronwright-Schreiner, *The Life of Olive Schreiner*, p. 265.
104 Ibid. p. 271.

3: THE USES OF PRINCIPLE – I: HAVELOCK AND EDITH

1   Ellis, *My Life*, p. 218.
2   Edith Ellis, *Stories and Essays*, 'Olive Schreiner', p. 1.
3   Ellis, *My Life*, p. 213.
4   Ibid. pp. 214–15.
5   Ibid. p. 246.
6   Edith Ellis, *Attainment*, pp. 175–7.
7   Quoted by Marguerite Tracy in her introduction to Edith Ellis, *The New Horizon in Love and Life*, p. xxx.
8   Ellis, *My Life*, p. 221.
9   Ibid. p. 219.
10 Ibid. p. 229.
11 Ibid. p. 237.
12 Ibid. pp. 237–8.
13 Havelock Ellis to Olive Schreiner, HRC.
14 Ellis, *My Life*, pp. 233–4.
15 Ibid. pp. 239–40.
16 Ibid. pp. 247–8.
17 Ibid. p. 251.
18 Ellis, *Man and Woman*, p. 522.
19 Elaine Showalter, *The Female Malady*, p. 55.
20 Ibid. p. 123.
21 Ellis, *My Life*, pp. 230–1.
22 Ibid. p. 231.
23 Ibid. p. 292.
24 Ibid. p. 256.
25 Ibid. p. 292.
26 Edith Ellis to Edward Carpenter, 1916, SCL.
27 Beatrice Webb, *The Diary of Beatrice Webb*, vol. 2, pp. 193, 207.

28 Jenny Longuet to Laura Lafargue, March 1882, *The Daughters of Karl Marx*, ed. O. Meier, p. 152.
29 May 1891: Ellis, *My Life*, p. 260.
30 Ibid. pp. 261–2.
31 Edith Ellis, *Stories and Essays*, p. 28.
32 Havelock Ellis to Olive Schreiner, 1885, HRC.
33 Ellis, *My Life*, pp. 227–8.
34 Ibid. p. 234.
35 Foucault, p. 118.
36 Ibid. p. 105.
37 Edith Ellis, *Kit's Woman*, pp. 160–1.
38 Ellis, *My Life*, p. 233.
39 Ibid. p. 263.
40 Ellis, *Studies in the Psychology of Sex*, vol. 2, *Sexual Inversion*, p. 226.
41 Ibid. p. 335.
42 Ellis, *My Life*, p. 264.
43 Ibid, p. 212.
44 Ibid. p. 265, 14 Feb. 1893.
45 Ibid. pp. 267–8.
46 Ibid. p. 291.
47 Ibid. p. 290.
48 Ibid. p. 254.
49 Havelock Ellis to Olive Schreiner, 1884, HRC.
50 Ellis, *My Life*, p. 264.
51 Ibid. pp. 270–1.
52 Ibid. p. 271.
53 Ibid. pp. 291–2.
54 Ibid. p. 292.
55 Ibid. p. 179.
56 J. Wortis, *Fragments of an Analysis with Freud*, p. 154.
57 Ellis, *My Life*, p. 43.
58 Ellis, *Impressions and Comments* series 3, p. 63, 'A Revelation'.
59 Ellis, *Impressions and Comments* series 2, pp. 195–6, 'Dorothy Richardson'.
60 Ellis, *My Life*, pp. 296–7.
61 *Justice*, 2 Nov. 1895.
62 J. Sweeney, *At Scotland Yard*, p. 181.
63 Ibid. p. 186.
64 Ibid. pp. 186–7.

65 Ellis, *My Life*, p. 305.
66 Ibid.
67 Ibid. p. 309.
68 J. Sweeney, *At Scotland Yard*, p. 193.
69 Ibid. p. 196.
70 Quoted Grosskurth, p. 228.
71 Foucault, p. 7.
72 J. Wortis, *Fragments of an Analysis with Freud*, p. 179.
73 Ibid. p. 156.
74 Ibid. pp. 177–8.
75 Ellis, *My Life*, p. 321.

4: ELEANOR AND EDWARD: END OF THE LONG, SAD YEARS

1   Havelock Ellis, 'Eleanor Marx', *The Adelphi*, Sept. 1935.
2   Eleanor Marx to Laura Lafargue, 10 December, 1895, *The Daughters of Karl Marx*, ed. O. Meier, p. 284.
3   Eleanor Marx to Liebknecht, 2 June 1897, Liebknecht, *Briefwechsel*, p. 453, quoted Tsuzuki, p. 297, Kapp, vol. 2, p. 678.
4   Quoted Kapp, vol. 2, p. 678.
5   Quoted Tsuzuki, p. 305.
6   Tsuzuki, p. 299.
7   Ibid.
8   Shaw, *The Doctor's Dilemma*, standard edition, p. 151.
9   Hesketh Pearson, *Bernard Shaw*, p. 124.
10 Shaw to Ellen Terry, 5 Jan. 1898, quoted Tsuzuki, p. 309.
11 E. P. Thompson, *William Morris*, appendix II, pp. 866–7.
12 *Reynolds News*, 7 Aug. 1898, quoted Tsuzuki p. 329.
13 Theodor Rosebury, 'Eleanor, Daughter of Karl Marx: personal reminiscences of Aaron Rosebury', *Monthly Review* (New York), vol. 24, no.8, Jan. 1973.
14 Tsuzuki, p. 298.
15 Ibid. pp. 300–301.
16 I have used Yvonne Kapp's version of these letters, which were written in English and sent by Freddy Demuth after Eleanor's death to Eduard Bernstein who published them in German in *Die Neue Zeit*. They were then retranslated for *Justice*, 30 July 1898. Keir Hardie wrote another article in the *Labour Leader* using the originals, but only in part. Kapp has reconstructed them from an amalgam of these

sources (Yvonne Kapp, *Eleanor Marx*, vol. 2, The Clouded Years, pp. 680 ff.)

17   Eduard Bernstein, 'What Drove Eleanor Marx to Suicide', *Justice*, 30 July 1898.
18   *Justice*, 30 July 1898.
19   Tsuzuki, p. 303; Kapp, vol. 2, p. 683.
20   *Justice*, 30 July 1898.
21   Quoted Kapp, vol. 2, p. 684.
22   Ibid.
23   Ibid. p. 685.
24   Ibid. pp. 684–5.
25   Tsuzuki, p. 306.
26   Ibid. p. 307.
27   *Hamburger Echo*, 20 Jan. 1898, quoted Tsuzuki, p. 307.
28   Eleanor Marx to Laura Lafargue, quoted Kapp, vol. 2, p. 686.
29   Quoted Kapp, vol. 2, p. 693.
30   Ibid. p. 694.
31   *Labour Leader*, 30 April 1898, quoted Tsuzuki, p. 316.
32   Kapp, vol. 2, p. 697.
33   *Forest Hill and Sydenham Examiner and Crystal Palace Intelligencer*, 8 April 1898, quoted Tsuzuki, p. 320.
34   Tsuzuki, p. 318.
35   *Justice*, 30 July 1898.
36   Eduard Bernstein to Adler, 5 April 1898, quoted Tsuzuki, p. 324.
37   Hyndman to Liebknecht, 10 Aug. 1898, quoted Tsuzuki, p. 325.
38   Eduard Bernstein to Laura Lafargue, April 1898, *The Daughters of Karl Marx*, ed. Meier.
39   Liebknecht to Laura Lafargue, 9 April 1898, *The Daughters of Karl Marx*, ed. Meier.
40   E. P. Thompson, *William Morris*, appendix II.
41   Kapp, vol. 2, pp. 707–8.
42   All quoted Kapp, vol. 2 pp. 642–3.
43   Rosebury, 'Eleanor, Daughter of Karl Marx,' *Monthly Review* (New York), vol. 24, no.8, Jan. 1973.

5: THE USES OF PRINCIPLE – 2: H.G.'S NEW UTOPIA

1   Shaw's Diary, quoted Holroyd, *Bernard Shaw*, p. 155.
2   H. G. Wells, *The Misery of Boots*, Fabian Society Tract, 1907.

3   Wells, *A Modern Utopia* (1905), quoted in *First and Last Things* (1908), pp. 139–41.

4   Olive Schreiner to Karl Pearson, 20 July 1886, Schreiner, *Letters*, ed. Rive, p. 98.

5   Quoted N. and J. Mackenzie, *The First Fabians*, p. 323.

6   Beatrice Webb, *The Diary of Beatrice Webb*, vol. 2, March 1902, pp. 240–1.

7   Wells, *The New Machiavelli*, p. 315.

8   Wells, *Experiment in Autobiography*, vol. 2, p. 464.

9   Ibid. pp. 464–5.

10   Ibid. p. 465.

11   Ibid. p. 436.

12   Wells, *First and Last Things*, pp. 216–17.

13   Wells, *Experiment in Autobiography*, vol. 2, p. 469.

14   *Dear Girl*, ed. Tierl Thompson, p. 158.

15   N. and J. Mackenzie, *The First Fabians*, pp. 334–5.

16   E. Bernstein, *My Life in Exile*, quoted Briggs, *A Woman of Passion*, p. 84.

17   Wells, *Experiment in Autobiography*, vol. 2, p. 605.

18   E. Nesbit, *Daphne in Fitzroy Street*, quoted Briggs, p. 91.

19   E. Nesbit, *Daphne in Fitzroy Street*, pp. 184–5.

20   Quoted Briggs, p. 105.

21   Wells, *Experiment in Autobiography*, p. 605.

22   Letter to Doris Langley Moore, quoted Briggs, pp. 114–15.

23   Olive Schreiner to Edward Carpenter, Dec. 1888, SCL.

24   Quoted Briggs, pp. 114–15.

25   Ibid. pp. 299–300.

26   Wells, *Experiment in Autobiography*, pp. 602–7.

27   Wells, *H. G. Wells in Love*, pp. 68–9.

28   Briggs, p. 309.

29   Ibid. p. 271.

30   Ibid. p. 208.

31   Ibid. p. 313.

32   Letter to Doris Langley Moore, ibid., p. 115.

33   Letters in Wells papers, University of Illinois, Champaign-Urbana.

34   Briggs, p. 310.

35   Wells, *Experiment in Autobiography*, pp. 606–7.

36   Wells, *H. G. Wells in Love*, p. 71.

37   Letter in Wells papers, University of Illinois.

38 Wells, *H. G. Wells in Love*, p. 73.

39 Letters in Wells papers, University of Illinois.

40 Wells, *H. G. Wells in Love*, p. 74.

41 Ibid. pp. 75–6.

42 Ibid. p. 76.

43 Ibid. p. 77.

44 This is at any rate what Justin Blanco-White, Amber's second daughter, told the author, so it is presumably what Amber told her family.

45 Wells, *The New Machiavelli*, p. 461.

46 Wells, *H. G. Wells in Love*, p. 78.

47 Rebecca West, *The Strange Necessity*, pp. 199–200.

48 Gordon Ray, *H. G. Wells and Rebecca West*, p. 178.

49 Wells, *The New Machiavelli*, p. 454.

50 Ibid. p. 456.

51 Berta Ruck, 'The Picture of an Optimist', in *H. G. Wells: Interviews and Recollections*, ed. J. R. Hammond, p. 33.

52 Quoted Ray, pp. 45–6.

53 Wells, *The New Machiavelli*, pp. 456–7.

54 Wells, *H. G. Wells in Love*, pp. 77–8.

55 Wells, *The Research Magnificent*, pp. 262–3.

56 Wells, *H. G. Wells in Love*, p. 79.

57 Compton Mackenzie, 'Dramatizing a Wells Novel', in *H. G. Wells: Interviews and Recollections*, ed. Hammond, p. 22.

58 Wells, *H. G. Wells in Love*, pp. 80–81.

59 Anthony West, *H. G. Wells: Aspects of a Life*, p. 8.

60 Ibid. p. 9.

61 M. Meyer, 'H. G. Wells and his Family', in *H. G. Wells, Interviews and Recollections*, ed. Hammond, p. 22.

62 Beatrice Webb, *The Diary of Beatrice Webb*, vol. 3, p. 120.

63 Beatrice Webb, *Our Partnership*, pp. 359–60.

64 Ibid. p. 366.

65 Beatrice Webb, *The Diary of Beatrice Webb*, vol. 3, pp. 121–2.

66 Ibid.

67 Wells, *H. G. Wells in Love*, pp. 82–3.

68 Beatrice Webb, *The Diary of Beatrice Webb*, vol. 3, pp. 125–6.

69 Beatrice Webb to Amber Blanco-White, 11 Sept 1909, Beatrice and Sidney Webb, *Letters*, p. 355.

70 Beatrice Webb, *The Diary of Beatrice Webb*, vol. 3, 4 Oct. 1909, p. 128.

71 Quoted N. and J. Mackenzie, *The First Fabians*, p. 373.

72 Wells, *H. G. Wells in Love*, p. 75.

73 G. B. Shaw, *Misalliance*, standard edition, p. 135.

74 Beatrice Webb, *The Diary of Beatrice Webb*, vol. 3, 27 Dec. 1909, p. 133.

75 Shaw, *Correspondence*, ed. Dan Laurence, pp. 869–70.

76 Wells, *H. G. Wells in Love*, p. 83.

77 Wells, *The Secret Places of the Heart*, pp. 114–17.

78 Personal communication with the author.

79 Wells, *H. G. Wells in Love*, p. 86.

80 Ibid. p. 35.

81 Arthur Salter, 'Apostle of a World Society', in *H. G. Wells: Interviews and Recollections*, ed. Hammond, p. 75.

82 Wells, *H. G. Wells in Love*, pp. 114–5.

83 Shaw, 'H. G. Wells and the Rest of Us', in *Pen Portraits and Reviews*, London, 1932, pp. 279–80.

6: THE SAGE AND THE WOMAN REBEL

1   H. G. Wells, *The New Machiavelli*, pp. 410–12.

2   *The Woman Rebel*, no.1 (February–August 1914, New York Public Library).

3   Margaret Sanger's plea to the New York Supreme Court 1917, p. 5.

4   Margaret Sanger, *An Autobiography*, p. 76.

5   Ibid. p. 85.

6   Ibid. p. 89.

7   Ibid. p. 94.

8   Sanger papers, Sophia Smith Collection, Smith College.

9   Sanger, *An Autobiography*, p. 68.

10 Sanger papers, SSC.

11 Quoted Lawrence Lader, *The Margaret Sanger Story*, p. 54.

12 Ibid.

13 Ibid. p. 58.

14 Ibid. p. 60.

15 Margaret Sanger's diary in Sanger Papers, Library of Congress. The following quotations are from the same source.

16 Sanger papers, LC.

17 Ellis, *Impressions and Comments*, 2nd Series, p. 64.

18 Ellis, *My Life*, p. 429.

19 Sanger papers, LC.
20 Ibid.
21 Ibid.
22 Ibid.
23 Sanger, *An Autobiography*, p. 185.
24 Sanger papers, LC.
25 Ibid.
26 Ibid.
27 Ellis, *My Life*, p. 430.
28 Ibid. p. 433.
29 Edith Ellis, *The New Horizon in Love and Life*, p. 25.
30 Edith Ellis, *Stories and Essays*, p. 33.
31 Ellis, *My Life*, p. 436.
32 Ibid. p. 433.
33 Sanger papers, LC.
34 Ellis, *My Life*, p. 447.
35 Ibid. p. 454.
36 Sanger papers, LC.
37 Ellis, *My Life*, p. 456.
38 Ibid. p. 459.
39 Sanger papers, LC.
40 Ibid.
41 Lader, p. 74.
42 12 Sept 1915 – Sanger papers, LC.
43 Lader, p. 80.
44 Ibid. pp. 80–81.
45 Ibid. p. 81.
46 Ibid. p. 82.
47 Sanger papers, SSC.
48 Lader, p. 93.
49 Ibid. p. 94.
50 Ibid.
51 Ibid. pp. 94–5.
52 Ellis, *My Life*, p. 471.
53 Ibid. p. 483.
54 Ibid. p. 496.
55 Ibid. p. 492.
56 Diary of Eva Slawson, 9 Aug. 1913, in *Dear Girl*, ed. Tierl Thompson, p. 178.

57 Françoise Lafitte-Cyon to Margaret Sanger, 1 Jan. 1954, 1 Feb. 1956,
    Sanger papers, LC.
58 Ibid.
59 Ibid.
60 Ibid.
61 Ibid.
62 Edward Carpenter, *My Days and Dreams*, p. 236.
63 G. B. Shaw, preface to S. Winsten, *Salt and His Circle*.
64 Ellis, *Studies in the Psychology of Sex*, vol. 2, *Sexual Inversion*,
    p. 226.
65 Edith Ellis to Edward Carpenter, 5 Dec. 1905, Carpenter papers,
    SCL.
66 Kate Salt to Edward Carpenter, 28 Jan. 1898, SCL.
67 Kate Salt to Edward Carpenter, Jan. 1903, SCL.
68 Olive Schreiner to Karl Pearson, 30 Jan. 1887, UCL; Schreiner, *Letters*,
    ed. Rive, p. 122.
69 Kate Salt to Edward Carpenter, Jan. 1892, SCL.
70 Kate Salt to Edward Carpenter, 17 Feb. 1897, SCL.
71 Edward Carpenter to Kate Salt, 1896, SCL.
72 Ellis, *My Life*, p. 296.
73 Ibid. p. 382.

CONCLUSION

1   Rosamund Sharp to H. G. Wells, 1929, U. of Illinois.
2   Beatrice Webb, *The Diary of Beatrice Webb*, vol. 1, p. 361.
3   Havelock Ellis, *The Objects of Marriage*, in 'Appellant's Plea to the
    New York Supreme Court 1917' in re Margaret Sanger.
4   Elaine Showalter, *The Female Malady*, p. 122.
5   Ibid. p. 123.
6   See the discussion of this in Showalter (though she does not mention
    Elizabeth Barrett).
7   Charlotte Perkins Gilman, *The Living of Charlotte Perkins Gilman*,
    pp. 94–5.
8   Gilman, p. 96.
9   Showalter, p. 141.
10 Margaret Sanger, *An Autobiography*, p. 59.
11 Ibid. p. 64.
12 Lader, p. 144.

13 Anthony West, *H. G. Wells: Aspects of a Life*, p. 56.
14 H. G. Wells to Margaret Sanger, 12 July 1921, Sanger papers, SSC.
15 Wells to Margaret Sanger, 30 November 1921, Sanger papers, SSC.
16 Margaret Sanger to Juliet Rublee, quoted Lader, p. 52.
17 Wells to Margaret Sanger, Sanger papers, SSC.

SELECT BIBLIOGRAPHY

Aveling, Edward, and Eleanor Marx: *Shelley's Socialism*, 1888, reprinted Manchester, 1947, preface by Frank Allaun.

Bebel, August: *Woman in the Past, Present and Future*, tr. H. B. Adams Walther, London, 1885.

Bernstein, Eduard: *My Years of Exile: Reminiscences of a Socialist*, tr. Bernard Miall, London, 1921.

Bland, Hubert: *Letters to a Daughter*, London, 1906

Briggs, Julia: *A Woman of Passion: The Life of E. Nesbit*, London, 1987.

Calder-Marshall, Arthur: *Havelock Ellis*, London, 1959.

Carpenter, Edward: *The Intermediate Sex: Study of Transitional Types of Men and Women*, London, 1912.

Carpenter, Edward: *Love's Coming of Age: Papers on the Sexes*, London, 1896.

Carpenter, Edward: *My Days and Dreams: Autobiographical Notes*, London, 1916.

Cronwright-Schreiner, S.C.: *The Life of Olive Schreiner*, London, 1924.

Ellis, Edith: *Attainment*, London, 1909.

Ellis, Edith: *Stories and Essays*, privately printed, Berkeley Heights, 1924.

Ellis, Edith: *Kit's Woman*, London, 1907.

Ellis, Edith: *The New Horizon in Love and Life*, preface by E. Carpenter, introduction by M. Tracy, London, 1921.

Ellis, Havelock: *The Dance of Life*, London, 1923.

Ellis, Havelock: *Impressions and Comments*, 2nd Series, London, 1921.

Ellis, Havelock: *Impressions and Comments*, 3rd Series, London, 1924.

Ellis, Havelock: *My Life*, London, 1940.

Ellis, Havelock: *The New Spirit*, London, 1890.

Ellis, Havelock: *Studies in the Psychology of Sex*, 3rd edition, 7 vols., Philadelphia, 1928.

Ellis, Havelock: *The Task of Social Hygiene*, London, new edition 1927.

First, Ruth and Ann Scott: *Olive Schreiner*, London, 1980.

Foucault, Michel: *The History of Sexuality*, vol. 1: *An Introduction*, tr. Robert Hurley, London, 1979.

Gilman, Charlotte Perkins: *The Living of Charlotte Perkins Gilman*, New York, 1935.

Glendinning, Victoria: *Rebecca West*, London, 1987.

Gregg, Frances Lyndall: *Memories of Olive Schreiner*, London, 1957.

Grosskurth, Phyllis: *Havelock Ellis*, London, 1980.

Hammond, J. R., ed.: *Wells: Interviews and Recollections*, London, 1980.

Hill, Mary A.: *Charlotte Perkins Gilman: The Making of a Radical Feminist, 1860–1896*, Philadelphia, 1980.

Hinton, James: *Life in Nature*, introduction by Havelock Ellis, London, 1932.

Hobman, Daisy Lucie: *Olive Schreiner: Her Friends and Times*, London, 1955.

Holroyd, Michael: *Bernard Shaw*, vol. 1: *The Search for Love*, London, 1988.

Hyndman, H. M.: *The Record of an Adventurous Life*, London, 1911.

Hyndman, H. M.: *Further Reminiscences*, London, 1920.

Kapp, Yvonne: *Eleanor Marx*, vol. 1: *Family Life, 1855–1883*, London, 1972.

Kapp, Yvonne: *Eleanor Marx*, vol. 2: *The Crowded Years, 1884–98*, London, 1976.

KP: 1857–1957, Speeches delivered by J. B. S. Haldane and others at a dinner held in University College, London, on the occasion of the Karl Pearson Centenary Celebration, May 1957 (privately issued, 1958).

Lader, Lawrence: *The Margaret Sanger Story*, New York, 1937.

Mackenzie, Norman and Jeanne: *The First Fabians*, London, 1979.

Mackenzie, Norman and Jeanne: *The Time Traveller: A Biography of H. G. Wells*, London, 1973.

Marsh, Jan: *Back to the Land: The Pastoral Impulse in Victorian England, 1880–1914*, London, 1982.

Marsh, Jan: *Jane and May Morris: A Biographical Story, 1839–1938*, London, 1986.

Meier, Olga, ed.: *The Daughters of Karl Marx: Family Correspondence, 1866–1898*, tr. and adapted by Faith Evans, introduction by Sheila Rowbotham, London, 1982.

Meyer, Mathilde M.: *H. G. Wells and his Family, as I have known them*, Edinburgh, 1956.

Morris, May: *Introductions to the Collected Works of William Morris*, New York, 1973.

Pearson, Hesketh: *Bernard Shaw: His Life and Personality*, London, 1943.

Pearson, Karl: *The Ethic of Freethought*, London, 1901.

Ray, Gordon N.: *H. G. Wells and Rebecca West*, New Haven, 1974.

Rowbotham, Sheila and Weeks, Jeffrey: *Socialism and the New Life: The Personal and Sexual Politics of Edward Carpenter and Havelock Ellis*, London, 1977.

Salt, Henry: *Seventy Years Among Savages*, London, 1921.

Sanger, Margaret: *An Autobiography*, London and New York, 1939.

Schreiner, Olive: *Dreams*, London, 1891.

Schreiner, Olive: *From Man to Man*, introduction by S. C. Cronwright-Schreiner, London, 1926.

Schreiner, Olive: *Letters 1876–1920*, ed. S. C. Cronwright-Schreiner, London, 1924.

Schreiner, Olive: *Letters*, vol. 1: *1871–1899*, ed. Richard Rive, Oxford, 1988.

Schreiner, Olive: *Stories, Dreams and Allegories*, London, 1923.

Schreiner, Olive: *The Story of an African Farm*, London, 1883 (Penguin, 1971).

Schreiner, Olive: *Woman and Labour*, London, 1911.

Shaw, Bernard: *Collected Letters*, 3 vols. ed. Dan Laurence, London, 1972–1985.

Shaw, Bernard and Mrs Patrick Campbell: *Correspondence*, ed. Alan Dent, London, 1952.

Shaw, Bernard: *The Diaries, 1885–1897*, ed. Stanley Weintraub, Philadelphia, 1986.

Showalter, Elaine: *The Female Malady: Women, Madness and English Culture, 1830–1980*, London, 1987.

Sweeney, John: *At Scotland Yard*, London, 1905.

Thompson, E. P.: *William Morris: Romantic to Revolutionary*, London, 1955.

Thompson, Tierl, ed.: *Dear Girl: The Diaries and Letters of Two Working Women, 1897–1917*, London, 1987.

Tsuzuki, C.: *The Life of Eleanor Marx, 1855–1898: A Socialist Tragedy*, Oxford, 1967.

Webb, Beatrice: *The Diary of Beatrice Webb*, ed. Norman and Jeanne Mackenzie, 3 vols., London, 1982–4.

Webb, Beatrice: *Our Partnership*, London, 1948.

Webb, Sidney and Beatrice, *Letters*, ed. Norman and Jeanne Mackenzie, vols. 1–3, Cambridge, 1978.

Wells, H. G.: *Ann Veronica*, London, 1909.

Wells, H. G.: *Experiment in Autobiography*, London, 1933.

Wells, H. G.: *First and Last Things*, London, 1908.

Wells, H. G.: *H. G. Wells in Love*, ed. G. P. Wells, London, 1984.

Wells, H. G.: *In the Days of the Comet*, London, 1906.

Wells, H. G.: *The New Machiavelli*, London, 1911.

Wells, H. G.: *The Research Magnificent*, London, 1915.

Wells, H. G.: *The Secret Places of the Heart*, London, 1922.

West, Anthony: *H. G. Wells: Aspects of a Life*, London, 1984.

West, Rebecca: *The Young Rebecca: Selected Essays of Rebecca West, 1911–1917*, ed. Jane Marcus, London, 1982.

Winsten, Stephen: *Salt and His Circle*, London, 1951.

Wortis, Joseph: *Fragments of an Analysis with Freud*, New York, 1954.

Yeats, W. B.: *Autobiographies*, London, 1926.

INDEX

Shelley, Percy Bysshe 243
Showalter, Elaine 106
Siemens, Alexander 135
'Singer, J. Astor' 123
'Singer, Mrs J. Astor' 123
Sivewright, Mrs 79
Slate, Ruth 171
Slawson, Eva 171
Slee, J. Noah H. 263
Smuts, Mrs Isie 88
Social Darwinism 105
Social-Democratic Federation (SDF) 19, 50, 124, 134, 140, 141, 143, 152, 155, 156
socialism/socialists 25, 26, 29, 42, 49, 60, 124, 135, 137, 138, 140, 146–7, 157, 162–4, 165, 171, 183, 185–6, 206, 208–9, 212, 216–17, 219, 228, 254, 257
'Socialism and the Middle Classes' (Wells) 171
Socialist Party (US) 212
Society for Psychical Research 4
South Africa 1, 4, 5–6, 27, 74, 76, 78–9, 81, 82–3, 84, 85–9, 90, 91, 95, 138
South African Telegraph 86
Spanish Atrocities Committee 141
Spencer, Herbert 12, 71, 252
spiritualism/psychic research 4–5
Stead, W.T. 57, 78–9, 83, 87, 88, 89
Steffens, Lincoln 212
Story of an African Farm, The (O. Schreiner) 1–2, 5–6, 7–8, 10, 15, 27, 30, 49, 50, 53, 70–1, 73, 83, 96, 223
Straight, Mrs Willard 234
strikes 74–5, 135, 146–7, 214
'strop bill' (flogging African servants) 81
Studies in the Psychology of Sex (Havelock Ellis) 107, 115–16, 120–3, 125–31, 241, 245; Vol. 1 *Sexual Inversion* 121–3, 125–31; Vol. 2 128
Study of Sociology (Spencer) 12
suffragette movement 1, 26, 51, 53, 172, 208–9
Sullivan, James 124
'Sunlight Lay Across My Bed, The' (O. Schreiner, allegory) 67
surrealism 3
Surrey (ship) 10
Swan, Sonnenschein, publishers 152
Sweeney, Inspector John 125–6, 129

symbolism 3
Symonds, John Addington 122

Tarbell, Ida 212
Tatler 181
Taylor, Ellen 96–7, 98
Ten Days that Shook the World (Reed) 212
Terry, Ellen 137, 198
theatre and drama 3, 16–17, 21–2, 96, 100, 140
Thorne, Will 156
Time Machine, The (Wells) 161
Tono-Bungay (Wells) 188
Towards Democracy (Carpenter) 245, 247
trades unions 42, 73–4, 82, 134–5, 141, 145, 146–7, 151, 152, 156, 214, 217
Treasure Seekers, The 176
Trooper Peter Halket of Mashonaland (O. Schreiner) 87
Tsuzuki, C. 152
Tuke, Dr Hack 105, 122–3

Undine (O. Schreiner) 70
undinism (urolagnia) 120–2, 130
University College, London 20, 45, 74, 150

Value, Price and Profit (Marx) 152
vegetarianism 101, 244, 245
Vezin, Mrs 16
Vienna Secession 3, 4
Vies des dames galantes (Brantôme) 11
'Villiers, Dr Roland de' (aka 'Dr Sinclair Roland'; aliases of Georg Ferdinand Springmuhl von Weissenfeld) 123–4, 125, 126, 128–9
Vindication of the Rights of Woman (Wollstonecraft) 73
Virginian, RMS 219
Vorwärts 135, 147
Voysey, Alfred 168

Wagner, Richard 244
Walker, Emery 244
Walker, Mrs 34, 35
Ward, Mrs 228
War of the Worlds, The (Wells) 161
Watford University Press 123–4, 125, 127, 129
Webb, Beatrice (née Potter) 4, 18–19, 47, 76–8, 82, 108–9, 110, 11, 160, 164–5, 171, 172, 183, 195–200, 249, 250, 254

Webb, Sidney 78, 82, 109, 110, 137, 160,
    161, 164, 171, 172, 183, 195, 197, 200,
    250
Weissenfeld, Georg von *see* 'Villiers, Dr
    Roland de'
Weldon, Maud 62
Wells, Frank 168, 253
Wells, Gip 168, 253
Wells, H.G. 161–72, 173–4, 176–210,
    249, 251, 252–3, 254, 259, 260–2
Wells, Isabel 165–6
Wells, Jane (née Amy Catherine Robbins)
    166–8, 176, 177, 178, 182–3, 185, 187,
    190, 192, 193–4, 200, 202–3, 204–5,
    253, 254
West, Anthony 193, 201, 204, 253, 260,
    261
West, Rebecca 188–9, 190, 193, 201, 202,
    203, 204, 249, 250, 252, 253, 260–1
Westphalen, Jenny von *see* Marx, Jenny
    Sr
What Every Girl Should Know (Sanger)
    212–13
What Every Mother Should Know (Sanger)
    212

Wilberforce, Bishop 162
Wilde, Oscar 3, 74, 241, 245
Wilhelm II, Kaiser 88
Wilkes, John 21
Williams and Norgate, publishers 122
Wilson, Charlotte 69
Wollstonecraft, Mary 69–70, 73, 227
Woman and Labour (O. Schreiner) 73, 90,
    91, 92, 223
Woman Question/New Woman ideas
    1–2, 3, 27, 38, 45–6, 50–2, 56, 57, 60,
    69, 73, 90, 91–3, 94, 95, 96, 124,
    160–1, 172, 208–10, 249–63
Woman Rebel, The (ed. Sanger) 209–10,
    216–18
'Woman's Question, The' (Pearson) 50–
    51
Women's Hospital (Seven Dials) 7
Woolf, Virginia 248
World Set Free, The (Wells) 162
Wortis, Joseph 120, 131

Yeats, W.B. 3
Yellow Book, The 3
Yellow Wallpaper, The (Gilman) 256